TRUE BLUE

TRANSFER PRINTED EARTHENWARE

Edited by Gaye Blake Roberts, FMA, FRSA

The catalogue of an exhibition of British Blue Transfer Printed Earthenware,
to celebrate the 25th Anniversary of the Friends of Blue.
Held at The Wedgwood Museum, Barlaston, Stoke-on-Trent, Staffordshire,
21st March to 12th July, 1998

CHRISTIE'S
SOUTH KENSINGTON

W
WEDGWOOD
ENGLAND 1759

'The Art (of transfer printing) has helped to make English
Pottery famous throughout the civilized world, and has done
much towards making its production one of the greatest
staple manufactures of the Country.'

On the Art of Pottery J. Mayer (1875)

Front Cover: **Coffee Pot** with 'Cottage Children' pattern. *Maker Unknown.* About 1815–1825.
Cat. Ref. Case 18/4.

Back Cover: **Pierced Stand** with the Prince of Wales' Feathers made by *Thomas Lakin, Stoke.*
About 1812–1817. Cat. Ref. Case 7/3.

Published by the Friends of Blue, East Hagbourne, Oxfordshire, 1998.
Supported by Christie's South Kensington, London.
Colour pictures by Brent Burgess Photography, Stone, Staffordshire.
Design and layout by Helen Gumn.
Printed by B.A.S. Printers Limited, Over Wallop, Hampshire

ISBN 0 9532736 0 1

Contents

Acknowledgements

The 'True Blue' exhibition has been mounted to celebrate the 25th anniversary of the Friends of Blue. The Society was founded in 1973 to promote an interest in blue and white transfer printed earthenware and to publish information about the subject. This publication would not have been possible without the generous sponsorship of Christie's South Kensington and of some of our members. We are extremely grateful to them and hope that they will be pleased with the result.

The exhibition would not have been possible without the generous, liberal and enthusiastic support of the Wedgwood company and the Trustees of the Wedgwood Museum. Not only have they given every possible assistance, but they have without stint provided the exhibition space and all aspects of the display as well as a vast amount of ancillary work which is generally taken for granted for example, storage, administration, insurance, publicity, expertise and many other things without which there could have been no exhibition at all. To them we owe a debt of gratitude which will, we hope, be repaid by the success of the exhibition.

Thanks are also due to the many other people who have been concerned in the organisation of the exhibition and in the production of this book, including Robin Gurnett, Ken and Margaret Linacre, Colin Parkes, Martin Pulver, Arthur and Julia Roberts, and most particularly John Potter who has worked tirelessly with the Museum staff to ensure the success of the project.

Our thanks are also due to all those collectors who have generously lent their objects for display, written introductory essays, helped with photography, transport and in so many other ways. Individual acknowledgement to items in the exhibition have been made only where requested, but we would also like to thank the many lenders who wished to remain anonymous. The following members and non-members have provided help and assistance with the exhibition and we are grateful to them all;

G.A. Amos; David & Linda Arman; V. Auchinachie; Anne & Graham Aylett; Shirley M. Barrett; J. & D. Beggs; Michael J. Benson; John Bentley; R.G. Bevan; Renard Broughton; Eric A. Bryan; Judith Busby; Margaret Buxton; Yvonne Buttimer; Joyce & Derek Chitty; Chenda Clark; L.M. Cole; B. Coleman; Rhoda Cope; Sydney Creed; Margaret & Peter Crumpton; John & Margaret Cushion; S.G. Elkington; Derek Ferrier; Christopher Fiorini; Geoffrey Fisk; Sheila French; Laurie Fuller; Dr David Furniss; Cliff Gazely; Mervyn Gibbs; Edward & Diana Goatham; Geoffrey Godden; D.C. Gowans; Allen Grace; W.I. Graham; Jonathan Gray; Dr David Greenbaum; Brian Hawtin; Helen Hallesey; Michael Hickman; Dr John Hicks; Lyn & Maurice Hillis; Tim & Minnie Holdaway; David Hoexter; Mr & Mrs M. Houlden; Peter Hyland; Margaret Ironside; Mr & Mrs S.F.N. Jenkins; J.M. Jenkins; Mr A. Kessel; K. Knapton; Barbara Lanning; J.E.M. Latham; Mr & Mrs J Leatherland; David Lewis; Ken & Margaret Linacre; Celia Lowe; P.L. & A.E. Maclean-Eltham; Catriona & David Maisels; Joyce McCarthy; Patrick McQuaid; Ralph Mears; Phillip Miller; Wendy Mitton; Peter & Gillian Mobbs; Jennifer Moody; Nancy Mortimer-Rudd; Joyce Mountain; Mrs D.M. Mugleston; A.J.L. Muir; Howard Mumford; Gabriel Newfield; Doreen Otto; Colin & Patricia Parkes; Colin & Ruby Pavor; Roger Pomfret; Barbara J. Pond; Jean & John Potter; Mr & Mrs John Price; Rosalind and Martin Pulver; Flora Rabinovitch; Alan Ricketts; Julia & Arthur Roberts; Joanne & Denis Blake Roberts; A.S. Rowe; John Samuels; Michael Sack; Jill Sandberg; Terry Sheppard; Mr & Mrs D.T. Sibson; Judie Siddall; The Stevenson Collection; John & Sally Storton; P. Stovin; The Strong Collection; Stella Swabey; Jill Turnbull; J.M.D. Walker; David Weake; J.B. Wilkinson; Anna Wolsey; Margaret Wood; J.L. Worrall; Norma Wright; The City Museum and Art Gallery, Stoke-on-Trent (Miranda Goodby, Keeper of Ceramics and Debbie Skinner Senior Assistant Keeper); and last and most of all the staff at the Wedgwood Museum, without whose hard and dedicated work neither book nor exhibition would have happened – Gaye Blake Roberts (Curator); Lynn Miller; Sharon Gater; Martin Chaplin; Sue Howdle; Joanne Riley; David Plant.

We would also wish to thank Shopfitting and Exhibition Services, Stone, for designing the exhibition. Brent Burgess for taking the colour illustrations for this catalogue, and Ellen McAdam for her work in the initial stages of preparing this book.

Preface

by Robin Gurnett, President and Founder of Friends of Blue

During the 1960's and 1970's interest in collecting blue and white transfer printed wares was beginning to gather momentum. There had always been enthusiasts, but the wide variety of designs, produced over a very long period, meant that here was a wealth of possibilities for both the avid and the new collector alike. It was possible to collect examples in the most general terms, or specialise in a particular maker, shape or theme, or in subject matter such as animals, birds, colleges, even patterns depicting popular dramas – which were available at quite reasonable prices. The average cost of a plate with an attractive view would not be much over £5. At that time examples of the famous 'Willow' pattern were just not wanted at all, but now there are Collectors' Clubs who are devoted entirely to the study of the 'Willow' pattern. Some of them go much further, in that their interests can cover examples that are produced even today, on all sorts of mediums like paper, plastic and cloth as well as ceramics.

Specific manufacturers were an obvious choice to collect and included such well known names as Spode, Masons, Leeds, Herculaneum, Davenport and Wedgwood. Before long, some lesser known makers started to be individually identified; Bathwell and Goodfellow; Goodwins and Harris; Heath; Rogers and Clews, to mention only a few. Some of these makers obviously produced other types of wares and one was already aware of them, but many emerged, having lain dormant for over a hundred years, with the production of blue and white transfer wares as their main output; they now began to be noticed and examples became avidly collected.

Probably the most popular types with collectors were those depicting views, often from a named series like 'English Scenery', or 'The Beauties of England and Wales'. The North American collectors were well catered for with numerous scenes made especially for export and often in a very dark blue colouring. Any examples of 'Old New York', the 'Coats of Arms of American States', or the 'Boston State House' had always commanded high prices in America. As most of them were specifically made for export, not so many examples remained here in the United Kingdom. Scenes from Canada were also to be found, some with polar bears and Eskimos; these are still in great demand.

One of the problems initially was that there were very few reference books on the subject, and a great deal of guesswork was involved in trying to designate makers to certain pieces. It was because of the huge variety of patterns that were being collected, without many books to refer to for attribution, that it was felt that there was an acute need for collectors to pool their knowledge and get all these patterns recorded in a central system. Against this background, the Friends of Blue was formed in 1973. Here, like-minded devotees would be able to call upon this information through the use of a magazine, or by contacting the Keeper of the Records. Members were asked to scrutinise their own collections and to forward details of anything of interest to the Records. In turn, other members could draw upon these collective records, and together as a group we could not only help each other, but add valuable documentation for posterity. A further attraction was that it would bring together fellow enthusiasts for mutual discussions, exchange of views and information. Many long-term friendships have resulted, and these have been cemented through local meetings which are still organised to this end, and are in addition to the Annual Meeting and the *Bulletin*. Through the medium of the *Bulletin* one could pose questions, often illustrated by the objects, which in turn would then generate various responses, from as far apart as India and the West Indies, and further relevant data could then be logged, thus building up and extending our knowledge.

The very first meeting (Figure 1), held in the Victoria & Albert Museum Lecture Theatre in 1973, attracted over 50 people from as far away as Devon, Wales and Scotland. Bill Coysh and W.L. Little, the two authors of the only specialist books on blue and white transfer printed wares then available, kindly offered the names of people who had corresponded with them through their publications, and these formed the very nucleus of those who, as interested parties, were invited to attend and become members of the society. Even by the publication of *Bulletin* 2, we had already been able to identify the makers of a particularly attractive series known as 'Metropolitan Scenery'. From these humble beginnings, a great deal of serious research has evolved, in particular the publication by two of our members of their own detailed research work on Rogers and Meir, which now forms an important addition to our source of knowledge of these manufacturers. This type of work

1. The first meeting of the Friends of Blue held at the Victoria and Albert Museum, London, in 1973

goes on, continually adding to the history of blue transfer printed earthenwares. Before long we had established the identity of numerous unnamed views, in particular the popular 'Wild Rose' pattern; in this case, unusually, the name refers to the border rather than the central design. The view was recognised, as having been taken from a contemporary print by W. Cooke after a painting by S. Owen (1811), depicting Nuneham Courtenay in Oxfordshire, with a punt on the Thames.

In the 1800's, certain Oxford Colleges did not receive ladies, not even Her Majesty the Queen! The following instances are taken from *Discovering Oxford* by Michael De-la-Noy:

'On 15th June 1841 the youthful and recently wed Prince Albert went to Oxford to receive an address of Commemoration, but although Queen Victoria could scarcely bear to let him out of her sight, she was compelled to spend the day alone, to her great grief, in the beautiful surroundings of Nuneham Courtney. The Prince was enthusiastically received'.

Another amazing story regarding this house concerns a visit by the first Professor of Geology at Oxford, Canon William Buckland. He had a reputation for having eaten his way through the entire range of British animals. The nastiest he ever tasted he declared, was the mole! On this occasion he was shown a silver casket which held the preserved heart of one of the Kings of France. 'I have eaten some strange things in my time' said the Professor, 'but never the heart of a King' and, loathe to let the opportunity slip by, popped it into his mouth and swallowed it. These little anecdotes serve not only to enhance the interest of the pieces concerned, but also improves one's knowledge of history!

Some of our members specialise in finding original prints and pictures from which blue and white designs were taken. Huge volumes of prints and illustrations were kept in libraries by some potters, and the actual locating of a source design is very rewarding. It can often take many hours of patient browsing to find one, and eventually to hang the picture and the plate together is very pleasing indeed. This use of other people's work was curtailed when the law of copyright came into effect, so that the scenes from 1842 onwards are often stilted in style, being imaginary rather than factual.

One of our first two Presidents, W.L. 'Tiny' Little, author of *Staffordshire Blue* had been collecting since before the War. He was also interested in early English porcelains and delftware, many of which he copied in watercolours. In those days the dress for meetings of the English Ceramic Circle was black tie and dinner jacket. As an Official of the Bank of England in London he was aware that there was somewhere an image of this famous building, known to be illustrated on a blue platter. So, being an artist, he set about compiling a picture of what the actual scene might look like. As there was no response to his pleas in this country, the challenge was then taken up in America, and eventually two different examples of the platter were located. After numerous letters back and forth, he was able to make an offer for one of them and purchased it for the Bank of England in 1938, when they paid £20, which at that time this was quite a high price, despite the rarity of the piece. It is still housed in the vaults at the Bank today.

Our other co-President Bill Coysh, had recently completed his own illustrated book, *Underglaze Blue Printed Earthenwares*; this was followed by a further similar volume. Since then he has produced *The Dictionary of Blue and White,* with a second volume; these were written in conjunction with Dr. Dick Henrywood, the first Keeper of the Records and another founder member. These two books are often referred to within the Society as the 'Blue and White Bibles'.

Wilfred 'Tiny' Little died in 1979 and 10 years later Bill Coysh relinquished the title of President due to a combination of poor health and other commitments.

Today there are more than 300 Friends of Blue scattered throughout the world, many of them in regular communication with the Keeper of the Records or the Editor of the *Bulletin*. The *Bulletin*, shortly approaching its 100th issue, continues to record recent finds and research and there is usually something new in every issue. The records contain fifteen thousand cards in two indices, one for manufacturers and their products and the other of pattern names.

Over the years the naming of patterns has proved somewhat complex, with some designs having several contrived titles given by various members at different times. When these are eventually matched up, a choice of name has to be made, except of course, where a genuine factory name can be identified. The records also hold thousands of photographs of members' pieces. A few years ago, it was found necessary to purchase a computer, mainly to facilitate searching for unidentified patterns. Now, with the increasing advances in the use of personal computers, the possibility of making these records directly available to members is under review.

In this year of 1998, our 25th Anniversary, the Friends of Blue are delighted and honoured to be able, with the help and co-operation of the Trustees of the Wedgwood Museum, Josiah Wedgwood & Sons Ltd and Christie's of South Kensington, to mount this celebratory exhibition, accompanied by this book, which contains both essays and a catalogue section and is intended to form a standard reference work on the subject. We hope that the exhibition proves surprising to some, enjoyable to most, and interesting to all its visitors. It is indeed a 'True Blue' exhibition, for this form of ceramic decoration was conceived and perfected in England. Additionally, because most of the pieces on display have been lent by members, an appropriate sub-title might have been 'Something borrowed, something blue'; certainly many Friends of Blue are virtually wedded to their hobby!

Introduction

by John Potter (Keeper of Records)

A short examination of the field of blue and white transfer printed earthenware will show that it is at least as large as any other in ceramics and in some respects a great deal more complex. Big, of course, is not necessarily beautiful, and only the most ardent fans of blue and white would contend that as a class it is anything more than of high quality at its best, generally striking to look at and often interesting even at the lower end of the market.

That last word is an important one. The entire concept of transfer printing in blue on white earthenware was originated in order to satisfy an emerging market by extending to the rising middle classes, as a whole, the opportunity to emulate the rich in possessing, and being able to use daily, decorative domestic crockery. In its way, this concept constituted a minor social revolution, and at the same time a commercial one, because it was naturally the aim of the manufacturers who first thought of it to make this new, cheaper ceramic product available to a huge market unable to afford the expensive Chinese porcelain originals or their Continental copies. So successful was the whole idea that after more than 200 years blue and white is still being produced (though by modern processes, of course) and along the way an incredible number of different designs have been made – probably upwards of ten thousand – practically every maker of earthenware contributing to this massive market.

Before the 1750's, fine porcelains (at that time obtainable from the Orient or, in lesser quantity, from the Continent) were only to be found in the establishments of the wealthy and the aristocracy, mainly because they were expensive but perhaps also because the masses were not fully aware of the variety of goods available to lovers of the finer decorative arts. The outlets for such items were limited to specialist establishments in the larger towns and cities. Around the beginning of the 18th century, porcelain was in fact considered an investment and was sometimes more highly prized than silver or even gold. Augustus II 'The Strong', Elector of Saxony and King of Poland, is reputed to have exchanged a company of his Dragoons for a garniture of Oriental vases, and it was he who was primarily responsible for the development of the European porcelain industry.

Like the majority of the Chinese ware imported into Europe and most of the tin-glazed earthenwares which had earlier copied the Chinese decorative style, a lot of early European porcelain was decorated in blue. This was perhaps because at that time only cobalt, among the metal oxides, had been sufficiently stabilised to withstand the high temperatures needed to fire the glazes. This gave the porcelain its finished look and

made it impervious to liquids, thus enabling a decoration to be incorporated in the original manufacturing process. This was opposed to the use of enamel colours on top of the glaze, which required additional firings at a much lower temperature. The blue decorated Oriental wares formed a large part of the china imported into England by the East India Company, and when the first English porcelain makers succeeded in making a passable substitute – albeit using different materials requiring different methods – their first commercial productions also tended to be blue decoration on a white background.

By 1750 there was a growing demand for decorated china in England. The application after about 1756 of the newly invented methods of transfer printing developed a year or two earlier at Battersea and other enamelling centres greatly facilitated production. At the same time this introduced a higher degree of standardisation than was possible using only hand painted designs. The time was ripe, and the scene was set for a breakthrough into a much wider market.

By the mid 18th century the English earthenware manufacturers, who had congregated mainly in the Staffordshire area where there were ample supplies of materials, fuel and labour, enjoyed some years of success through a series of changes and improvements. These included white salt-glazed earthenware and stoneware, marbled bodies and glaze effects, coloured glazes and, by the end of the 1760's, cream coloured earthenware. The potters had no decorative line which, in terms of cost to themselves and price to their customers, could sweep the huge market constituted by the emerging middle classes. To be able to bring within reach of this market a ware resembling that used by the wealthy but at a fraction of the cost had to be a recipe for triumph.

The first manufacturers of earthenware to attempt the use of transfer printing called on the engraving and printing expertise which already existed in the porcelain factories and some relocation of staff took place, mostly from Worcester and Caughley. Josiah Spode drew benefit from this movement, his first printer being a man named Rickett from Caughley, but he was not the first to use the process. According to Simeon Shaw's *History of the Staffordshire Potteries*, Josiah Spode I used from 1784, 'the improved methods successfully adopted by Mr Ralph Baddeley of Shelton'. Indeed, the honour of being the first potter in this field is usually dated around 1779/1780 and attributed either to William Adams of Greengates, Tunstall or to John Turner of Lane End, Fenton. Later on, as the demand for engraving skills extended to small manufacturers who could not afford to employ full-time technicians, specialist firms of engravers grew up and contributed to the rapid expansion in the production of blue and white which took place between the 1790's and the 1820's.

Whereas most of the early porcelain factories and their wares can be pinpointed as to date because of the sterling work done over the years by several generations of dedicated ceramic researchers, it is not easy to do the same for blue and white. However, if there is no certainty within a year as to the date of the first production, there is no doubt that by 1790 the flood-gates had opened and many manufacturers large and small throughout the Potteries and elsewhere were producing transfer printed earthenwares, often of high quality and nearly always in the Chinese style.

The technicalities of engraving and transfer printing will be covered elsewhere in this book, but it should be mentioned here that the development of engraving techniques had a substantial influence on the appearance of blue and white printed pieces. The earliest items were all line engraved, with cross-hatching coming in a little later and enabling the illusion of solid colour to be produced. It was not until about 1800 that the stipple engraving technique made possible much more sophisticated effects in depth and perspective. Partial etching was also used in this way. All this progress, and the improvements to the fineness of ceramic bodies and glazes, resulted at least until the 1820's in a continued refinement of the product, and the period between about 1815 and 1830 is usually referred to as the 'Golden Age' of blue and white transfer printed earthenware.

Thereafter, as social conditions and competition in the market became fiercer, production tended to be dictated by more commercial pressure and less artistic sensitivity. Much as we may deplore this nearly 200 years later, it was after all only the natural order of things once the age of competitive trading was firmly established. Gradually the public taste changed; the customer, conditioned by what was available to him, came to expect less refinement as the manufacturers geared their production down to a price rather than up to a quality. The blues became paler, no doubt influenced by the rising price of cobalt, and the subject matter grew less definite. By the 1840's most of the popular patterns were nondescript, make-believe romanticised scenes and the work of art on the plate had degenerated to the point where anything blue would do. In fairness to the manufacturers, let it be said that they were in business to make a living and they had little option but to gear the quality of their products to the price at which they could maintain sufficient turnover.

By the 1850's and 1860's the wheel had turned full circle and instead of makers striving to produce crisper and clearer images they were deliberately blurring outlines by contriving to have the cobalt pigment flow into the glaze; this 'flow' or 'flown' blue had quite a period of popularity, especially in America where today it is highly collectable.

Through all these years a few designs remained in demand and scarcely changed over a long period of time (Cat. Ref. Case 23). The 'Willow' pattern is an inexplicable phenomenon – a standardised hotchpotch of Chinese inspired subjects which has lasted for well over 200 years, its invention being attributed to Thomas Turner, who founded the Caughley porcelain factory near Ironbridge in Shropshire. A possible explanation for the success of this – probably the best known ceramic design of all time – may lie in its combination of a busy pattern around which was woven a plausible though fictitious story and, above all, the fact that at the time it must have epitomised the popular idea of Chinese porcelain. It certainly engendered a most amazing quirk of public taste, from which came a belief that 'Willow' was the definitive blue and white pattern, even to the extent of substituting 'Willow' for 'blue and white'; as witnessed by the order received by the Wedgwood factory in June 1824; 'It must be blue willow in any pattern,' as cited by Una des Fontaines in her paper on 'Early Printed Patterns at Etruria', given to the Wedgwood Society, London in 1975.

There have of course been other long-running patterns, such as 'Wild Rose', which lasted from the early 1820's well into the 1850's, when it was superseded by 'Asiatic Pheasants', a relatively insignificant pattern always printed in pale blue and made by at least sixty factories over a period of 40 years.

The longest-running design in constant use, apart from 'Willow', is probably Spode's 'Italian' which was first produced in 1816 and is still popular today. Originating from the 'Golden Age', it is taken from a drawing of an unidentified classical landscape. There is a perverse but inexorable logic in this fact that all four of the longest-running patterns are fairly uninspired. However, the success of these designs may well have been due to the very fact that they were not too definite and tended therefore to be compatible with the tastes of the greatest number of potential customers. The 'Italian' design was copied by a few other makers, as it was introduced before any enforceable form of copyright law began to appear.

The first blue and white patterns tended to imitate the Oriental (Cat. Ref. Case 1), were naturally in the Chinese idiom and continued to be fashionable from the early 1780's until the first decade of the 19th century. Many examples can be traced back directly to imported Chinese originals. Several revivals of the Oriental influence took place over the years, one of Chinoiserie in the 1820's and a strong taste for the Japanese design style in the 1880's. However, soon after 1800, engravers were becoming less bound by the Chinese influence and other elements began to emerge, including a movement towards European sources. The years between approximately 1800 and 1815 are known as the 'Transitional' period, wherein the subject matter widened dramatically, mixing for instance Gothic buildings with a Chinese landscape (Cat. Ref. Case 3).

Around 1815 the 'Transitional' period began to merge smoothly into the 'Golden Age', which is typified in the many and varied series of patterns taken from volumes of prints illustrating such themes as Oriental scenery, sporting subjects, British and Continental views, churches, public buildings and stately homes and many others. Literary, classical, historical, botanical, nautical, zoological, ornithological and commemorative subjects also provided a vast reservoir of design sources, none of them at the time protected against direct imitation. These series of prints, which sometimes extended to over fifty different patterns, were more than matched in number by the proliferation of one-off designs issued according to the ideas of each manufacturer as to what was likely to achieve good sales. By the middle 1820's a further dimension had been added by the rapid opening up of the American market, aided by advances in the speed, size and safety of the cargo ships which crossed the Atlantic. This market encouraged a totally new style of design, catering specially for the American taste, both in subject matter and in the patterns themselves, which tended to cover the surface more completely and to be printed in a very deep, dark blue (Cat. Ref. Case 35). Relatively few examples of this type of ware have been available in England until fairly recently, when a mysterious reverse movement across the Atlantic was noted in the antiques market, perhaps encouraged by relative price movements in the two countries.

The 'Golden Age' was well and truly over by the late 1830's and within ten years the 'Romantic' period was in full swing (Cat. Ref. Case 36). Blue and white was still produced in vast quantities but gradually the patterns grew less distinguished and the indeterminate pale blues began to give way to the indistinct darker colours of the flow blue era. The 1920's and 1930's saw a few re-issues of 19th century designs, but only very recently has there been a small revival of some of the early patterns, printed of course by modern processes and therefore to some extent lacking the majestic appearance of the originals. The making and decoration of pots is an industry in which even the tremendous advances in techniques and materials which have taken place over the years cannot reproduce the exact look of pieces made by the old hands-on methods and skills of the 'Golden Age'.

The appeal of blue and white transfer printed earthenware to the collector is something which is almost as old as the technique itself. Here we have a large body of ware which was mass-produced for the domestic market yet was generally handsome in its own right and, in its various periods, offered a variety sufficient to attract many different eyes. Although to some collectors it is the fine products of the 'Golden Age' which have the greatest allure, the later wares must not be dismissed as, apart from anything else, they are closer to the present and associations and even documentation can be much fresher. And, at least in theory, blue and white is not difficult to come by, though as a ware it was in daily use and subject to all the many hazards of domestic life. Vast quantities were made, but these were consumer goods and therefore expendable, and vast quantities also were broken and discarded. Consequently we have today a class of collectable ware whose field is extremely wide yet which contains numerous pockets of relative rarity. Within this wide field there are many opportunities for specialisation; medical wares, kitchen and dairy pieces, individual series, animal prints, botanical patterns, shapes, commemoratives, miniatures and a whole host of others.

Collecting is a hobby which dates back into antiquity. For instance we are told that after the taking of Alexandria in 30 B.C. the Emperor Augustus retained only 'a porcelain vessel' for himself (an inadequate translation as neither the word nor the material then existed). Blue and white collecting itself dates back a long way into the Victorian period, and many of the books published in the last quarter of the 19th century devoted some space to the subject. By the early 1900's, specialist books on transfer printed earthenware were beginning to appear.

Collectors tend to be a breed apart. Horace Walpole once wrote of a collector of his acquaintance;
'China's the passion of his soul.
A cup, a plate, a dish, a bowl
Can kindle wishes in his breast,
Inflame with joy, or break his rest.'

In the *Pottery Gazette* of April 1881 there appears a letter under the pen-name 'Old Fogey';
'I have spent some years and much money collecting blue china and now I am told that it is not fashionable. Is Art a fashion and not a fact? Is it a term for something I have and another cannot get? Must it be scarce and in a few hands? Can anything be artistic that is plentiful? Must a thing to be beautiful be limited?'
That could be paraphrased, very broadly, as 'Beauty is in the eye of the beholder', which must surely be the best possible precept for the collector. On the other hand, and from a totally different viewpoint, there have to be standards of execution in any art form, and a piece of mass-produced blue and white earthenware from the late 19th century does not look particularly good when displayed beside a quality piece from the 'Golden Age'. In the May 1881 issue of the *Pottery Gazette* (presumably continuing the previous correspondence), 'Peter Teazle' wrote; 'Blue china is not fashionable. It was getting hideous both in shape and design. Potters live by tempting the taste with novelty which is too often a burlesque on the beauty of Art'. These are points of view, but no collector worthy of the name should be swayed by either. He must continue along his own chosen route, following the dictates not of his conscience but of his instinct.

Notes on the Essay Section

Plate. refers to the colour pictures located between pages 64 and 65.

Figure. refers to the black and white pictures within the text.

Cat. Ref. Indicates a reference to an object which is illustrated and described fully in the catalogue section by case number and object number, for example: Case 10/5.

Manuscript references to the Wedgwood papers are quoted by kind permission of The Trustees of The Wedgwood Museum, Barlaston, Stoke-on-Trent, Staffordshire, England.
Figures 12 to 17 inclusive are published with the kind permission of the Guildhall Library, London.

All the authors have asserted and given notice of their right under Section 77 of the Copyright, Design and Patent Act 1988 to be identified as the Author of the foregoing articles.

How blue printed transfer wares were made

by David Drakard

A blue derived from cobalt for the decoration of pottery and porcelain was in use long before its appearance transferred onto earthenware from about 1780 in England. Found painted on early Persian pottery, it was taken up by the Chinese during the Yuan dynasty about AD 1300, and was used extensively both on glaze and underglaze to decorate Ming porcelain as well as all later Chinese wares.

Cobalt is a silvery-white metal element, which is found in two natural forms of which one, smaltite, a greyish mineral of cobalt arsenide, occurs in veins associated with silver. The English name cobalt is taken from the middle high German 'Kobolt', meaning a goblin, named from the German silver miners' belief that malicious goblins placed it in the silver ore. It was used in Europe as a blue painted decoration on tin glazed pottery and other earthenware and from about 1725 on European porcelain and continues in use as a painted and enamel decoration both on and under glaze. In the United Kingdom the earlier supplies of cobalt were imported from Saxony in the form of 'Zaffre', an impure cobalt oxide, or further refined as 'Smalt', a fused body of 'Zaffre', potassium carbonate and silica. In 1815–1816 cobalt was found in Cornwall and British cobalt oxide, known as 'Calx', became available for use by the potters.

The first record of the establishment of a transfer printing process is found in the three unsuccessful patent applications of John Brooks, a Dubliner, who served an apprenticeship in Birmingham as an engraver. In his first petition for a patent dated 10th September 1751, he described himself as John Brooks, 'of Birmingham in the County of Warwickshire, engraver' and he claimed to have:

> 'Found out a method of printing,
> impressing and reversing upon enamel
> and china from engraved, etched and mezzotinto
> plates and from cuttings on wood and mettle,
> impressions of History, Portraits, Landscapes,
> Foliages, Coats of Arms, Cyphers, Letters,
> Decorations, and Other Devises.(sic)'

Brooks left Birmingham in 1753 to manage the Battersea Enamel Works in London and from there made further patent applications in January 1754 and April 1755 both equally unsuccessful.

The second claim for invention of transfer printing was by John Sadler, a printer of Liverpool, who on 2nd August 1756 swore an affidavit, as a preliminary step to a patent application. The statement states that, assisted by Guy Green and in the space of six hours, he had printed upwards of twelve hundred tiles of different patterns and that he had been upwards of seven years finding out the method. Although supported by John Poole, member of Parliament for Liverpool, in his intention to obtain a patent, no such application appears to have been lodged. Thus, despite four attempts at patents, none were ever granted in the 18th century for transfer printing on ceramics.

The printing by Sadler at Liverpool was always made upon the already fired glaze using a glue bat as the transfer medium. From 1756 until 1761 he continued printing on tiles and occasionally on porcelain and enamels with black, the most frequently used printing colour.

On 23rd September 1761 he came to an agreement with Josiah Wedgwood to transfer print on the glaze of Wedgwood's creamware. This Sadler/Wedgwood connection in 1761 influenced Wedgwood's Staffordshire competitors to adopt Sadler's glue bat printing methods for on glaze print decoration of earthenware and the later porcelains as soon as they could discover his methods. By the end of the century the skill of black printing, as it was known in the 18th century, or bat printing as it became known in the 19th, was practised throughout the pottery industry in the United Kingdom. However Sadler's methods were not and could not be used for underglaze blue printing.

Simeon Shaw, in his *History of the Staffordshire Potteries* published in 1829, attributes the first blue printing to Thomas Turner at Caughley, near Broseley, in Shropshire. Born in 1749, Turner is described as a pottery chemist and engraver. Turner left Worcester for Caughley in 1772 by which time Worcester was the leading porcelain manufacturer using blue printed decoration. At Caughley, Turner introduced a range of soapstone porcelain following Worcester shapes and traditions so that Worcester should probably be recognised as the originators of cobalt blue transfer printing rather than Caughley.

Returning to the *History of the Staffordshire Potteries*, Simeon Shaw reported that, in an endeavour to facilitate the great demand for blue painted and enamelled pottery in Staffordshire William Adams of Cobridge employed William Davis who 'had learned engraving and copperplate printing, at Worcester; and had practised Blue Painting and Black Printing in Shropshire, from which he came to the Potteries.' At Cobridge Davis formed the outline in blue on the ware from a glue bat, similar to black printing, which could be readily filled in by the painters. 'The method of printing with glue bats was also practised by Harry Baker, for Mr. Baddeley of Shelton, about 1777 and very little progress was made in the practice for some time.'

As further reported by Simeon Shaw, 'The next stage in its improvement was employing paper and transferring it to the Pottery; but in this the printer proceeded very differently from the present method. The paper was different in texture and quality, and was used in a dry state.' Shaw continues by describing the copper plates which were deeply engraved by a burin, or graver, and without punching, and were of an even tone using a dark colour blue with no delicate shades being preserved. The transfer printed papers were most difficult to remove from the ware and designs to cover a twenty inch dish were engraved on two copper plates since a large single transfer, because of its dry state, could not be removed from the dish sufficiently quickly to be satisfactory. This difficulty was subsequently overcome by printing with a wet transfer paper first undertaken by John Turner, senior, of Lane End.

Improvements in the glaze and body of the ware including the addition of a little cobalt in the glaze, induced several other manufacturers to commence to make blue printed pottery. Simeon Shaw comments that, 'about 1783, John Rickett, John Ainsworth and John Lucock, an engraver, left the service of Mr. Turner at Caughley, and engaged with the Staffordshire manufacturers, Rickett and Lucock with the first Mr. Spode and Ainsworth with the first Mr. John Yates, of Shelton. These two printers first introduced the Composition called <u>Oils</u>, and the method of washing the paper off the bisquet pottery, and hardening on the colours previous to the immersion in the fluid glaze.'

During the next thirty years the craft of underglaze blue printing was subject to continuous small improvements in the body and glazes of the ware, in the preparation of the colour, in the variations of the copperplate engraving techniques, in the transfer printing presses and the paper upon which the transfers were printed, all of which brought the ware so decorated to the technical excellence found on wares manufactured from about 1805–1810. From this time variations in fashion and style of the decorative designs and the shapes of the wares continued, but the basic techniques of production of blue printed earthenwares remained little changed for more than a century.

Having briefly examined the history of cobalt blue and the antecedents and beginnings of transfer printing with the aid of Simeon Shaw's reminiscences of the years before 1829, an endeavour now will be made to offer a view of a 19th century British pottery and, in particular, its blue transfer printing department. Reference will be made to a supplement issued in May 1843 by *The Penny Magazine* entitled *A Day at the Staffordshire Potteries* and a special supplement issued by *The Illustrated London News* on 30th August 1884, *The Staffordshire Potteries*. The first supplement is perhaps better written but sparsely illustrated with the second better illustrated by a very competent artist Harry Furniss to which has been added a later photograph from this century.

The Penny Magazine supplement of 1843 acknowledges that the Pot Bank being described was the Spode Works then in the hands of Copeland and

2. Aerial view of the Spode Factory

Garrett, employing nearly a thousand persons and 'appearing more like a small town than a manufactory.' It consisted of a 'labyrinth of passages and courts, intersecting each other at angles, and bounded by other buildings' with 'altogether nearly a hundred and twenty separate workshops' and 'in different parts of the Works, seven biscuit-ovens, fourteen glaze-ovens and sixteen kilns for enamelling and other processes'. The aerial photograph of 1929 (Figure 2), taken during the smoke free atmosphere of the Potteries Wakes Week, shows little change some eighty years later. The Spode Works remains on the same site but all the bottle ovens have now gone, replaced by gas-fired tunnel ovens, but blue transfer printed ware remains a staple production of fine quality.

During the period of manufacture covered by the exhibition, preparation of the clay remained heavy work. In the traditional method the clay was first left to 'weather' in banks at the pottery, as can be seen at the rear of the Works in Figure 2. For the earthenware body most used for blue printed ware, local clays had been superseded by finer clays from Dorset and Devon shipped to Liverpool and brought into the Potteries by the Trent and Mersey Canal. That stalwart trade unionist William Evans issued a seventy-two page booklet in August 1846, entitled *The Art and History of the Potting Business*, listing formulas of the various bodies, glazes, decoration and details of every craft and process used within the Staffordshire potting industry. Of the bodies he lists eleven formulas for the preparation of the earthenware body for blue printed ware. All include blue clay, china clay and flint and either black or brown clay.

3. Mixing the clay, taken from Furniss' illustration 1884

Each grade of clay was treated separately, first being cleaned by a process known as blunging. The clay, having been mixed with water in a vat, was kept in agitation by large paddles so that the finer clay particles were in suspension whilst the heavier sand and stone sank to the bottom and so remained when the blunged clay and water was run off into settling tanks through a sieved orifice placed a little above the bottom of the blunging vat. Although since mechanised, this was still a manual process in 1884 as can be seen by Furniss' illustration of that year. The various cleaned clays were combined (Figure 3), according to the recipe adopted, as a mixture of clay and water before being run into a slip kiln of open troughs some sixty feet long, heated from below, where the water evaporated leaving a stiffish clay. From there the clay passed through the pug mill to be further compacted and to expel the minute bubbles of air, and finally, to be held in moderately humid cells ready for the hands of the potter.

With underglaze printed earthenware, the largest aspect of production by far was the dinner service. Of this the plain dinner plate outnumbered all other pieces by at least four to one. In consequence the basic forms of all new printed dinner ware patterns were made to fit this shape and size. Plate makers are illustrated at work in both the 1843 *Penny Magazine* supplement and that of *The Illustrated London News*. As might be expected, the description in the *Penny Magazine* is clearer than that in *The Illustrated London News*; the former is quoted whilst the latter is used for the illustration (Figure 4). The 1843 description of making a plate reads: 'Beneath the workman's hands is a vertical pillar on top of which is a horizontal wheel bearing a reverse copy of the plate made in plaster of Paris; that is, the upper surface is the same size and shape as the inside or face of the plate that is to be made.'

After covering this mould with clay the plate maker's boy set it into rotary motion and beneath the potter's hands the bottom of the plate was formed by gauges, ribs or profiles. The plate and mould were then placed in drying stoves and, after some shrinkage by evaporation, was later trimmed and separated from the moulds before being placed into saggars for firing in the coal fired biscuit ovens at about 1250 degrees centigrade

4. Plate makers – taken from
The Illustrated London News

Successful decoration by transfer printing depends first on the skill of the copperplate engraver, whose copperplate must meet two needs. The engraving must accept the printing liquid quickly, easily and evenly. Second, the same liquid must as easily and quickly be lifted out with a sharp clear print when the flexible transfer is pressed firmly on the copperplate. If these criteria are met, a good printed decoration can be produced quickly and with a minimum of wastage, both necessities for efficient, swift production. The most successful engraving forms that meet these needs are a 'V' cut line and a dot that is an inverted cone, again a 'V' form. There is nothing in the shape to impede easy entry or removal of the printing liquid, and by increasing the depth of the cut additional colour can be held to give a darker shade of blue when printing with a cobalt mixture. The tool used to make a cut line in a copperplate, named the burin or graver, is a sharpened length of steel of triangular section held in a mushroom shaped wooden handle. This is pushed through the flat copperplate to make the required 'V' cut line removing the surplus copper as it goes. A tap on the head of the punch forms the inverted 'V' dot but leaves a raised rim around the impression which must be cut away by a sharpened steel scraper and finally made smooth by rubbing with a wet stone and water, a process known as 'planishing' in the Potteries.

The following description of the transfer printing process is taken from Volume III of *Chemical Essays* by Samuel Parkes published in 1815, a time when underglaze blue printing had reached its peak of excellence. It reads:

'The mode of imparting designs to the surface of earthenware or porcelain, and which is known in the trade by the appellation of BLUE PRINTING, is managed somewhat in the following manner. One man constantly attends the press, which is very similar to our common copperplate press; and as soon as he has applied the colour, for blue printing being oxide of cobalt, which is laid on the copper in the same manner as the copperplate printers apply the ink; he lays it upon a hot iron, to thin the oil with which the colour is always mixed for this purpose, it being a peculiar preparation of boiled linseed oil. When the colour upon the copperplate is thus reduced to a proper consistence, a sheet of thin paper is laid over it, and the workman passes it, with the paper through the press.

When the paper comes from the press, it is, of course, stamped with the intended pattern. It is then delivered while wet with colour, to a girl, who cuts the superfluous paper with a pair of scissors, and passes it to another girl, who immediately applies it to a piece of biscuit ware, and then delivers it to a third, who fixes it more firmly by rubbing it very hard with a piece of flannel tightly rolled up in the form of a short cylinder.

The design of this hard rubbing is to force the colour into the pores of the ware. When the papers which have been thus applied have been lain on for about an hour, the colour is generally found to be sufficiently fixed to admit of their being detached. This is effected by putting the articles into a tub of water, where the paper soon becomes soft and pulpy enough to allow of its being peeled off by gentle friction, leaving the full impression of the pattern on the biscuit.

The papers having been removed, the ware is suffered to stand a sufficient time to become dry, and then it is put into an oven at a low heat, for the purpose of dissipating the oil, and prepare it for receiving the glaze.'

Figure 5, showing a print shop, was drawn by Harry Furniss in 1884, and illustrates much of the basic process which had remained virtually unchanged since its introduction the century before. The printer on the left is shown forcing the warmed mixture of colour and oil into the engraving on the heated copperplate using a wooden tool called a dabber. The woman on the right is fixing the transfer to the biscuit body by vigorously rubbing with a roll of printers' flannel. The underglaze process was completed by dipping the ware in a liquid lead glaze before a final firing in the oven to harden the glaze and produce an underglaze blue printed dinner plate ready for long hard wearing service.

5. View of a printing shop drawn by Harry Furniss in 1884

The Marketing of Blue and White Wares
by Robert Copeland

Many people have a narrow interpretation of the term 'marketing'. It is most often thought to refer only to the selling activities of advertising, publicity, merchandising and, of course, selling. But it embraces much more. In a nutshell, marketing is the meeting of the needs and wants of the market and providing the goods and services with pleasure to the consumer and profit to the provider.

With this in mind, let us consider the background to the market for blue and white ware. Ever since the late 17th century the East India Company had been importing teas from China, and Chinese porcelain teawares from which to enjoy drinking them. In the 18th century millions of pieces of Chinese blue and white porcelain entered Britain as well as Europe.

Why was blue and white so popular? Chinese porcelain is true porcelain, often called 'hard paste', and was fired to about 1400 degrees centigrade (2550 degrees Fahrenheit). The cobalt compound which yielded the blue colour was the only mineral which would withstand that high temperature and give an attractive colour. Unlike English blue and white decorations, the Chinese artists painted in blue direct onto the unfired clayware. When the painting was finished, a glaze was applied swiftly, the piece was dried thoroughly and then fired once only. These blue decorated wares were produced in Ching-tê-chên in Kiangsi Province. If on-glaze decorations were required, these would most likely have been applied by china painters in Canton where lower temperature kilns were allowed.

So Western Europe developed a taste for blue and white. The appearance of food was enhanced when presented on plates of blue and white, and this quality ensures its continued popularity to this day. The market, therefore, was conditioned to blue and white. The other side of marketing to selling is production. Marketing involves market research – what people want, or need – and then the production of those goods which the manufacturer hopes will meet those desires. Josiah Wedgwood was the finest example of the complete marketing man. The Josiah Spodes – father and son – weren't bad either!

Caughley, in Shropshire detected a desire for Chinese style patterns. Why was this so? The English East India Company directors were seeing a decline in the profits on the chinaware (their term for Chinese porcelain) which they imported. The wealthy classes in England were now entranced with the Palladian style of architecture – Georgian – with its tall windows, high ceilings and often Neo-classical plaster mouldings. Their furniture, too, which once was of heavy oak (which enhanced the appearance of blue and white) was changed to the fashionable mahogany and other fine-grained hardwoods imported from abroad.

Furniture design, led by Thomas Chippendale (1718–1779) and Thomas Sheraton (1751–1806) was now of more delicate proportions and demanded tablewares with more classical shapes and patterns, like those supplied by Wedgwood. Chinese blue and white porcelain services were often disposed of. However, there still were masses of people who had services of their own, or had acquired 'cast-offs', who needed replacements or extra pieces for expanding families. If the East India Company would not import them what were they to do? Turn to an English potter. So Caughley, who had retail premises in Lincoln's Inn Fields, London, was the first to oblige with matchings. But Caughley was making porcelain; this was not inexpensive. The market need was for a less expensive product – earthenware.

By the early 1780's, it seems, there may have been several potters in Staffordshire experimenting with a transfer printing process. There were already potters painting on biscuit earthenware in blue with naive 'House and Fence' style patterns as well as patterns with small flower sprays.

Early transferring media tended to be unsatisfactory, and it may have been Ralph Baddeley in Staffordshire who found the first secret of how to transfer successfully onto biscuit earthenware. It should be understood that the surface of biscuit earthenware is nothing like as fine as biscuit porcelain; rather it was pitted all over, which presented a difficulty in transferring all the image perfectly. It is believed that, in 1784, Josiah Spode discovered the complete answer by wetting the transfer paper with soft soap and water and rubbing the paper down very thoroughly. Why Spode? Because Josiah II was in London in 1778 and, listening to his customers' requests for replacements of Chinese blue and white porcelain, he urged his father to consider developing the process whereby such replacements could be supplied at reasonable cost. The two Spodes, especially Josiah II, were marketing men like the first Josiah Wedgwood. They discerned a need in the market and set out to satisfy it with great success. The first essays into transfer printed underglaze blue which they marked with the name SPODE were copies of Chinese landscape designs, coarsely engraved, transferred as well as possible, bearing in mind that with only a few copper plates the transferrer had to cut up the design to make the pattern fit a variety of objects. The cobalt blue, too, was impure, tending to be dark. Perhaps the coarse engraving contributed to this. Gradually, however, the engraving technique improved and the colour ingredients became purer. Soon Spode set the highest standard of draughtsmanship, skill of engraving and the luminous quality of the blue. Other potters followed his lead swiftly, amongst whom were

Rogers, Riley, Clews, Don Pottery, Minton, Davenport, Ridgway, Turner and eventually Wedgwood. There were many other manufacturers who, seeing the opportunities, began to adopt the process with varying degrees of quality and price.

The main growth in this market was around the turn of the century while Britain was at war with the French. Imports of Chinese porcelain by the East India Company ceased in 1799. Blue and white is the least expensive, durable and decorative tableware, and as the population of Britain increased it is understandable that the demand for such tableware increased in step. Spode's adaptation of a widely known Chinese design ('Mandarin') to create the 'Willow' pattern in about 1790 proved so popular that many potters copied it. It was so important a product that when manufacturers combined to try to regulate prices within the pottery industry, 'Willow' was one of the categories along with 'CC (Cream Colour), edged, dipt (sic) and painted', for which price scales were set.

But there were many Chinese designs on the market which Spode and the other potters copied, 'Two Temples variation Broseley' and 'Mandarin' being the most popular. Then there were interpretations of Chinese landscapes like 'Long Bridge' (Cat. Ref. Case 1/12), 'Chinoiserie Bridgeless', the 'Elephant' pattern, 'Forest Landscape', 'Lady with Parasol', and very many more. The market, or some parts of it, still wanted Chinese-style patterns. Some patterns were really exotic inventions, like 'Curling Palm' (Cat. Ref. Case 1/4).

Taste was bound to change eventually. The potters were better able to cater for this when the technique of engraving included the ability to provide tonal qualities by varying the texture by stipple punchwork and by varying the depth of cut. While Chinese landscapes scarcely needed these skills, English flowers, figures, landscapes and buildings certainly gained enormously from it.

Interest in the Grand Tour brought patterns like Spode's 'Tower', 'Italian', 'Lucano', 'Rome' and 'Castle', and several series of Italian scenery by Don Pottery, Meir, and Enoch Wood, for example, while the British interests in India encouraged potters to use printed sources of sporting and topographical scenes to decorate their tablewares.

Floral patterns of all sorts, and topographical subjects like Cathedrals, University Colleges, famous stately houses, all provided the market with a truly enormous choice to suit anyone's fancy and pocket. Some patterns became 'common property'; the patterns 'Wild Rose' (Cat. Ref. Case 23/18) and 'Asiatic Pheasants' being widely produced by potters in different centres of pottery manufacture.

Blue and white, being so durable, was used by many institutions like City Livery Companies and Regimental messes (Cat. Ref. Case 7/2). Unfortunately very little of these types of wares remain available for collectors today, mainly because much was damaged and thrown away when some new ware was adopted.

These wares often had a badge or armorial device in the centre of a pattern which had a standard border (Cat. Ref. Case 7/5), that is, the regular central flower or other feature was replaced by a crest; Spode's 'Geranium' is a good example.

The turn of the century saw not only the cessation of imports of Chinese porcelain, but also Britain deeply engaged in war with the French Republic. A duty of £47.10.0d per £100 worth of goods was imposed on imports. Despite this it seems that some low-priced French porcelain continued to be imported into England; although this would not have affected the Staffordshire earthenware trade in the 1790s, it apparently did injure the sales of the English porcelain manufactories like Derby and Worcester. This duty was increased in 1799 to £109.8.6d on the same volume of ware. The war caused the supply of European corn to be cut off, and the poor suffered dreadfully because of the tripling of its price. But the 'poor' had not yet become the potters' market – not for blue and white, at any rate. The landed gentry, however, had seldom been wealthier. It was this class who, at first, bought blue and white for everyday use, especially for tableware and toiletware, while porcelain or china was preferred for serving tea. The consumption of tea was an important factor. After the Commutation Act of 1784, by which the duty on tea was cut from 119% to 12½% ad valorem, the demand increased rapidly to the point where the population of North Staffordshire rose from about eight thousand in 1780 to about sixty thousand in 1840. This followed the increase in the consumption of tea from 8 million pounds weight in 1780 to 50 million pounds weight in 1840. All this increase in population was not just in pottery workers, but coal miners, foundry workers, potters' millers were all needed to sustain the increased demand for pottery of all kinds. In fact, pottery workers rose to 24,724 in 1841, two fifths of the population of the district.

Unfortunately, I do not know of any studies of the wholesale and retail trade in pottery and glass in the United Kingdom. In Britain, almost all research has been into the potters and their products. The names of a few retail shops are known, but the framework of distribution in the 18th and 19th centuries remains to be researched.

Communications had an impact upon distribution. Until the development of the canal system in the late 1700s and early decades of the 1800s, most earthenwares were manufactured in areas inland from ports so needed to be transported overland in horsedrawn wagons. Between 1757 and 1790 sixteen hundred Road Acts were passed in Parliament. As turnpikes and other roads improved and more canals were navigated, so towns grew in size, and some developed into major centres of affluent population, like Bath, Chester, Norwich, York and many more. Also, centres of manufacturing like Manchester, Birmingham and Liverpool developed city centres with better than average retail shops for the wealthy mill and manufactory owners and their families. English earthenware replaced pewter, and blue and white earthenware steadily dominated the market, especially after about 1800.

The better retailers often demanded that a pattern which they held in stock should be exclusive or 'reserved', to them for the trading area which they served. This resulted in a manufacturer having to produce a large range of patterns, which led to a larger and more fragmented production than was really economically sensible. This was so that six, say, retailers in a major town each could have at least one reserved pattern. Indeed, there was over-production in the pottery industry during the first half of the 19th century and this led to ferocious competition and price-cutting. This, of course, resulted in bankruptcies, and corner-cutting and lowering of quality.

With limited communications the manufacturer would rely on two principal methods of selling: firstly his own salesman visiting the important towns, travelling either by coach with his bags of samples, or on horseback to the more remote locations, or secondly from a local wholesaler from whom the smaller retailer, general store and market trader probably obtained their supplies and from whom they could withdraw smaller quantities to suit their needs. Naturally a higher price would have had to be paid, but the capital tied up was the burden of the wholesaler, who had to charge for the service.

In later years, when the railway network was established, the principle of stockrooms was adopted by the big manufacturers. Certain hotels in large towns and cities set aside large rooms in which the manufacturer or importer could display his wares on tables covered with white table-cloths. The retailers were invited in to inspect the wares and to place their orders; the best customer being invited in first so that he could pick what he thought to be the best of the 'new lines'. This pattern would be put below the table hidden by the table-cloth and the display adjusted to fill the gap! The other retailers would come in order of importance – or hoped-for importance – and make their selection. After the 1939–1945 war and when decorated ware was permitted to be offered on the United Kingdom market, stockrooms gradually were superseded by trade fairs, notably the one held at Blackpool, the Gifts and Fancy Goods Fair. There were also sales by auction. The porcelain houses used this method, and the sales' records provide useful information on the wares and the prices attained. Certainly, Charles James Mason used this method, and in doing so, incurred the extreme displeasure of his retail shop customers in the towns where he conducted auctions, because the prices often undercut those of the shops. It seems less likely that blue and white earthenwares were sold in this manner because the prices were too low to interest the auctioneer, for the amount of merchandise would be great but of relatively low value.

Collectors of blue and white tend to concentrate on wares made for the domestic market, and mainly tablewares. The probable reason is that wares made for other markets are extremely rare today, and toilet and medical ceramics are none too plentiful. But these goods were made in boatloads and supplied to hospitals (Cat. Ref. Case 27/12), railway companies, shipping lines (through ships' victuallers like Stonier's of Liverpool and Southampton), hotels, tea rooms and restaurants as well as institutions of all sorts. Mostly these wares were lightly decorated with a simple bead, perhaps a line, and a ribbon with the name of the establishment. An interesting study could be made of manufacturers' records, but most institutional ware today carries no applied decoration, let alone blue printed ones. One reason for the scarcity of this type of ware is that it does not look good in a display with so much undecorated surface – and most of the ware were plates and dishes (platters).

The North American market was enormously important to British manufacturers of pottery, especially transfer printed earthenwares. While Copeland and Garrett, and Copeland, supplied large quantities of printed earthenwares to the Hudson's Bay Company, many potters shipped earthenwares to the United States. After the European market for English pottery collapsed during the wars with France it was replaced by the American market. 'The United States was the largest customer every year between the end of the War of 1812 and the eve of the Civil War (1860), generally purchasing between 40 and 50 percent of the ware exported from Staffordshire.' (From J. Potter *Atlantic Economy, 1815–1860* quoted by George L. Miller in *Marketing Ceramics in North America – An Introduction*.) Three major Staffordshire potters, Enoch Wood, William Adams, and Thomas Mayer even used marks on their ware that incorporated the American eagle! (see Appendix B). And these and many other potters produced patterns specifically aimed at the American market: scenes depicting American places and views, heroes, historical events and military battles – even victories over the British! Apart from these wares made especially with American subject matter, other designs were named appropriately in the belief that the name would help to attract custom. Indeed, it may have done! 'Columbia' was a popular name for romantic scenes, and my favourite is a chinoiserie design by Enoch Wood and Sons which was named 'Detroit'!

For reasons unknown to me, after about 1840 the flood of flow blue patterns seems to have been prodigious, judging from the popularity of that class among collectors in the United States in the 1990's. Most flow blue patterns must have been cheap, or at least not expensive, low in both price and quality. Could its popularity have started when inferior ware was dumped on the American market in large quantities, and this might have led to a demand for more? Certainly America was used as a dumping ground for pottery that was either not up to standard or had gone out of fashion.

In the early years, pottery was sold to importers, but later some manufacturers visited America to sell their wares. Most employed agents or sold direct to those retailers who had buying agents in Britain or who sent over their own buyers. The East Coast market was well established and quite good quality merchandise was sold there, but the expanding inland markets could only afford the most inexpensive goods for many years.

In the United States the other main player in the early 1800's was China, who after the War of Independence, began to supply porcelain direct to American merchants. Later a hand painted adaptation of a Chinese landscape, called 'Canton', competed with English blue and white. This version of the 'Willow' pattern was very cheap, but undercut Staffordshire severely.

Blue and white faced growing competition from other underglaze colours. In about 1824, chrome green became a stable underglaze colour, and in about 1831 chrome-tin pink was possible underglaze. The many other colours – mauve, brown, various hues of green, grey, cranberry or mulberry, and quite pale blue – became more in demand. Mulberry and brown were especially liked in the United States.

Finally, a special category of blue and white is that known as 'Historic China', or 'American Views on British Pottery', which sold in the United States. Unlike the earlier American subjects these were printed in a very dark royal blue, and were manufactured by just a few British potters to capture the market. In the 19th and 20th centuries there grew up many firms of potters in the United States; most of them manufactured blue transfer printed wares, about fifty making the 'Willow' pattern.

Sources of Design – Introduction

by Judith Busby

The primary source of designs for the potters venturing into the new popular market were the Chinese ceramics which had been a major import into England for many years. The blue and white ware of the English potters of the late 18th and early 19th centuries was largely decorated with copies and variations of the Chinese patterns on these imported goods, but also with the European interpretations of them. Having exhausted the Chinese theme the potters turned their attention to other possibilities – what could they use next? We, who are so familiar with photography tend to forget that in the period under discussion there was a wealth of existing printed illustrative material – woodcuts, line engravings and etchings. These were used in two ways – to copy paintings and drawings and to produce original work, which, in their view, would be a commercial success.

There was indeed a multitude of subjects from which to choose. The spirit of the age was one of exploration in many fields, one of which being travelling, both in England and further afield, to admire the grandeur and romance of nature and architecture. The Grand Tour was the culmination of any gentleman's education and took the travellers through France and Switzerland, down to the toe of Italy and across the sea to Sicily. Some ventured further to the Middle East, India and China. There was also exploration in America and to the frozen wastes of the Arctic. The result of all this activity was a continual flow of drawings, sketches and, in some cases, illustrated books, all presenting possible source material.

Another fruitful source was the many representations of rural life and pursuits. Among them were hunting, shooting and fishing, hay-making, milking, gleaning, hop-picking, tending the sheep and moving the bee-hives. The lame traveller was offered food and the blind boy cared for; as a group these scenes present an idyllic picture of rural life, although actuality may not have been so rosy.

Scenic patterns aside, there still remained natural history, literature and historic events. There was a wide interest in botany in the early 19th century and the use of flower patterns suitable for transfer printing was a natural progression from the floral painting on porcelain. Instead of small sprays of flowers and single blooms, the flowers were arranged in fairly loose bunches so that the design covered as large an area as possible, and sometimes an all-over pattern was created. The foundation of the Royal Horticultural Society in 1804 had a marked influence on this fashion, which was possibly not unconnected with the fact that Josiah Wedgwood's eldest son, John, was a founder member and the first treasurer.

As a source for animals and birds two books, amongst others, were used extensively, one on 'Quadrupeds' and the other on 'British Birds', by Thomas Bewick both of which had been published in the last decade of the 18th century. Another interesting series entitled 'Zoological Gardens' was based on the London Zoo which had opened in 1829.

In addition to these there were many more subjects on which the potters could draw. One pottery produced a whole dinner service illustrated with scenes from British history and another chose scenes from the literary works of Sir Walter Scott. Yet another factory issued a splendid series of ships and naval battles, with a particularly inspired border. City Livery companies ordered crockery decorated with the appropriate coats of arms and the armed services ordered ware for their messes (Cat. Ref Case 7/2).

Events merited commemoration – the death of George III in 1820 probably inspired a particularly attractive pattern with a plough and other agricultural implements, alluding to his popular nickname 'Farmer George'. Feats of engineering were recognised in a series entitled 'Railway' and another called 'Bridges', while the Crystal Palace, erected for the Great Exhibition of 1851, duly appeared on pieces from more than one factory.

Ecclesiastes tells us that; 'of making many books there is no end'; he would have undoubtedly said the same about blue and white patterns!

Sources of Design – British and European Patterns

by John Potter (Keeper of Records)

During the first decade of the 19th century the fashion for transfer printed earthenware as a substitute for the more expensive porcelains caused a market explosion of which the earthenware manufacturers of Staffordshire and other, smaller centres were able to take full advantage. The day of the full Chinoiserie design was coming to an end and influences from closer to home were rapidly taking over. This shift owed a good deal to the fact that the 'Grand Tour' of Europe was still in fashion for those who could afford it, while those who could not were being catered for by having the tour brought to them here at home in England through the medium of many volumes of topographical prints, usually engraved from drawings done on site and often with the long and ponderous names which we associate with the end of the 18th century.

This was nothing new, for as early as 1707 there had been published *Britannia Illustrata, or Views of several of the Queen's Palaces also of the Principal Seats of the Nobility and Gentry of Great Britain*, a volume of eighty views drawn by Leonard Knyff and engraved by Jan Kip. Although it had no relevance to blue and white earthenware, mention should also be made of the mammoth work of Josiah Wedgwood in gathering prints, drawings or camera obscura representations of over twelve hundred different landscape pictures to be processed by his draughtsmen for the Frog Service in 1773–1774.

Quite obviously the Staffordshire manufacturers had a great deal of luck in finding the sudden huge demand for their wares coinciding with a vast supply of design sources, thus enabling them to offer interesting and striking patterns which would have been costly and time-consuming to have produced from scratch. The main element of this luck was of course that until 1842 no copyright law existed to prevent them from descending like vultures on these volumes of topographical engravings and copying them shamelessly, frequently in exact detail. The ready availability of this material encouraged the production of a large series of related designs, sometimes extending to over sixty different patterns and usually linked by a common border, for example the 'Grapevine Border' series produced by Enoch Wood. (Plate I).

For some reason collectors did not appreciate until quite recently the fact that here was a most interesting and rewarding sideline to a mainstream collection – the identification of source prints, and even their acquisition and display together with the appropriate pattern on earthenware. Now there is an increasing body of research on this subject and a great deal appears in the two volumes of the Coysh and Henrywood *Dictionary of Blue and White Printed Pottery* – the 'Bible' of the blue and white collector. In this important work appear two appendices listing sources known to have been used for transfer printed wares, and there are also examples of copies of well known paintings, either direct or through engravings of them. This article is largely a cull from the mass of information contained in the *Dictionary*, but a much fuller understanding of the subject will certainly be gained by consulting the original.

Among the earliest identified examples of sources is Grose's *The Antiquities of England and Wales*, first published around 1773. This is known to have been used for the Minton 'Miniature' series (Cat. Ref. Case 17/26 & 17/28), together with Cooke's *Views on the Thames*, and *The Beauties of England and Wales* as well as Storer and Greig's *The Antiquarian and Topographical Cabinet* published between 1807 and 1811. The latter work also turns up as the source of a pattern in the 'Belle Vue Views' series made by the Belle Vue Pottery in Hull. In 1797 came a large work which was used, probably exclusively, by John Ridgway for the 'Angus Seats' series, (Cat. Ref. Case Kitchen/9 & 38 and 25/1); the publication certainly ranks high in the long names category with *Seats of the Nobility and Gentry in Great Britain and Wales in a collection of Select Views engraved by W. Angus from Pictures and Drawings by the most Eminent Artists with descriptions of each View*.

The Beauties of England and Wales, or Delineations Topographical, Historical and Descriptive, by John Britton and Edward Brayley, appeared between 1801 and 1808 and was later copied by Pountney and Allies of Bristol for some of the scenes in their 'Bristol Views' series (Cat. Ref. Case 26/1 & 2), while a maker still unidentified with certainty drew for the 'Antique Scenery' series on both W. Marshall's *Select Views in Great Britain*, of which Part II was issued in 1825, and *The Antiquities of Great Britain, illustrated in Views of Monasteries, Castles and Churches now existing*, engraved by W. Byrne from drawings by Thomas Hearne and published in 1807. The Marshall book was also used for the 'Pineapple Border' series, now attributed to John Meir (Cat. Ref. Kitchen/21).

Perhaps one of the largest of these topographical works was *Views of the Seats of Noblemen and Gentlemen in England and Wales, Scotland and Ireland*, engraved by John Preston Neale and issued in eleven volumes between 1818 and 1829. Prints from this publication appear on J. & R. Riley's 'Large Scroll Border' series (Cat. Ref. Case 25/12) and on other wares produced by J. & R. Clews, the Elkin Partnerships, William Adams and Ralph Stevenson.

Among the many other volumes of prints published were some whose scope was rather narrower, which was reflected in their use by the earthenware producers. John Britton's 1828 *Picturesque Views of the English Cities* formed the basis of Enoch Wood's 'English Cities' series, and *Metroplitan Improvements, or London in the Nineteenth Century*, published in 1827 from drawings by Thomas Shepherd, was used on Enoch Wood's 'London Views' (Cat. Ref. Case 35/3), the 'Regents Park' series from the Adams' factory (Cat. Ref. Case Kitchen/30, 26/4, 35/2 & 3), and also the 'Flower Medallion Border' series by an unknown maker. A view from *Lancashire Illustrated*, engraved by E. Wallis from drawings by T. Harwood, appears among Herculaneum's 'Liverpool Views', and the T. & J. Carey series of 'Titled Seats' seems to stem in part from Jones & Company's *Views of the Seats, Mansions, Castles etc. of Noblemen and Gentlemen in Scotland* of 1827 (Cat. Ref. Case 25/8, 9 & 10). Also in Scotland, R.A. Kidston & Co used *Twenty Views of the City and Environs of Edinburgh drawn by T.H. Baynes* (1823) in their 'United Kingdom' series and John Meir & Son turned to William Beattie's *Scotland; Illustrated in a Series of Views Taken Expressly for this Work by Messrs Allen, W.H. Bartlett and H. McCulloch* (1838) for their 'Northern Scenery' series. The list, if not endless, is still far from complete, taking in regional works covering Wales, East Anglia and specific rivers like the Thames and the Clyde.

Among the individual landscape views printed on earthenware, some have been identified as copies of original works of art. The 'Beemaster' pattern (Cat. Ref. Case 6/1, 5 & 6), well known but by an unidentified maker, is taken from a painting by George Robertson (1742–1788) entitled 'Swarm of Bees, Autumn' which now hangs in the Cecil Higgins Art Gallery in Bedford. Spode's 'Bridge of Lucano' comes from an undated print, 'The Tomb of Plautius Lucanus,' engraved by A.H. Payne after a painting by H. Bibby, and the 'Castle' pattern made by Spode and others comes from 18th century aquatints by Merigot (Cat. Ref. Case 16/5 and 27/4). The source of Spode's 'Italian' pattern (Cat. Ref. Case 22/8 and 37/4A), remained a mystery for many years but in 1989 an unidentified drawing, which was obviously the origin of the design, turned up and was purchased for the Spode Museum.

Perhaps some of the most striking of the classical landscape patterns are those based on the paintings of Claude Lorraine. These include 'Europa' (J. & R. Riley, Cat. Ref. Case 33/3), 'Scene after Claude Lorraine' (Leeds Pottery and also J. & R. Riley), 'Ponte Molle' (maker unknown) and, probably best of all, Wedgwood's 'Blue Claude', engraved by Thomas Sparkes in about 1822.

The William Adams' 'Lions' was taken from a print in the 1807 publication *The Cyclopaedia of Arts, Sciences and Literature* (Cat. Ref. Case 21/5), and 'Going to Market', from the J. & M. P. Bell factory, came from an engraving by William Finden of 'Returning from Market', after a painting by A.W. Callcott.

J. & R. Clews issued a series named 'Wilkie's Designs,' based on paintings of family scenes by Sir David Wilkie, while the woodcuts of Thomas Bewick were also in great demand, mainly for the birds and animals. Even the small end scenes in Bewick's books were used, for instance the 'Kite-flying' pattern was taken directly from the tailpiece to the *History of British Birds*. In the Goodwins and Harris series known as 'Metropolitan Scenery' there is a particularly interesting pattern showing a cricket match with Windsor Castle in the background, taken from a print in the *Sporting Magazine* of 1793. Perhaps most unusual of all is the 'Diorama' series, by an unknown maker, which was based on panorama pictures shown in London in the early 19th century by Daguerre and Boulton.

The literary scene, past and current, afforded another design stream which, judging by the number of series produced, must have been quite popular. Even the Holy Bible was used, with Thomas Mayer's 'Illustrations of the Bible' apparently coming from William Finden's *Landscape Illustrations of the Bible* (1830) and other similar sources. Finden's *Landscape and Portrait Illustrations to the Life and Works of Lord Byron* was also copied extensively for the Copeland and Garrett series of 'Byron Views' (Cat. Ref. Case 22/15 and 33/12). The popularity (or perhaps notoriety) of Byron is also evidenced by two other series of patterns on earthenwares, both entitled 'Byron Gallery' and depicting scenes from the poet's works, and a further series of 'Byron's Illustrations', by John Meir & Son from the Finden source. *The Seasons* by the poet Francis Thomson, one of the most illustrated poems in English literature, found its way onto earthenware in the 'Thomson's Seasons' series made possibly by Samuel Alcock. Scenes from a variety of plays were used by J. & G. Rogers in their 'Drama' series (Cat. Ref. Case Kitchen/23), copied later by Pountney and Golding, a possible source for these being a lengthy series of paintings done between 1789 and 1800 by William Hamilton and Robert Smirke. *Don Quixote* was another very popular subject and a series was produced by Brameld (Rockingham) and possibly by J. & R. Clews.

Aesop's *Fables* spawned various ceramic designs, from early porcelain onwards (Cat. Ref. Case 33/2). Spode produced a lengthy series probably based on Samuel Croxall's *Fables of Aesop* (1793) and Minton used the Samuel Howitt engravings of *Fables of Aesop and Phaedras* on tiles. Contemporary satire featured in the 'Dr. Syntax' series produced by J & R Clews in the 1820's and reissued in this century by the Adams' factory; this was based on Thomas Rowlandson drawings in the *Poetical Magazine* around 1810. Other books and authors were featured in series based on the works of Charles Dickens and Sir Walter Scott. Even a children's book found its way onto ceramics, Mary Elliott's 1820's version of *The Progress of a Quartern Loaf* (Cat. Ref. Case 33/5).

The variety available for the adornment of the Englishman's table in the early part of the 19th century even included Greek and Etruscan patterns taken mainly from the catalogue of the Sir William Hamilton collection of antiquities, by d' Hancarville, and botanical designs (especially by Wedgwood) from magazines such as *The Botanical Magazine*, started by William Curtis in

1787, and *The Botanical Repository* of 1804.

For those people who perhaps liked to be a bit different (or maybe create an impression), series based on European landscapes were available – the 'French Series'(Cat. Ref. Case 16/10) and 'Italian Scenery' by Enoch Wood (the latter title also being used by John Meir & Son), 'Polish Views' from E. & G. Phillips and (later and somewhat idealised) – Ralph Hall's 'Italian Buildings'. Probably the largest and best-known European series was 'Named Italian Views' (Cat. Ref. Case 11/3, 14 & 15; 16/6, 9 & 11), produced originally by the Don Pottery and later by Joseph Twigg, of Swinton in Yorkshire, who bought the copper plates when the Don works closed down. The source for this was a well-known French topographical publication by L' Abbé de St Non, entitled *Voyage Pittoresque ou Description des Royaumes de Naples et de Sicile*, published in the 1780's. Even the Spode pattern known generally as 'The Tiber', but actually named as 'Rome' in the factory pattern book has been tracked down, to *Views and Ruins in Rome and its Vicinity* (1797–1798) by J Merigot.

This is of necessity a factual list, but hopefully it will serve to illustrate something of the background to the remarkable variety of design which went into the blue and white earthenware market up to the 1840's, and to show how the opportunist manufacturers of the day were quick to take advantage of prevailing trends and fashions. In 1842, with the introduction of copyright, all this changed and the change was quickly reflected in a dramatic reduction in the artistic standards of subsequent patterns. All new designs then had to be drawn from the imagination, a creative task which was mostly beyond the capabilities of even the skilled engraver, and the public was treated to an interminable deluge of romantic patterns frequently with strong Swiss scenic overtones. At this point the source print became a thing of the past, but the legacy of those previous forty years remains to give an idea of how splendid (not to mention educational) a full blue and white dinner service of the 1820's must have looked.

Sources of Design – Oriental and Middle Eastern Patterns

by Laurie Fuller (Editor of Bulletin)

The early years of the 19th century saw a fundamental change in the sources chosen by the potters for decorating their wares. Gone, for the most part by 1805, were the copies of the Chinese export patterns and the English variations in the same stylised manner, and the manufacturers now began to look for more naturalistic sources such as the volumes of prints and aquatints which were then being published, presenting to the public, views of far-away places recently visited by travellers, explorers, and the draughtsmen they took with them to record their journeys.

Such a publication was Luigi Mayer's *Views in Egypt, Palestine and the Ottoman Empire* which were mainly in Caramania, originally published in three volumes, in 1801, 1803 and 1804. The second volume, *Views in the Ottoman Empire. Chiefly in Caramania*, was to provide the scenes for perhaps the most famous and, arguably, the earliest of all the multi-print table services ever produced with under-glaze transfer printed decoration. Josiah Spode II's 'Caramanian' series (Cat. Ref. Case 15/13) dates to about 1809 and comprises at least twenty-one different patterns, each of which was used to decorate a particular size of dish, shape of tureen or other items in the service, sometimes more than one, (Cat. Ref. Case 15/11 & 12).

The region then known as Caramania now forms part of south-west Turkey, and the towns Boudron, Macri, Castel Rosso and Cacamo, the sites in Caramania of most of the scenes used on the Spode service, were all to be found around the south-western seaboard. The names of the scenes are not stamped on the wares, however, an early identification of many of them by the source print names was described and published by S.B. Williams in *Antique Blue and White Spode* (1943). Thus we have, for example, 'Ancient Granary at Cacamo', 'The Harbour at Macri' and 'The Castle of Boudron'. The Caramanian table service was obviously viewed as a special production by Spode. For the dishes, an oval shape was chosen, having a rim edge with four pairs of widely spaced indentations. The plates were also distinctive, having six pairs of indentations to the rim. The transferrers were prevailed upon to take pains to set the patterns straight on the plates so that, when placed around a table, the distinctive outline of each plate would be similarly placed.

The choice of Mayer's prints had been inspired. The scenes were not only intriguing views of far-off parts, but were full of life as well. Wherever possible the engravers for Spode retained all the people present on the source. In some cases, they brought together bits taken from more than one source print to form a composite scene which they found satisfying. And they often added trees, usually in order to cover up areas which would otherwise have remained white and undecorated, particularly areas of sky.

The border pattern, which is common to all the scenes in the Caramanian table service, was not, however, taken from the same source as the central patterns. It is a repeat strip scene border made up from bits taken from two or more prints in Thomas Williamson's *Oriental Field Sports, Wild Sports of the East* (1807). It is possible that the 'Caramanian' series did not remain in production long, certainly the unusual oval shapes and double indentations were replaced at some stage by the more normal eight-sided (oblong) shape dishes and normally indented plates. This may have coincided with the introduction of another Spode multi-print table service based on the *Oriental Field Sports'* prints mentioned above. The 'Indian Sporting' series, as it was called (Cat. Ref. Case 14), may have been introduced within a year of the Caramanian.

October 4th, 1811 saw the introduction by Wedgwood, of a table service decorated with a view of the tomb of Absalom at Petra. The source for this pattern is also to be found in Mayer. The tomb itself comes from a print in Volume III, 'Views in Palestine', and is titled 'The Sepulchre of Absalom'. The background has its source in the print 'City of Corinth' in Volume II, while parts taken from four more engravings can be found in the figures and stone columns. The border pattern is of crocuses. Interestingly, despite the probably erroneous title by which the pattern is now known, 'Absalom's Pillar', it was known as 'Blue Corinth' when first introduced at the factory. This was to be Wedgwood's only excursion to exotic parts for the next ten years but the fascination with such places was continued by the Herculaneum Pottery at Liverpool, where a group of five patterns known as the 'India Series' was introduced in about 1815. These patterns showed views in Northern India and, again, had their source in published aquatints, in this case in a work of six volumes called *Oriental Scenery*, published by Thomas & William Daniell, uncle and nephew, between 1795 and 1808 as a record of the ten years they had spent travelling in India.

The pattern names are not stamped on the wares, but are identified by the source print names, from *Oriental Scenery*:

'The Chalees Satoon in the Fort of Allahabad on the River Jumna' (Volume I, No. 6)
'Mausoleum of Sultan Purveis near Allahabad' (Volume I, No. 22)
'View in the Fort, Madura' (Volume II, No. 14)
'Gate of a Mosque built by Hafiz Ramut, Pillibeat' (Volume III, No. 10)
'Mausoleum of Nawaub Assoph Khan, Rajmahal' (Volume III, No. 24)

According to Michael Archer (1980), this last print is probably wrongly named. It is probably not the tomb of Assoph Khan but of his brother, Ibrahim Khan. It is possible that two of the patterns, 'View in the Fort, Madura' and 'Mausoleum of Sultan Purveiz, near Allahabad', may also have been produced by William Walsh, who was potting at Burslem at this time.

The scenes chosen show the grandeur of Indian Palaces and tombs and each portrays a striking building taken from a Daniell aquatint, but all contain added details taken from other aquatints in the series. One of these details, the hilltop fort of Tritchinopoly, is common to all five patterns in the group, appearing as part of the backdrop to each view and rising, as it does, to cover otherwise undecorated areas of sky. In addition, all the patterns include figures and animals, often also taken from several different prints. Each design has its own individual border. Two are floral, one is of leaves, one has a border consisting of the foliage of framing trees on either side of the scene, and the fifth is of sea shells and small Indian scenes. These magnificent views are seen to best advantage on Herculaneum's unusually broad meat dishes (Cat. Ref. Case Kitchen 28), and a complete table service decorated with any one of them would have lent an almost overpowering richness to a middle-class Regency dining room.

The Daniell publications were not only taken up by Herculaneum. At much the same time, in Staffordshire, John Rogers & Son made use of three of the Daniell scenes, plus details from others. The main building on the Rogers' pattern known as 'Camel' (Cat. Ref. Case 15/10) was subsequently shown to have come from a Daniell aquatint entitled 'Gate leading to a Musjed, at Chunar Ghur'. Other elements, including the camel, had come, in reverse, from another Daniell source. The 'Camel' pattern was also used by Dixon Austin & Co at Sunderland and at the Leeds Pottery, where the camel had been turned round again and moved to the left of the Gate!

The building on Rogers' 'Musketeer' pattern also appears to have been adapted from the Daniell source, 'View in the Fort, Madura', with additions and alterations from elsewhere and, in the background again, Tritchinopoly.

Rogers' 'Monopteros' pattern (Cat. Ref. Case Techniques 1) is a faithful copy of the Daniell aquatint 'Remains of an Ancient Building near Firoz Shah's Cotilla, Delhi', the only additions being the trees to either side which spread around and over the top of the design to frame the buildings. The tree on the left appears to owe its origin to another Daniell source, 'The Sacred Tree of the Hindoos at Gyah Bahar'. Framing trees are common to all three of the Rogers' patterns, replacing the normal border, which is reduced to a narrow band hugging the edge of the rim. Another version of 'Monopteros' was produced at the Swansea Cambrian Pottery in about 1821 (Cat. Ref. Case 17/25 & 12/13). The view is from a slightly different angle and may, therefore, have had a different source.

The Staffordshire firm of John & Richard Riley also produced a table service using Daniell aquatints. The Riley pattern 'Eastern Street Scene' (Cat. Ref. Case 3/9) takes the tree on the left from 'The Sacred Tree of the Hindoos . . .' mentioned above, and the main central building from 'View on the Chitpore Road, Calcutta.' The tree again spreads its branches over the sky, but the Rileys also gave the pattern a full width border of Sweet Williams and Orchids.

A Daniell aquatint, 'Near Currah on the River Ganges', seems to have been the source for a marked Leeds Pottery pattern and also for a similar fanciful unmarked version with a different border, which may also be Leeds. Yet another Daniell print, 'An Ancient Hindoo Temple in the Fort of Rotas Bahar', is found on an unmarked soup plate with a border of flowers and scrolls totally different from any other bearing these prints. Finally, a plate marked 'Asiatic Scenery' in a printed cartouche which includes the maker's name J. HARDING actually bears a pattern whose source is also in Daniell, 'Gate of the Tomb of the Emperor Akbar at Secundra, near Agra.' This is a later use of an Indian scene, since Harding potted at Navigation Road, Burslem from about 1850–1851.

About 1820, a multi-print table service dubbed the 'Ottoman Empire' series was produced, most probably by John and William Ridgway, although no marked pieces have been found. Items do, however, for the most part bear a printed cartouche with the pattern title, and the source for nearly all the sixteen patterns recorded is a publication of 1810, *Views in the Ottoman Dominions, in Europe, in Asia and some of the Mediterranean Islands, from the Original Drawings taken for Sir Robert Ainslie by Luigi Mayer*. The scenes range from the magnificent 'Mosque of Sultan Achmet in Istanbul' to a view simply titled 'Near Bucharest.' There are three scenes involving the port of 'Latachia' on the Mediterranean seaboard of Syria, looking across at the northern tip of Cyprus (Cat. Ref. Case 15/4), and others may be around the Bulgarian and Romanian Black Sea seaboard. Remarkably, a small tureen in this series carries, in reverse, a print from Mayer's 'Views in Caramania', the view being 'A Colossal Sarcophagus at Cacamo in Caramania'. The 'Ottoman Empire' series sports a distinctive border of flowers and scrolls interspersed with incense-burners. This major series is almost certainly a J. & W. Ridgway product.

On 1 July 1824 a series of aquatints was published in a volume entitled *A Picturesque Tour along the Rivers Ganges and Jumna in India*. It was written by Lt. Col. C.R. Forrest, late of His Majesty's Service in India. The aquatints were engraved by G. Hunt and T. Sutherland. The publication of these aquatints soon found them appearing as decoration on items in at least four more multi-print table services. Two of the series of prints are titled 'Oriental Scenery'. Both use the same printed cartouche mark, but one also bears the maker's name, I. HALL & SON, below the cartouche. Despite the odd fact that both series use the same cartouche and some views appear in both series, the style of engraving makes it obvious that they are in fact different and most probably made by two different manufacturers, one known and the other not. These are both extensive table services and run to at least sixteen different views. Most of the patterns in the unmarked service have their source in the Forrest aquatints, possibly all can be attributed to Forrest. Fewer of the John Hall series have, so far, been linked to their source but those that have, also seem to come from the same source.

A third series, dubbed 'Indian Scenery', was used on a table service by T. & B. Godwin (Cat. Ref. Case 15/8) and some much later examples, from the 1860's, are found marked C.E. & M, for Cork, Edge & Malkin. Ten of the patterns in this series have so far been identified but fewer than half linked for certain to their source prints. Forrest, however, features again and we owe a debt to Patrick Latham for his work on the sources. Apart from Forrest, he found a further source in *Travels in India* (1786) by William Hodges, which provides at least one source print in the 'Parrot Border' table service. This 'Parrot Border' (or 'Pecking Parrot') series' table service is the fourth multi-print service to have been identified from about 1825 with views in India and, as its name suggests, all the prints used on the wares share the same border of fruit, berries and roses interspersed with perching parrots about to peck at some fruit below their right wing. It is a most distinctive border. Eleven titles are known of which four have their source in Forrest, one in Daniell and one in Hodge. The pattern titles appear on the wares in a printed rock cartouche.

Between about 1825 and 1830, table services printed with English views dominated the market, and with such interest in things close to home, the Eastern sources were laid aside.

Sources of Design – North American Patterns
by Elizabeth Collard

It is just a little over a hundred years ago that American collectors began taking an interest in 19th century British earthenware transfer printed with North American scenes. At that time the earliest of these wares were scarcely half a century old.

Among the first to relate identifiable views to the history of a developing country was the fictional (or semi-fictional) 'Mr. Whitney'. In 1878 'the youngest member of the China Hunters Club' (Annie Trumbull Slosson) was writing; 'one of our members, Mr. Whitney, entered the club only when he found that ceramic art had some connection with American history.' It was American collectors who began calling this ware 'historical china'.

Canadian interest came later. Early in the present century David Ross McCord of Montreal, an indefatigable collector of Canadiana, was considering this ceramic ware important enough to merit at least some place in the vast collection he gave to McGill University in 1919. His Canadiana formed the basis of what is now the McCord Museum of Canadian History.

Recognising a scene as North American was the initial step; the search for the sources of the views used by potters came next. The sources were published engravings, whether found as illustrations in travel books or published as sets of engravings (or a single engraving) issued apart from books. The engravings were after drawings, water-colours or paintings, but the engravings were far more likely to have been the potters' source material. For the maker of printed earthenware engraving was a medium closer to his own, and engravings were more easily accessible to the potter than an original work of art.

Not all sources for recorded North American ceramic views have been traced. Much remains for the collector to discover, and there is not, nor can be a 'definitive' list of these views. Hitherto unrecorded ones turn up unexpectedly, including a 'View of Montreal' found in 1981. The view was related but not identical to another ceramic view known to collectors since at least the 1890's, Davenport's 'Montreal', listed by E.A. Barber in *Anglo-American Pottery* in 1899. Both the new view and the Davenport one were taken from an engraving entitled 'View of Montreal from St Helens Island,' one of a set of six views of Montreal after water-colours by the Irish artist Robert Sproule. Advertised in the *Montreal Gazette* at the end of 1829 they were readily available by 1830.

The Davenport view may be used as a typical example of problems that confront the researcher when trying to ascertain the potters' sources for North American scenes. Though clearly based on the published engraving, it departed from the engraving in a significant point. A steamboat in the river between Montreal and the island, unidentified in both the original water-colour and in the engraving copied from

it was given a name 'British America'. Why did the pottery engraver choose the 'British America' and where did he get his information? No engraving or water-colour of the 'British America' has been found that would supply the answer. Whenever this type of puzzle arises (and it frequently does) there is always the temptation to resort to speculation. Purely speculative is the suggestion that the answer may lie in the publisher of the set of engravings, Staffordshire-born Adolphus Bourne who had settled in Montreal in the 1820's. He was known to be on business in London in 1832; did he, perhaps, visit relations in Staffordshire at that time and furnish a pottery engraver with the information?

The Montreal View discovered in 1981 was not just a copy of Davenport. It had features not present in Davenport's 'Montreal' and was closer in a number of details to the published engraving. There was, however, a readily perceptible link between the two. Both added a canoe taken from another of the six engravings published in 1830. This type of interpolation often occurs in North American ceramic views. Highly unsuitable borders occasionally appeared with these views. The unidentified potter's 'View of Montreal' had a border of vignettes of tropical palm trees, a strange surround to a view of a city where ice and snow are normal weather conditions for six months of the year. In this particular case the border is explained by the fact that the Montreal view was part of a multi-scene series that included West Indian scenes.

Known sources for most (but not all) North American views belong to the first half of the 19th century. It was a period when the United States and Canada were regarded as lands of opportunity. Transatlantic travel conditions improved, immigrants, topographical artists, and tourists (Charles Dickens among them) came across the ocean in rapidly increasing numbers. Illustrated travel books proliferated, their illustrators hailing from Great Britain, Europe and North America itself.

Potters had a wide choice when they went looking for geography for the dinner table. In a single service of ceramic views a potter might draw upon a surprising variety of sources. Enoch Wood, who strenuously cultivated the American market (bigger and more lucrative than the Canadian) provides a typical example. In the 1930's, and later, Ellouise Baker Larsen made an extensive study of potters' source materials for North American views, including Wood's shell-bordered series marked with an American eagle and the United States motto, 'E PLURIBUS UNUM' ('one out of many'). Much of her material stands, though new research has changed some of it, which is to be expected and welcomed. Wood included in this series so obviously intended for the United States' market three Canadian views (all of places popular even then with American tourists). For his view of Montmorency Falls ('Fall of Montmorenci Near Quebec') Mrs Larsen suggested Wood may have drawn upon a view by W.H. Bartlett published in *Canadian Scenery*, but this could not have been the case. The ceramic picture is not in Bartlett's style; moreover, it contained a feature that Bartlett never saw. The little summer house jutting out over the water as erected in 1792 by Sir Frederick Haldimand, when Governor of Quebec. The beams supporting it rotted, and it was gone before Bartlett was there in the 1830's. Wood's 'Montmorenci' is one of the North American views that has proved difficult to relate to a source.

A ceramic view might be a composite picture, taking bits and pieces not just from one particular set of engravings but from different books on travel and exploration. 'Arctic Scenery', examples of which the American President Millard Fillmore (1800–1874) had in his personal china, was such a multi-scene series which has been tentatively attributed to Thomas Godwin on the basis of the tureen and platter shapes (Cat. Ref. Case Kitchen/40 and 21/1). This series reflected the sustained interest, throughout most of the 19th century, in Arctic exploration. Already several sources have been cited, including Sir W.E. Parry's *Journal of a Voyage for the Discovery of a North West Passage...*, published in London in 1821, and the *Journal of a Second Voyage...*, published in 1824; on dinner and soup plates the potter combined elements taken from both the Parry Journals. Sir John Franklin's *Narrative of a Journey to the Shores of the Polar Sea...*, published in 1823, was more recently added to the list of sources.

The 'Arctic Scenery' borders surrounding the views depicting scenes in the region of snows and permafrost are composed of flowers and a parade of animals and birds from lands that never know a flake of snow (Cat. Ref. Case 21/1). Some of them occur in Sir William Jardine's *Naturalists' Library*. Illustrations in this series of works, issued in a small format and relatively inexpensive in their day, were often borrowed from earlier sources. It is impossible to say whether a potter drew from the original source or from one closer to his own times and more easily available.

The potters' sources extended to works that endeavoured to bring the world, not just North America, to the public. For teaware decoration another still-to-be-identified potter turned to *A Voyage Round the World Performed in the Years 1785, 1786, 1787 and 1788, by the Boussole and Astrolabe under the Command of J.F.G. de la Perouse*. The view selected was entitled in French 'Vue d'un Établissement des Habitans du Port des Français pour la Saison de la Pêche.' The French naval officer, the Comte de la Perouse, gave the name Port des Français to what today is Lituya Bay, but Russia claimed jurisdiction over the area and her claim was recognised by treaty early in the 19th century. It became American territory when the United States purchased Alaska from Russia in 1867. Whether the potter worked from the French or from an English edition of the *Journal* is impossible to say as there were a number of editions.

Material drawn upon by potters for North American views was so varied, sometimes so unexpected, that it might almost seem as if no journal of exploration, no illustrated travel book, no set of published engravings that would have been known during the period of these wares can be ignored in the search for some elusive source. There was, however, one source of North American views that became easily available, was immensely popular and was made use of by more potters than any other. This was the work of the English topographical artist W.H. Bartlett. Between the years 1836 and 1852 (he died in 1854) Bartlett was to visit North America four times. The sepia drawings he made in the United States and Canada appeared as steel engravings in *American Scenery* and *Canadian Scenery*, both available to the potters by about 1840. Issued first in parts, they were published by Virtue in London with texts supplied by the American journalist N.P. Willis. In North America they were advertised as books 'suitable for the centre table', the coffee table books of their day. Many more American scenes than Canadian were selected by the potters and more than a dozen manufacturers produced them on dinner, tea and toilet ware; they even appeared on toyware. Bartlett's style as well as the subject matter accounted for the popularity of his work. It was in what Prince Albert described as 'the softer tone' that appealed to Victorian romanticism. In using these views the potters often altered them slightly, making it necessary at times to consult a number of Bartlett engravings to establish the source materials for one ceramic view. Bartlett continued to be a source for pottery decoration even after the turn of the century as successors to earlier firms re-issued old patterns based on these views.

Printed material that had not been a source for potters in the first years of the century attracted a Scottish pottery in the 1880's. John Marshall & Co of Bo'ness introduced a pattern called 'Canadian Sports' that was a direct translation of scenes that appeared on printed Christmas and New Year cards published in Montreal early in the 1880's. The cards were without doubt the potter's source and there was virtually no alteration in the views, but it is nonetheless interesting to note that at least one of the cards (showing snowshoers negotiating a hurdle) can be traced back to a wood engraving in a Canadian magazine that antedates the cards. Though arranged differently, the snowshoers, the hurdle, and the distinctive fence in the background were all in an engraving depicting a snowshoe steeplechase.

Without the artists the potters would not have had their fund of source material and it would have been difficult to have come upon this almost limitless source had not the engravers and the publishers been there to make the work of artists widely available. North American views, of one kind or another, enlarged the British potters' export trade. They appealed in North America not only because they met the taste of the times but because they catered to a growing sense of national pride in both the United States and Canada.

Sources of Design – Sporting Patterns
by Peter Hyland

The hunting of animals for enjoyment, rather than as a mere necessity, has been popular in Britain since the Roman occupation. Even today, the landscape bears traces of the vast vanished game parks of Norman and Plantagenet Kings. Despite the savage penalties imposed in the Middle Ages on commoners who killed deer, boar and other beasts in the royal forests, hunting was widespread, and in time came to be enjoyed legally by the rising breed of squires and yeomen farmers who formed the basis of rural communities during the later Medieval period. It was this 'landed gentry' who conceived the idea of 'field sports', that is, the pursuit of the gamebirds, fish and smaller mammals to be found in a landscape in the process of changing from forest and wilderness to arable fields and parkland.

The 18th and early 19th centuries saw field sports at their height. By that time, the sporting gun had been developed and specialist breeds of dog introduced, enabling birds and small animals to be hunted with a fair chance of success. Fox-hunting with packs of hounds began, combining sport with predator control. Hares were either pursued with hounds, or 'coursed', an activity more akin to modern sheepdog trials but involving heavy wagering, during which the hares mostly got away. Angling had also now acquired a competitive aspect, with caught fish being returned to the water after weighing. In fact, it was of the essence of good sport that the quarry was allowed an opportunity, however limited, to escape (literally a 'sporting chance').

By the end of the 18th century the popularity of field sports had created a demand for pictorial representation (Cat. Ref. Case 30). Hunting, with its lively action and promise of imminent feasting, has inspired artists from the days of the cave paintings. Ancient Greek and Roman artists depicted scenes of the chase, inspiring the pot-makers in turn to depict leaping deer, boar and dogs on the moulded or painted sides of their vessels. The tapestries and paintings of the Medieval period continued this tradition, and by the late 18th century, the new school of artists inspired by George Stubbs (1724–1806) were specialising in animals and game. The development of engraving and printing techniques meant that reproductions of sporting scenes could be made available to the general public, and to satisfy the ever-growing demand for this type of illustration a host of specialist magazines and part-works were published from around 1780 onwards; these included *The Sportsman's Dictionary, Rural Sports, Orme's Collection of British Field Sports, The Sportsman's Directory, The Sportsman's Cabinet,* and the most popular and long-lasting of all, *The Sporting Magazine*, issued monthly from 1792 to 1870. Its purpose was made plain by its subtitle: *Monthly Calendar of the Transactions of the Turf, the Chace, and every other Diversion Interesting to the Man of Pleasure and Enterprize. The Sporting Magazine* and *The Sportsman's Cabinet* regularly carried prints derived from the work of such sporting artists as J.F. Sartorius, George Morland, James Barenger, Philip Reinagle, Samuel Howitt and others, including George Stubbs himself, and were the source of most of the sporting patterns used by the potters of Staffordshire and elsewhere for the purposes of transfer printing.

One of the earliest sporting scenes to be transfer printed on a ceramic body in England appears on tiles printed in Liverpool by Sadler and Green about 1770, and depicts two sportsmen recharging their muzzle-loading guns accompanied by two pointers, a design derived from a painting by George Stubbs entitled, 'Two Gentlemen Going a-Shooting'. By the end of the century, the rising enthusiasm for such views, combined with the continuing interest in Asian customs and topography, prompted the publication in 1807 of 'Oriental Field Sports', a series of coloured engravings after the designs of Samuel Howitt and Captain T. Williamson. These were chosen by Josiah Spode's factory at Stoke as the source for the first multi-pattern series of transfer printed wares featuring sporting designs, the 'Indian Sporting' series, first produced around 1812. The wares issued in these patterns, all superbly potted and printed, were extraordinarily successful, and of all sporting patterns on ceramics are the most avidly collected and prized today. The sight of an 'Indian Sporting' service (Cat. Ref. Case 14) laid out on a mahogany table, with the wild animals and huntsmen of the Indian subcontinent leaping all over the dishes and the title of each scene printed on the reverse, ('The Hog at Bay', 'Hunting a Buffalo' etc.), is every blue collector's dream. Needless to say, most of the views in the series were copied by other potters at one time or another.

As the public taste switched to views of rural Britain and its country houses and estates, domestic hunting scenes began to appear in the great outpouring of blue printed patterns between 1810 and 1820, although it is fair to say that only a few managed to recapture the verve of the Spode 'Indian Sporting' series. Multi-pattern services were rare, as most manufacturers economised by choosing one good view and using it on all shapes. A typical and eye-catching example, by a maker as yet unknown, features a gamekeeper training, or 'breaking', four pointers in open country within sight of a large country house (now identified as Goodwood House in Sussex). The keeper, dressed in top hat, cravat, hunting coat and gaiters, has his right arm raised vertically in the visual stop command, or 'Toho'. In his left hand he carries a whip, the mere sight of which by the dogs was apparently effective, although it could be cracked over their heads if all else failed. This instructional view is taken from an illustration by John Landseer (father of Sir Edwin) published in the Reverend W. Daniel's *Rural Sports* of 1812. The copper plate engraver has added the Goodwood background and provided the printed mark GAME KEEPER on a coiled belt (Cat. Ref. Case 30/3).

By 1815, field sports were so much a part of rural life that no transfer printed view of a large house and park was complete without the inclusion of gentlemen sportsmen and their dogs, usually resting, or perhaps a couple of anglers. A scene in the 'British Views' series produced by Henshall & Co of Longport, Staffordshire, is typical: a large Palladian house stands behind a lake and three-arched bridge, while in the foreground sit two sportsmen with their pointers and modest 'bag' of two brace of pheasants, all surrounded by a rich border design of fruit and flowers. One or two manufacturers were more adventurous and, relying on the perennial popularity of animals, reproduced close-up views of dogs and their quarry in action. Ralph Stevenson of Cobridge, Staffordshire, issued a lively single-pattern series comprising a spaniel 'springing' a woodcock at the edge of woodland (Cat. Ref. Case 30/16), taken from an illustration by Philip Reinagle R.A. in *The Sportsman's Cabinet* (1803). Reinagle (1749–1833) was an outstanding painter of dogs, and several of his studies for *The Sportsman's Cabinet* (including 'Pointer and Quail', 'English Setter' and 'Duck Shooting') were reproduced about 1820 by Enoch Wood and Sons of Burslem in a fine multi-pattern series of hunting scenes in Britain and overseas surrounded by a distinctive Rococo scroll and flower border. Only top quality designs were used; other patterns in the series were taken from the work of Luke Clennell (1781–1840), a Northumberland artist and engraver who had been apprenticed to Thomas Bewick. A Clennell view ('Hunter Shooting Fox'), appears on a dinner plate, and shows a fleeing fox, having dropped its goose, about to be blasted by a top-hatted gamekeeper under a full moon.

Views of fox hunting proper are surprisingly uncommon on transfer printed wares of this period, and horse-racing scenes unknown, despite the growing popularity of both activities. Possibly the rectangular 'landscape' format required to depict a hunt or race in full cry did not adapt easily to ceramic shapes. However, some fox-hunting views appeared towards 1830; a blue printed platter of this date carries an impressive view of a 'kill', with the huntsman holding aloft the fox as the top-hatted Master of Fox Hounds gallops up with the rest of the field. Coursing with greyhounds was evidently more acceptable, as prints of twin greyhounds in action occur frequently on both earthenware services and bone china tewares. The short-lived partnership of Toft and May of Hanley (1825–1829) produced a multi-pattern series of coursing scenes based on designs again by Philip

Reinagle. This series was unusual in having no border apart from a narrow stringing, thus giving a startling immediacy to the views of greyhounds at full stretch before mounted onlookers, set among the grassy banks and solitary oaks and elms of pre-industrial England.

At this later period, the Herculaneum Pottery at Liverpool produced a fine multi-pattern series, (Cat. Ref. Case 30/2), which was virtually a compendium of British hunting customs of the time. These patterns, aptly labelled 'Field Sports' on a printed mark, were issued on gadroon edge moulded wares in both blue and black between 1825 and 1835, and were derived from illustrations in *The Sporting Magazine*. The most common pattern in this series (seen on dinner and soup plates) depicts two hunters (probably gamekeeper and squire) setting out on a shoot, and, like the 'Game Keeper' pattern, (Figure 6; Cat. Ref. 30/3), provides much information on contemporary sporting procedure and dress. Three dogs are shown, cocker spaniels by appearance, trained to flush snipe and woodcock from overgrown habitats. The squire has his right arm outstretched horizontally, directing the dogs to 'seek' to the right. Two of the dogs have already started forward, while the third looks up hesitantly, perhaps only partially trained and unused to commands. The dress of the gesticulating figure is clearly drawn: 'flower-pot' hat (sometimes known as a 'turf'), cravat, single-breasted hunting coat with 'hare pockets', and gaiters. A vegetable dish in the same series shows a pack of foxhounds flushing a covert, a large platter has a foxhunt in full cry with one of the mounted followers urging on the pack with a wave of his riding cap, while other shapes depict gamebird shooting, duck shooting, fishing, and pointers at work in a formation similar to that shown in the 'Game Keeper' pattern.

Patterns which concentrate on details of the hunt in this way are rare and highly sought after. For the most part, the British potters were content to use designs which blended sporting activities into the landscape. Anglers, for instance, occur in countless views of the 'rural scenery' type (the Davenport 'Fishermen' series being perhaps the best known), but rarely achieve foreground status. When they do, as in the 'Boys Fishing' pattern produced by the Bramelds at Swinton, Yorkshire (1806–1826), the participants tend to be village lads using simple fishing poles without reels or specialised equipment. Fishermen with nets are depicted on a pattern produced by Robert Hamilton of Stoke (1811–1826); this type of activity is more a trade rather than a sport, and is just one component of an attractive landscape.

Organised games or pastimes, in the modern sense of 'sport', occur rarely on ceramics of this period and generate enormous interest when they are discovered. Most of the team games we know today had not yet been devised or were in their infancy. The centuries-old game of cricket, however, was becoming widely popular, and a scene from a match played at Lords'

Ground, Mary-le-bone published in *The Sporting Magazine* in 1793 appears, somewhat relocated, in the foreground to a view of Windsor Castle in the Goodwins and Harris 'Metropolitan Scenery' series, further proof that sports and pastimes were generally considered only worthy of being a component in an overall composition. There are occasional exceptions to this: 'The Archery Lesson', a charming pattern used by the Turners of Lane End, Staffordshire, about 1800, concentrates on a lady and gentleman instructor at the butts in a simple classical landscape.

Sporting themes outlived the general decline in blue transfer printing around 1830, and appeared regularly throughout the 19th century, particularly on moulded stonewares. Fox-hunting designs came into their own, reaching even into the 20th century in the form of blue printed views after George Morland issued on earthenwares by Royal Doulton in 1906. More recently, however, the sharp decline in popularity of field sports for environmental and sociological reasons has been reflected by their absence from ceramic decoration. Now that even the continuance of fox-hunting is in doubt, the blue printed sporting patterns of the 19th century will be collected not only as vivid and attractive portrayals of animals and countryside, but as a record of yet another vanished part of British rural life.

6. Soup plate, 'Gamekeeper' pattern adapted from an engraving in 'Rural Sports' by the Rev. W.B. Daniel, published between 1805–1812. Maker unknown. Date 1820–1825. Diameter 25.3 cms (see Cat. Ref. Case 30/3).

Sources of Design – Botanical Patterns
by Minnie Holdaway

Prints of fruit and flowers on very early blue printed earthenwares, are used as subsidiary prints in between, and to augment, other major patterns. Eventually, and probably just before the turn of the 18th century, the better known Spode's, 'Chantilly Sprig' and Turner's 'Daffodil' patterns, were introduced where small flowers are scattered all over the wares. These were probably closely followed by 'sheet' patterns where small devices, including shells and flowers, were repeated throughout the designs with some kind of background filling the spaces between them.

In the 1780's and early 1790's flowers were used to embellish landscapes and chinoiseries, and this practise seems to have been relatively common amongst the earliest pieces of blue printed earthenware. A large bunch of flowers on the front of the jug seen in Figure 7 (Cat. Ref. Case 1/21), lies in between the main designs of 'Broseley' pattern. Flowers are seen around the handle of the LA GUILLOTINE mug (Cat. Ref. Case 4/8) and between the 'Woman on a Llama' and the 'Precarious Chinaman' patterns on a bowl. Inside the bowl are five sprays of flowers surrounding a piece of fruit, perhaps a Medlar seen in Figure 8. This fruit may have been taken originally from *The Ladies Amusement* printed for John Sayer in 1762 and perhaps the Caughley porcelain decorators took the Medlar which they also used for decoration from this source. However, since a slightly different arrangement of paired leaves appears in both the Caughley and earthenware versions, it is possible that the earthenware potters were copying this style of decoration from contemporary porcelains. The Medlar appears again in between the two Chinoiserie designs on the outside together with another botanical group 'Figs with Pink' (Figure 9), which owes something to the 'Pine Cone Group' printed on Worcester porcelains between 1770 and 1785 and the so called 'Pine Cone' or 'Mulberry'

pattern on Caughley porcelains (Holdaway, 1991). A similar bowl with the same Chinoiseries, has the Caughley 'Two Plums on a Twig' design between them instead of the fruit and flowers seen in Figures 8 and 9. Whether these particular flowers were copied directly from porcelain examples or from a source also used by the porcelain decorators, we shall probably never know.

The fruit and flowers on the bowls can be identified, to genus, at least like the carnations printed on earthenware which are reminiscent of those found on Caughley and the 'Gilliflower' or 'Carnation' patterns on Worcester porcelains. Sometimes, as on the acanthus-moulded jug seen in Figure 10 (Cat. Ref. Case 19/4), early engravings are rather flat. This jug is a rare example of printing in underglaze blue and overglaze black on the same piece. Two of the 'Bunches of Flowers' and part of the outer border are printed in black. Other earthenware potters used flowers which were not at all realistic and they appear wooden and diagrammatic. Spode used a similar arrangement of small scattered flowers called the 'Gloucester' pattern. More small flowers, engraved in this diagrammatic fashion, are frequently found as decoration on the handles and spouts of early tea and coffee pots.

This style of late 18th century decoration comes from the Continent, where flowers were widely used. Some of the finest large flowers were painted on, for example, Ludwigsburg porcelains of the 1770's, then later in the century smaller bunches of flowers, 'Deutsche Blumen', were painted on German porcelains. At the same time, small flower sprigs were being used to

8. Bowl with 'Medlar' and 'Five Flower Sprays' inside (main Patterns of 'Woman on a Llama' and 'The Precarious Chinaman'). Diameter 23.5 cms.

7. Jug with large bunch of flowers on the front (main pattern of 'Broseley'). Height 19.8 cms.

9. Bowl with 'Figs with Pink' on the outside between two chinoiserie scenes.

12.. Engraving from *The Botanical Magazine* 1806 showing *Nelumbium Speciosum*.

13. Engraving from *The Botanical Magazine* 1804 showing *Nymphaea Lotus*.

10. Jug, acanthus moulded with 'Flower Bunches' in underglaze blue and overglaze black. Height 14.8 cms (Cat. Ref. Case 19/4).

decorate French porcelains including 'Chantilly Sprigs' and these were copied on blue printed earthenwares by several potters including Spode. The larger bunches of flowers on the moulded jug (Figure 10), are more like 'Deutsche Blumen'.

Flowers of all kinds were used as decorative features throughout the 18th century and there are many examples provided in *The Ladies Amusement* (1762) including a basket of flowers. By about 1805 a basket or a vase of flowers in one form or another had become a popular motif on blue printed earthenware and were produced by several factories including, for example, Minton and Rogers who used 'Bowpot' and 'Fruit and Flowers' patterns respectively. On the latter pattern there is a figure printed within a bottle or vase (Holdaway, 1992) and when Josiah Wedgwood started production in 1805–1806 (Cat. Ref. Case 24 et seq), his first pattern was 'Blue Bamboo' (des Fontaines, 1975). The vase of flowers in this pattern, which also contains a figure, stands on a table surrounded by bamboos and a peony, all in an Oriental style (Figure 11). Wedgwood quickly followed with 'Blue Basket', which has radiating basket-weave interspersed with simple leaves and flowers, then 'Hibiscus' in 1806–1807, 'Peony' in 1807, 'Chrysanthemum' and 'Water Lily' in 1808, and 'Botanical Flowers' in 1809–1810. Here, then, is ample evidence of the popularity of flower patterns in the first decade of the 19th century and although some of

them, such as 'Blue Basket' and 'Chrysanthemum', are in a more geometric style, they are all quality products for they require an engraving of a particular size and shape for each piece that was made.

Perhaps the reason for the variety and accuracy of the Wedgwood patterns lies with John Wedgwood (1766–1844) who was an active partner in the firm from 1800 to 1812. Amongst his various aptitudes was botany, and it was as a result of his suggestion to one of George III's gardeners that, three years later in 1804 and after many discussions, he chaired the inaugural meeting of what later became the Royal Horticultural Society.

Wedgwood's 'Water Lily' (Plate XIV; Cat. Ref. Case 24/6) is a truly remarkable design for no less than four different prints from two different botanical journals are used in its composition (des Fontaines 1966). Three different botanical species are involved. A print of 'The Sacred Bean of India, *Nelumbium speciosum*' (Figure 12), from *Curtis's Botanical Magazine* (1806) appears in its entirety for the largest flower in the group and part of a print of the 'Lotus of India, *Nymphaea lotus*' (Figure 13), taken from the same journal of two years earlier, appears immediately to the right of it. The flower and bud on the left hand side represent half of a print of the 'Starry Water Lily, *Nymphaea stellata*' (Figure 14), in Sowerby's *Botanist's Repository* for 1803 and the flower and bud on the extreme right hand side are part of another print of the 'Lotus of Egypt, *Nymphaea lotus*' (Figure 15) in the same publication a year later. The 'Water Lily' pattern was printed in brown between 1807–1808 and 1811 and a dinner service was ordered by Dr Robert

11. Square dish, decorated with 'Blue Bamboo' pattern. Mark WEDGWOOD impressed. Width 19.7 cms (Cat. Ref. Case 24/32).

14. Engraving from *The Botanist's Repository* 1803 showing *Nymphaea Stellata*.

15. Engraving from *The Botanist's Repository* 1804, plate 391.

16. Engraving from *Paradisus Londinensis* 1804/1805 showing *Hibiscus Tiliaefolius*.

17. Engraving from *The Botanist's Repository* 1804, plate 362 showing *Crocus Biflora* or the 'Yellow-Bottomed Crocus'.

18. Can and saucer, with a 'Circle of Garlanded Roses' pattern. Mark 'Ridgway' impressed. Height of can 6cms, diameter of saucer 13.2 cms (Cat. Ref. Case 19/10).

Darwin. Subsequently, it was printed in blue and the border was changed to a series of narrow overlapping ovals. It was an extremely popular design which was used at the end of the 19th and beginning of the 20th century in other palettes.

Learned journals began to be published just before the end of the 18th century as a result of increasing public interest in botany and gardening, including hot houses. Several could have been used by Wedgwood for his 'Botanical Flowers' services. Many species are represented on these wares and sometimes printed numerals appear towards the base of the stems as an aid to identification at the factory. One of them, *Hibiscus tiliaefolius* (Figure 16), was copied from *Paradisus Londinensis* published by Richard Salisbury (des Fontaines, 1966). James Sowerby was another able and prolific engraver illustrating his *English Botany* with mainly wild flowers in thirty-six volumes published between 1790 and 1814. He had worked for Curtis prior to this, illustrating *Curtis's Botanical Magazine or Flower Garden Displayed* when it first appeared in 1787. So far, no Sowerby prints have been found which match blue printed earthenwares.

Recently we discovered the source print of another flower used by Wedgwood on his dinner wares decorated with 'Botanical Flowers' and the same border of overlapping ovals that was used on blue printed 'Water Lily' pattern. The 'Yellow-Bottomed Crocus, *Crocus Biflora*' (Figure 17) illustrated on a plate by Kelly (1970) is taken from *The Botanist's Repository* Volume 6, plate 362. *The Botanist's Repository* was published in ten volumes between 1797 and 1814 by Henry Andrews.

It should be appreciated that the engravers were using the same sources for their prints on blue printed earthenwares as the finest painters on English porcelain such as, for example, on the dessert wares of the Derby factory between 1791 and 1811 (Ledger 1991).

Not only the main designs were taken from learned journals. Some of the flamboyant borders of this period have identifiable flowers in them. The wonderful crocus border for 'Corinth' (or 'Absolom's Pillar') is somewhat similar to *Crocus lagenflorus* from *Paradisus Londinensis*, 1805–1808. However, taste played a great part in the precise nature of the border and in

1814 Josiah Byerley in charge of Wedgwood's London Showroom writes to the factory about a design with;

'a large blue flower in the centre and the Corinth border around the rim – those colours which have the most colour and broadest shades are to be preferred, as our customers do not like much of the white to be seen' (des Fontaines, 1975).

We cannot be certain which large blue flower is referred to but there is no doubting that the wonderful border of crocuses was popular.

Some of Wedgwood's later patterns such as 'The Chinese Economy of Time' (or 'Scroll'), introduced in 1811 with a background filled in with leaves, and 'Blue Rose' which covers the wares completely almost in the manner of a sheet pattern, would have fulfilled the customers' wishes of not wanting to see 'too much of the white'. However, 'Blue Rose' with pale floral shadows in the background is thought to have been introduced a decade later.

Spode's 'British Flowers' are printed in blue on a white background in the normal way but, when the flowers and leaves (only) were outlined in white with a completely engraved blue background, Spode's 'Botanicals' would have satisfied the same criteria. Despite the obvious high quality of these engravings no source prints have been found although it is just possible that 'Geranium' pattern (Cat. Ref. Case 17/4) could be the 'Largest Flowered Crane's-bill, *Geranium grandiflorum*', illustrated on plate 12, Volume 1 of the *Botanist's Repository* published in 1798 by Henry Andrews.

Flower patterns were very popular at different periods throughout the 19th century and it seems that the all-over blue designs were in demand more than once. Flowers were incorporated in a way not unlike a 'sheet' pattern earlier in the century. For example, an early Ridgway impressed saucer (Figure 18) has a design consisting of a 'Circle of Garlanded Roses' on a background of 'Cracked Ice' (Cat. Ref. Case 19/10) which is reminiscent of Bristol tin glazed earthenwares of the 1760's. This rare Ridgway mark is also found on 'Eastern Port Scene' (Cat. Ref. Case 18/11) and the two patterns were probably in production at about the same time showing that both chinoiserie and floral patterns had a role in the market place.

Sources of Design – Animal Patterns
by Tim Holdaway

Interest in natural history was widespread in the 18th and 19th centuries. This interest was fuelled by the number of natural history books (see footnote 1). In addition to these books on natural history, there were many encyclopaedias and cyclopaedias which carried large illustrated sections on quadrupeds, birds, and other subjects related to natural history, as well as other publications such as *The Sporting Magazine* (1793–1828) which contained articles and illustrations of natural historical subjects. This meant that there were a whole range of prints which the ceramic engraver could use as subjects for decorating ceramics.

Some porcelain manufactories produced services decorated from a single source such as Coalport's animal service decorated with Bewick prints about 1805 (see footnote 2). Derby made a service principally painted with animals taken from Church (see footnote 3). The Chelsea porcelain factory decorated many wares using Edwards (see footnote 4).

Some earthenware manufactories produced services decorated with underglaze blue and white prints taken from a mixture of sources such as, Hall's 'Quadruped' series about 1815, Meigh's 'Zoological Sketches' about 1820 (Cat. Ref. Case 21/2 & 20/9), and Enoch Wood's 'Sporting' series about 1820 (Cat. Ref. Case 21/8 & 30/9) and yet others used prints taken from a variety of sources, which were used as a form of decoration bearing little or no relevance to the main decoration. The 'Arctic Scenery' service (Cat. Ref. Case 21/1) possibly made by George Phillips, Longport, 1834–1848 has the principal decoration of Arctic scenes including Eskimos, whilst the borders are decorated with animals and birds, in many cases from a tropical background. Yet others used animal prints as decoration on wares not necessarily forming part of complete services.

Hall's 'Quadruped' series.

This is a large dinner service(s) (Holdaway 1984) of many pieces including a number of sauce tureens and soup tureens. Most of the pieces are marked with HALL and QUADRUPEDS printed in a cartouche (Cat. Ref. Case 20/1 et seq), and most of the prints are taken from Church (see footnote 3). The known animals used by this potter, taken from Church are the Tibetan musk, seal, hedgehog and mole, genet and civet cat, rabbits, rhinoceros, horse, nylghau, elk, beaver, goats, brown bear, raccoon, lion dog and zebra. The large soup tureen stand (Figure 19, Cat. Ref. Case 20/5) has three prints from Church. The centre is a rhinoceros, whilst the border has prints of the Arabian horse and the nylghau. The other two prints are taken from sources not yet identified. Another large tureen stand has only the print of the hare (Cat. Ref. Case 20/8). A dinner plate is decorated with five prints from Church (Figure 20). The centre shows an otter, whilst the border is decorated with the mole and hedgehog, rabbits, a seal, and a civet cat and genet. The sauce tureen stand is decorated with the pointer from Church (Cat. Ref. Case 20/4), and the prints in the border have still to be identified. Among the other prints used on this service from Church is that of the fox (Cat. Ref. Case 20/2). Although the vast majority of prints are taken from Church, some of the plates are taken from Bewick (see footnote 2). Figure 21 shows a small plate on which the prints of the common antelope, the jackal, the suricate, the ground squirrel and the raccoon, are all taken from Bewick. Other plates (Figure 22) have (on the right hand side), a water shrew mouse, the English setter, the monax and the stoat; the left hand side of Figure 22 has four more prints from Bewick. These are the dalmatian or coach dog, the weasel, the pine weasel or yellow breasted martin and the ichneumon. Another print taken from Bewick in this series is that of the striped hyena (Cat. Ref. Case 20/1).

Some potters only used one print from Church. A Roger's teapot (Cat. Ref. Case 21/7) is decorated with a zebra from Church, as far as we know the only time this potter used a Church print. Figure 23 shows two unidentified pieces using the frontispiece from Volume 2 of Church.

19. Stand, decorated with a Rhinoceros, made by John Hall of Burslem. Date about 1822–1832. Measurements 43 cms × 36 cms (Cat. Ref. Case 20/5).

20. Plate, decorated with an Otter, made by John Hall of Burslem. Date about 1822–1832. Diameter 22 cms (Cat. Ref. Case 20/6).

21. Plate, decorated with a Deer, made by John Hall of Burslem. Date about 1822–1832. Diameter 19 cms (Cat. Ref. Case 20/7).

22. Two small plates, decorated on the left, with 'The Dalmation or Coach Dog' and on the right with 'The English Setter', made by John Hall of Burslem. Date about 1822–1832. Diameter of plate on the left 15 cms, and on the right 13 cms (Cat. Ref. Case 20/3).

23. Two dishes, decorated with designs taken from the frontispiece of Volume 2 of *A Cabinet of Quadrupeds* by J. Church, published 1805. Maker Unknown. Diameter of left 14 cms; Diameter of right 20 cms.

Meigh's 'Zoological Sketches'.

The 'Zoological Sketches' produced by Meigh, differ from Hall's 'Quadrupeds' in that only one print is used as the central decoration, the border decoration always being a Rococo mixture of flowers and birds within a gadrooned edge. The known animals taken from Church (Holdaway 1984 and 1992) are the otter, fox, skunk, reindeer, elephant (Cat. Ref. Case 20/9), rhinoceros, tiger, hunting leopard (Cat. Ref. Case 21/2), zebra, camel, raccoon, nylghau, and armadillo. In some cases, where the same print is used by both Hall and Meigh, the manner of treatment is different, for example, the rhinoceros on the Meigh platter is a faithful copy from Church, the Hall version (Figure 19) is embellished with a ship and the boy climbing the palm tree has been omitted. Although many of the wares are decorated with under glaze blue and white prints, some are printed in black. Examples are known of the same wares with both types of decoration.

Enoch Wood & Sons (1818–1846)

This manufactory used many of Church's prints, not on a named series, like the two previous factories, but on many dessert and dinner wares. Not only were Church prints used, for example the lion, polar bear, tiger, beaver, elephant, leopard, tibetan musk, squirrel, goat, and spotted hyena, but also animals from other sources. Usually only one print was used and the border of the Enoch Wood's ware is distinctive.

Some of the prints used by Enoch Wood are taken from Bewick. The vegetable dish (Cat. Ref. Case 21/8) has the wolf and the bear from Bewick on the cover and a Bewick vignette on the dish (see footnote 2).

Enoch Wood is unusual in that some of his source prints are taken from a book entitled *Recreations in Natural History* (see footnote 8). Figure 24 (Cat. Ref. Case 21/13) and Figure 25 (Cat. Ref. Case 30/9) shows the prints which are by Luke Clennell, one of Bewick's apprentices. As far as is known these prints are unique to Enoch Wood. Other, as yet unidentified, potters have also used other prints from this source

Bewick Prints on Earthenware

Bewick prints are used on a variety of wares, not usually on a named series from any one potter. Some of the animals in the borders of the 'Arctic Scenery' service (Cat. Ref. Case 21/1) are from Bewick (Holdaway 1987), but others come from more unusual sources. The ostrich in the border of the platter (Cat. Ref. Case/Kitchen 40) is taken from *The Naturalist's Cabinet*, Volume 3, published in 1806 (Figure 26). Many of the prints decorating single known pieces are from Bewick, with some also taken from *Bewick's Bird's* (1797) for example; the dusky grebe, or dobchick (Cat. Ref. Case 30/8). As I have already mentioned some of the prints on Hall's 'Quadrupeds' and Meigh's 'Zoological Sketches' are taken from Bewick. Some of his vignettes are used as ceramic decoration, more commonly on creamware (Holdaway 1989), but five

24. Engraving of Deer from *Recreations in Natural History* or *Popular Sketches of British Quadrupeds* drawn by L. Clennell in 1815.

25. Engraving of The Fox from *Recreations in Natural History* or *Popular Sketches of British Quadrupeds* drawn by L. Clennell in 1815.

26. Engraving of an Ostrich from *The Naturalist's Cabinet* in six volumes by The Rev. Thomas Small published 1806.

27. Frog mug decorated with various animals taken mainly from Bewick prints. Maker unknown. Date about 1825. Height 9 cms; Diameter 13 cms (Cat. Ref. Case 21/12).

28. Engraving of The Varied Monkey, or Mona, from Bewick's *A General History of Quadrupeds* published in 1790.

29. Engraving of The Ouistiti or Cagvi, from Bewick's *A General History of Quadrupeds* published in 1790.

30. Engraving of The Mico, or Fair Monkey, from Bewick's *A General History of Quadrupeds* published in 1790.

31. Detail of a tureen lid showing a Sucatorio, an animal apparently found in the East Indies. Maker unknown. Date about 1795–1810 (Cat. Ref. Case 21/6).

examples are known on blue and white printed earthenware. These are 'Old Age and Heedless Youth', only known on miniatures, 'The Boy on a Goat', 'The Crouching Leopard', known in at least two versions, 'The Midnight Cavalry' and the vegetable dish (Cat. Ref. Case 21/8), by Enoch Wood already mentioned.

Primates on ceramics are unusual but several Bewick examples are known. The frog mug (Figure 27, Cat. Ref. Case 21/12), is decorated with Bewick animals viz. the lion, tiger, zebra and horse, and more unusually with The Varied Monkey or Mona (Figure 28), the Ouistiti, or Cagvi (Figure 29), and The Mico or Fair Monkey (Figure 30). The larger jug (Cat. Ref. Case 21/15) is decorated with three of these prints, the Ouistiti, zebra and lion, whilst the base has a further print of a monkey. This is the Talapoin, taken from Smellie's translation of Buffon of 1791 (see footnote 9). Why there is such a mixture of prints of chinoiserie and animals on this piece is puzzling.

Other Sources of ceramic decoration.

In addition to the prolific sources mentioned above, there is a range of sources which are used but infrequently. Howitt (see footnote 5) has four of the Fables used in the border of one of Hall's 'Quadrupeds' plates and on no other. The only other time a Howitt's *Fable* is used is on a Minton tile about 1880.

Prints from *The Sporting Magazine*, published monthly from 1793 onwards, are occasionally used. The frontispiece to Volume 25, 1805 is used in the

border of one of the 'Arctic Scenery' plates (Cat. Ref. Case 21/1) and at no other time.

The sucatorio or sukatoryo, was first described in the *Journal of John Nieuhoff of His Journeys to the East and West Indies* (1642). This was used on a few pieces of early blue printed ware about 1795 (Figure 31). Doubt was cast on the authenticity of this species in Shaw (see footnote 7), but was still mentioned in Oliver Rees' *Cyclopaedia of Arts and Sciences*, 1819, and *The Encyclopedaedia Londiniensis* of 1824. After this date there is no record of this animal.

The Rev. Daniels (see footnote 6) shows many prints of hunting and related topics. Two are used on blue and white earthenware, the coursing scene showing Czarina and Maria, and the 'Game keeper' (Figure 6, Cat. Ref. Case 30/3). Many of his other prints are used by other porcelain factories, for example the Derby manufactory (Holdaway 1996).

The sources used to decorate blue printed earthenware were many and varied. Some of the original prints were copied accurately, some less so. Why some were used and not others will always remain an enigma. Why only one was chosen from a series, for example the elk from *The Sporting Magazine*, remains mysterious, when there were many other more typical examples from contemporary zoological or natural history books. Many of the potters produced wares with animals as the main decoration and this is perhaps indicative of the then current interest in all aspects of the natural world.

Footnotes

1. Boreman, T. 1730 *A Description of three hundred animals*, London.
Edwards, G. 1743 *The Natural History of some uncommon Birds*, London 1743–1751.
Brookes, R. 1763 *A New System of Natural History*, London.
Pennant, T. 1771 *Synopsis of Quadrupeds*, Chester.
Goldsmith, O. 1774 *A History of The Earth and Animated Nature*, London.
White, G. 1789 *The Natural History and Antiquities of Selborne*, London.
2. Bewick, T. 1790 *A General History of Quadrupeds*, Newcastle upon Tyne.
       1797 *History of British Birds*.
       1797 *Volume I Land Birds*,
       Newcastle upon Tyne.
       1805 *Volume II Water Birds*,
       Newcastle upon Tyne.
3. Church, J. 1805 *A Cabinet of Quadrupeds*, London.
4. Edwards, G. 1743 *The Natural History of some uncommon Birds and of some rare and undescribed Animals*, London.
5. Howitt, S. 1809 *A New Work of Animals*, London.
6. Daniels, The Rev. W.B. 1805 *Rural Sports*, Volume 1 and 2, London.
1813 *Rural Sports*, Volume 3, London.
7. Shaw, G. 1800 *General Zoology*, London.
8. Anon. 1815 *Recreations in Natural History*, London
9. Buffon, Count de, 1791, *Natural History, General and Particular* (Translated by William Smellie), London.

Sources of Design – Historical and Literary Patterns
by Martin Pulver

Historical Patterns

With the exception of some 'mythical' patterns, which have only tenuous claims to be regarded as historical at all, it seems that the arrival of patterns which can truly be regarded as such, was relatively late. Patterns which included mythical figures such as 'The Fates', produced by Wedgwood & Co at the Ferrybridge factory, Yorkshire, are probably the earliest, dating to around 1800. These were followed shortly by the so-called 'Greek' patterns by Spode (Cat. Ref. Case 34/5) and Herculaneum. We can only keep these under the historical umbrella by regarding some of the figures depicted as representing heroes and demi-gods (such as Achilles and Ajax), stemming from a time when myths may indeed have possessed a kernel of historical truth. Many of these figures were taken from a bygone era, as they came through the medium of such volumes as Baron Pierre d'Hancarville's lavish illustrations of Sir William Hamilton's collection. We could therefore maintain that the works of Homer can not be entirely dismissed from the canon of history and could be allowed to remain as our jumping-off point, particularly since the very early patterns – almost totally Chinoiserie – do not bear on this subject at all.

However, when we look at the great explosion of non-Chinoiserie patterns from about 1805, it is clear that the preference of the potters (who were presumably in touch with the desires of the customers) was for classical scenes, exotic Oriental activities and, most of all, British rural scenes with backgrounds of well-known country houses and ruins. True historical patterns did not emerge to any extent until the 1820's at the earliest and even then were not widespread.

It is quite possible that potters played safe by investing their resources heavily in patterns which required only to attract attention by just being there and looking pretty. The modicum of enforced thought which might be stimulated by presenting a historical scene, could work against product popularity, and so it was not surprising that the incidents used were well-known and could be relied upon to enlist patriotic approval.

The series which illustrates this most clearly and indeed stands almost alone as an attempt to depict factual history in quantity on transfer printed pottery was the 'British History' series by Jones & Son (Cat. Ref. Case 33/18). However, the short stay in the market place by this company (1826–1828) can be perceived as an adverse comment on its popularity. Nevertheless, while the standard of printing is not of the highest, the scenes chosen were those most likely to persuade purchasers to cheer or to weep out loud. A full list of titles can be found in Volume 1 of the *Dictionary of Blue and White Printed Pottery*, and includes such stirring scenes as 'Signing of Magna Carta', 'Elizabeth Addressing the Troops', 'Death of General Wolfe' and 'Death of Lord Nelson'.

Although each of the scenes was chosen with an eye to patriotic approval, it is interesting to speculate how the choice was made from the depictions provided by the printers of the source volume, *Dolby's Universal Histories, Hume and Smollett's England* (1825, illustrated edition). It seems that, while the earlier scenes had to be the products of individual imaginations, the potters, very sensibly, copied the Dolby illustrations of well-known paintings when they could. Interestingly, Boswell's *London Journal* for 1762–1763 mentions, under Wednesday 16th March;

'. . . we went and saw the Exhibition of the pictures in the Strand'.

His footnote to this describes some of the pictures he saw. They included;

'The Death of General Wolfe' by Robert Edge Pine – won First Prize of 100 guineas; 'Canute Reproving his Flattering Courtiers', by George Romney – won special prize of 25 Guineas; and 'Caractacus before the Roman Emperor Claudius'.

The correspondence of these three titles to the Jones' list is too great for coincidence. Naturally, the incidents which occurred after Boswell's visit could also have formed the subject of famous paintings ('Death of Lord Nelson' certainly did) and these might well have created the bases of other named Jones' historical patterns. A fine platter depicting 'The Death of General Wolfe' is on display, very fittingly, in Quebec House at Westerham in Kent.

Equally late in the field of history as depicted on transfer printed pottery was the Teesside firm of W. Smith & Co. (1825–1855), which did not hesitate, only about 15 years after the battle of Waterloo, to produce a historical pattern which was more suitable for patriotic Frenchmen. This was 'Napoleon's Victories', which named his famous triumphs at Austerlitz, Jena, Marengo etc. Presumably, to Smith, history was history (and business was certainly business).

There were other historical and quasi-historical incidents offered by various potters. Knight, Elkin & Co. (1826–1846), depicted 'Hannibal Passing the Alps', while Ridgway, Morley Wear & Co. (1836–1842), produced the 'Eglintoun' pattern. This hardly world-shattering incident was caused by Queen Victoria's refusal to allow a 'champion' to 'throw down his gage' at her Coronation, offering to fight any person objecting to the succession, as had been done at all previous Coronations. The Earl of Eglintoun took it very badly and, as consolation, organised in 1839 a mediaeval tournament at his Gothic castle in Argyll, where there would be 'jousting, mead-drinking, wenching, etc.' All went well at the rehearsal, but on the day the British weather had the last word and the tournament sank without trace in a sea of mud (see *The Knight and the Umbrella*, by Ian Anstruther, published in 1963).

By now, potters seemed convinced that there were no particularly large profits to be made by persisting with historical patterns on transfer printed wares, and those we do see appear to be part of the huge market for commemoratives – in itself a subject for an entire book. No potter achieved exclusivity in this field. Rather, there was haphazard printing by anyone prepared to take the risk; naturally, the more important the event, the more manufacturers were attracted to it. Royal commemoratives, then as now, were popular, but the more truly historical incidents which were taken up were such things as agitation over Reform Law, repeal of the Corn Laws, rioting, conflict and wars generally. The many surviving pieces portray the attitudes of the general public at the time. Two good examples exist in the Shorthose pattern 'Wellington Hotel, Waterloo' (Cat. Ref. Case 16/4) and a fine, patriotic mug commemorating the Battle of Trafalgar showing a portrait of Admiral Lord Nelson on one side and a picture of the Victory under sail on the reverse (Cat. Ref. Case 5/6).

In addition, highly specialised subjects such as railway history, shipping history and slavery found their way onto pots, and the last notable outburst of activity in historical transfer printed wares commemorated the Great Exhibition of 1851.

Literary Patterns

Although the market for literary patterns does not seem to have fared a great deal better than the historical, there were certainly more series issued in this genre. Indeed, the various 'Greek' series already mentioned might qualify as literary just as much as historical, but once again there was a twenty year delay before designs firmly based on literary sources began to appear.

James & Ralph Clews (1815–1834) produced a series of more than twenty scenes based on *The Adventures of Don Quixote*, written by Miguel Cervantes in 1605–1615. This partnership's interest in literary-inspired series went even further. In 1810 there appeared a new English publication called *The Poetical Magazine*, which published a rhymed tale by William Combe (known as 'the English Lesage'), entitled 'The Schoolmaster's Tour'. This was later republished as 'Dr. Syntax's Three Tours' and illustrated by Thomas Rowlandson. Clews produced at least thirty scenes based on these illustrations (Cat. Ref. 33/14), which apparently so suited the mood of the time that they were among the most popular series ever produced and have remained as popular with today's collectors. Some of the scenes have in fact been re-issued this century by the Adams' factory. In the second decade of the 18th century, one of the buzz-words was 'picturesque' and the fact that one of the Dr. Syntax tours was '... in Search of the Picturesque' gave the series the appearance

of being the last word in up-to-the-minute fashion.

Brameld & Co. (1806–1842) traded from 1826 as the famous Rockingham China factory, but they continued to make good earthenwares also, producing a series based on Don Quixote which was, however, of markedly inferior quality and inspiration to that issued by Clews.

Another fruitful source of inspiration was the work of two very famous Scots – Robert Burns and Sir Walter Scott. Brameld produced a piece showing some of the characters from Burns' poem *The Cotter's Saturday Night* and it is thought that the firm of Thomas & John Carey (1823–1842) made a version of the same scene. 'Tam o'Shanter' also appears on pots (Cat. Ref. Case 33/17, see plate 7).

The Careys certainly produced a pattern taken from two prints after Richard Westall, R.A., which they combined to form a scene from Scott's *Lady of the Lake*. However, the best-known instance of this author's work appearing on pottery was a series produced by the major potters Davenport (1794–1887). It was entitled 'Scott's Illustrations' and scenes, made from 1836 onwards, include (so far as is known) three from *Bride of Lammermoor*, two from *Waverley* and one each from *Guy Mannering*, *The Heart of Midlothian*, *Legend o' Montrose*, *Old Mortality* and *Rob Roy*. The choices do not seem to follow the pattern of Scott's most popular works today. An unknown maker copied part of this series fairly quickly after its issue (Cat. Ref. Case 33/15).

The Spode company too judged it useful to employ a literary source. From the very end of their early period (about 1832), all the way through the Copeland & Garrett partnership (1833–1847) and well into the Copeland period, they produced a series based on Aesop's *Fables*, of which at least twenty-five are known to have been illustrated. In fact, the Copeland & Garrett period seems generally to have presumed a much higher standard of literacy among its customers than would have been the case as little as twenty years previously. A social historian might find much of interest there if investigating a possible surge in basic educational standards in the 1820's and 1830's. The partnership issued the 'Byron Views' series (Cat. Ref. Case 33/12) based on engravings in Finden's *Landscape and Portrait Illustrations to the Life and Works of Lord Byron* (1832–1834). 'Bad' Lord Byron was the dashing romantic figure of the period, and this series illustrated the areas of Europe associated with his wanderings, cashing in on his name to seize the opportunity of marketing scenes of the high picturesque school at the peak of its popularity. As usual, in that age when businesses were relatively unprotected by law from plagiarism, others were not slow in jumping on the bandwagon. John Meir (1836–1897) produced 'Byron's Illustrations' and 'Simplon' as very close copies of Copeland and Garrett. Goodwins & Harris (1831–1838) and their subsequent partnerships issued a series entitled 'Byron Gallery', with scenes illustrating many of Byron's works.

A later literary giant given his chance on transfer printed wares was Charles Dickens. The firm of William Ridgway, Son & Co. (1836–1848) issued a series entitled 'Humphrey's Clock' (Cat. Ref. Case 33/16), referring to *Master Humphrey's Clock*, a book which Dickens used for his early publication of *The Old Curiosity Shop* and *Barnaby Rudge* (1840–1841). By this time, the picturesque movement was degenerating into the maudlin, as reflected in scenes like 'Little Nell by the River'. However, Dickens' undoubted genius as an author helped to keep the series afloat. Later again, firms like Joseph Clementson (1839–1864) rediscovered the possibilities of illustrating the Greek classics. He produced the 'Classical Antiquities' series with patterns like 'Phemius singing to the Suitors'. However, these nostalgic glimpses of earlier attempts to popularise literary patterns proved to be the swan song of this particular area of illustration.

There are indeed many passing references to historical and literary matters on transfer printed wares, but the conclusion cannot be escaped that, as a whole, these two subjects comprised a very small percentage of the overall mass. It was rare for any series in this genre to gain the front rank of customer popularity and it must be confessed that their issue in general sprang either from a mistaken optimism unproven by market research, or from a deliberate self-indulgence on the part of the potter concerned, attempting to improve minds which had no wish to be improved.

The Early Wares 1780–1805

by Minnie Holdaway

Early blue printed earthenwares were born of enterprise and necessity with a rising demand for middle priced tea and table wares. A market for tea and dessert wares must have been present for the New Hall consortium to be established in 1782 and for the likes of Neale, Turner and Leeds to consider making porcelain before the century was out. On the other hand, extraordinarily cheap dinner wares had been available during the third quarter of the 18th century following Wedgwood's success with his Queen's Ware. Undecorated and elegant creamwares were freely available by virtue of their price (15/- or 75 pence a dozen plates: Shaw 1829), and would continue to dominate many outlets well into the 19th century.

Next in price to undecorated creamware were underglaze blue painted wares. These must have been very popular, with their copious and often vibrant freehand painting, and were probably produced by all or almost all earthenware manufactories. These wares are intrinsically interesting because of the market and time period which they occupy. It is more difficult to pin down their introduction but probably they were commonplace by 1780, and like the creamware they continued in production well into the 1820's and perhaps later. Blue printed earthenwares were even more expensive and sometimes almost ten times the price of undecorated creamware.

When and where did the manufacture of blue and white printed wares begin? For Staffordshire we have the statements of Simeon Shaw writing in 1829 and describing what happened half a century earlier. Following improvements in the technique of blue print-ing on porcelain by Thomas Turner at Caughley, several manufacturers in Staffordshire began blue printing, employing engravers and printers with experience gained in the leading porcelain manufactories of the day such as Worcester and Caughley. About 1783 and 1784 are the dates given by Shaw for these developments in Staffordshire. Jas Keeling of Hanley, Josiah Spode in Stoke and John Yates of Shelton being the names associated with the early development of blue printed earthen-wares in Staffordshire, together with R. Baddeley of Shelton, who continued to make improvements in the technique with the help of an engraver from Liverpool and a printer from Worcester.

Shaw suggests that the earliest pattern used by Spode for table wares was 'Old Willow', with a border of willow and dagger, and for tea services 'Broseley' from a pattern used at Caughley. All of the blue printed earthen-ware patterns attributable to the 18th century are hard to find, but identifying these two categories of wares is beset with pitfalls. What exactly were these patterns? In one sense 'Broseley' is perhaps easier to identify, for the pattern is routinely referred to in porcelain manufactories

as being like the pattern on the jug (Cat. Ref. Case 1/21). As for 'Old Willow' with a border of willow and dagger then it is tempting to think in terms of Caughley's 'Willow Nankin', a pattern with a small two-storied house to one side, a large willow tree in the centre and no bridge. However, this pattern was not used with a simple border of brocade with daggers within at Caughley (Godden 1969). On the other hand, dinner services in Chinese porcelain are well known and that, ultimately, was the source of the design. Nowadays we look to Spode for 'Dagger' borders with 'Trophies Dagger', 'Dagger Landscapes' I, II and III illustrated by Whiter (1970). Of these only the last-named has a large willow tree as part of the design - a design which became known as 'Mandarin' at Spode. However, 'Mandarin' complete with dagger border is found only on Spode bone china and stone china which belong to the next century and not the 1780's. The main design called 'Willow Nankin' at Caughley and 'Mandarin' at Spode had a different border (without dagger) at both factories and 'Mandarin' is well known to collectors of Spode's blue printed earthenwares (Copeland 1980 and 1990).

There is an earlier version of 'Willow Nankin' or 'Mandarin' on earthenware tablewares which has received little attention as potentially the earliest form of 'Willow' pattern. It has a border of 'Dagger and Drop' inside a different kind of border from the Chinese original and the Spode copy. The brocade border is still present but it is interrupted by paired 'Curves' and 'Key' elements. Pieces decorated in this way are early and a mug (Figure 32, Cat. Ref. Case 4/4) has 'W.Morshall, Sedburgh 1790' on the base (Plate 29). Neither the engraving nor the proportions of the buildings are the same as Caughley's 'Willow Nankin' and Spode's 'Mandarin'. The second building is more prominent and if anything, the willow tree is larger on the 'Morshall' mug and there are three, not two, birds flying overhead. Certainly the two ships to the left hand side are more obvious than the single vessel seen in Spode's 'Mandarin' pattern; they are reminiscent of light house ships. But what to call the pattern? Perhaps

32. Mug in 'Willow Mandarin I' dated 1790 on the base. Height 9 cms (Cat. Ref. Case 4/4).

'Willow Mandarin' thereby indicating that this may be the first willow pattern design and that it links with earlier Caughley porcelain and the later Spode 'Mandarin'.

'Willow Mandarin I' appears in a slightly different version, 'Willow Mandarin II' on a blue printed earthenware globular teapot (Cat. Ref. Case 4/3) with 'S. Tonnill 1789' painted in underglaze blue beneath the spout (Plate 29). There are no large birds flying overhead and the subsidiary design of an island is extended across the top in their place. Also, the border is quite different; the brocade is gone and instead there is a series of complex elements for which there are no words in the English language.

Let us leave the chinoiseries for the moment, for it should be realised that in the beginning the patterns used to decorate these earthenwares were not exclusively chinoiseries. Indeed, there were many kinds of different patterns in the first decade of production, and this is hardly surprising remembering that they were produced by engravers and printers who had come from Worcester, Caughley and Liverpool (Shaw 1829), where so many different kinds of design, not only chinoiseries, were painted and printed on porcelain. These included landscapes with figures, both European and classical, animals, fruit and flowers. The rare earthenware pieces decorated with these patterns are more or less confined to the 1780's perhaps until 1791 or 1792, after which it seems that almost all of the blue and white earthenware was decorated with chinoiserie designs during the closing years of the 18th century. Exceptionally, there are some examples of wares specially printed to commemorate historical events of the period, and just before the turn of the century one or more geometric patterns appear.

Some of the 18th century patterns have received attention in published works but they are few in number. Perhaps the most sophisticated of the late 18th century designs are those involving human figures in period dress in a European landscape. They may be printed in blue or in black. Wearing a frock coat and garters a European gentleman is offering a garlanded shepherdess some flowers: items of a picnic lie about their feet and there are poplar trees to the right over a variety of animals including sheep (Figure 33). Another pattern may be used on the reverse which consists of five farm animals – four with horns and mostly supine. Traditionally, these engravings have been attributed to Rothwell working in Swansea although there is a lack of evidence in support of this attribution. This pattern I propose calling 'Period Gentleman & Shepherdess'.

A similarly bewigged gentleman is seated alongside a lady in contemporary costume on the coffee pot (Cat. Ref. Case 18/3), so that the pattern could be called 'Seated Period Figures'. There is a tree to the left and a concoction of buildings to the right. On the reverse two cows are lying down with similar trees to the right and left. The 'brocade border' on this example has a particular form of 'dagger and drop' on the inside. Both 'Period Gentleman & Shepherdess' and 'Seated Period Figures' are used with borders other than those illustrated here.

33. Bowl with 'Period Gentleman and Shepherdess'. Diameter 16.4 cms.

Another design which was given to Swansea by Williams & Price (1972) is shown on Plate 9 (Cat. Ref. Case 38). This landscape, consisting of a house and shed with cattle being herded in the foreground, is well known on the creamwares of both Josiah Wedgwood and Ralph Wedgwood (Holdaway 1986), but in this example the house has been somewhat modernised with two chimneys over a tiled roof instead of thatch. It is proposed that these should be called 'Landscape with House and Shed I' and 'II'. The very large jug with modernised house, 'Landscape with House and Shed II' has the same border as a large punch bowl (Cat. Ref. Case 5/8) which has profiles of George III and Queen Charlotte in the bottom with 'A KING REVERED A QUEEN BELOVED' above and 'LONG MAY THEY LIVE' below. There are chinoiserie designs on the outside. A similar pattern incorporating the profiles of their Majesties beneath a crown and what may be an anti-Jacobin slogan 'KING and CONSTITUTION' sweeping around below them is illustrated inside a bowl with a different border by May (1972). It is reasonable to suppose that these designs were created at the time of the outbreak of war with France in 1793. Another bowl with the border of the first described here (i.e. without 'KING and CONSTITUTION') shows a Commander mounted on horseback with sword drawn and surrounded by his troops and 'His Royal Highnefs FREDERICK DUKE OF YORK' below. This second son of George III was the Duke of York of our childhood song, 'who had 10,000 men . . .' For a mug of the same design see (Cat. Ref. Case 4/7).

In contrast to the patriotic support shown by these pieces for the home market an event abroad was commemorated on a rare piece of Staffordshire blue printed ware impressed IH on the reverse. The plate shows 'PRESIDENT WASHINGTON' in one roundel and a print of the 'Seal of the United States' in another alongside (Plate 28) (Cat. Ref. Case 35/5). There are flowers and a cornucopia above and a shell and flowers below. Probably this design is linked to the death of the First President of the United States of America in 1799.

Somewhat earlier, is the better known 'LA GUILLOTINE' mug seen in Figure 34. A befrocked figure is operating the device, on which lies a hapless victim. Above the victim's legs is the date 1793 and at his feet stand two gentlemen in breeches. The printed words state:

34. Mug with 'LA GUILLOTINE' print. Height 9 cms
(Cat. Ref. Case 4/8)

35. Supper dish with 'Procession with Elephant'
Mark WEDGWOOD & CO impressed. Width 32 cms
(Cat. Ref. Case 3/12).

36. Small bowl with Elephant pattern. Diameter 11 cms.

'View of LA GUILLOTINE or modern beheading machine at PARIS by which LOUIS XVI late king of France suffered on the Scaffold Jan 21'.
To the extreme right and left of the design are four individual sprays of flowers, two on either side of the handle (Cat. Ref. Case 4/8). These flower sprays are not the same as in the bowl with the royal profiles (Cat. Ref. Case 5/8), although traditionally both are given to Swansea. A lack of evidence prevails and they remain unidentified.

On the whole fruit and flowers on early blue printed earthenwares are used between and to augment other patterns as we have seen already on the bowl (Cat. Ref. Case 5/8). There are flowers inside this bowl and on the 'LA GUILLOTINE' mug, and flowers and fruit inside and in between the chinoiseries on the outside of another bowl. The sources of these flowers are discussed in detail in the section on botanical patterns. The main patterns are the 'Precarious Chinaman' (Cat. Ref. Case 4/2), who sits under a parasol held by an attendant, and the 'Figure on a Llama', who is accompanied by a figure with a parasol whose position has been modified compared to the original print of a procession signed 'J.June sculp'. Both of these chinoiseries are taken from *The Ladies Amusement* which was printed in 1762 for John Sayer, a map and print seller in Fleet Street, London. What is interesting about these designs is that, remarkably, the building to the right and the groups of either bamboos or rocks above the figures are both major components of the well known 'Boy on the Buffalo Pattern' (Cat. Ref. Case 8). This pattern, which was copied from Chinese export porcelain, is found on the wares by many different potters (Copeland 1980; Holdaway 1980). It was probably in use before the end of the century until, perhaps, about 1805.

Less common are the patterns where the figures and animal in the 'Boy on the Buffalo' pattern are replaced by elephants in various forms. The elephant may have a castle, or a howdah, or nothing at all on its back and all of the marked pieces seem to belong to the 18th century.

A supper dish showing a 'Processional Elephant & Howdah' is seen in Figure 35, with a teabowl and saucer (Cat. Ref. Case 13/3) with an 'Elephant & Castle'. Both were made by Ralph Wedgwood. Examples of elephants without anything on their back are known on blue printed earthenware (Figure 36) and this particular 'Elephant' pattern is an example of a design which is found also on porcelain; there is a small Coalport jug with 1795 in gilt in the Godden Reference Collection. The 'Processional Elephant & Howdah' and the 'Elephant & Castle' patterns are common in the 'Shape & Pattern Book of Ralph Wedgwood' (Holdaway 1985). A great variety of well known porcelain patterns are used to decorate the earliest of the blue printed earthenwares (Holdaway 1991), and they are not necessarily contemporary porcelain designs. For example, 'Two Women Choosing Accessories' which was used on Bow porcelain (Watney 1973), is seen on a rare earthenware mug (Cat. Ref. Case 1/29). A creamware example is known and in each of the ceramic patterns the woman standing at the left hand end of the long display case has a single long sash falling from the bow at the back of her gown. In the print from which the pattern is taken, Edwards & Darley's *New Book of Designs* (1754) there are two sashes. This indicates that the earthenware engravers were probably seeking inspiration directly from porcelain pieces, although it is possible that an intermediate print, taken from the Edwards & Darley source with slight modifications, may come to light. Incidentally, there is no doubt that this is one of the finest and most detailed ceramic engravings in existence with a full and faithfully copied composition.

Some other patterns taken from more contemporary porcelains are equally rare. The rare border of the jug (Cat. Ref. Case 1/21) is found on Coalport porcelains and the 'Fence' pattern used to decorate Worcester, Caughley and Lowestoft porcelains is used on blue printed earthenwares, but it is very rare. The covered butter dish in Figure 37 is decorated with this pattern; the body of this and the tea canister decorated with

'Birds in Branches' are very white. The tea canister has a printed crescent mark which provides further evidence that, initially, the blue printed earthenware potters were making teawares like the contemporary porcelains and/or that the engraver came from Worcester or Caughley where such marks were used. The very large engraved bird on the reverse of the canister suggests that this 'Birds in Branches' design was taken from Worcester rather than Caughley porcelain. The earlier Hancock version of this print is known on contemporary black printed earthenwares and is likely to be discovered printed in blue in due course. The 'Milkmaids' pattern seen on earthenware (Cat. Ref. Case 18/2) was taken first from a Hancock print to decorate Worcester porcelains.

There are a number of patterns used on blue printed earthenwares which are also found on New Hall or New Hall related porcelains. This is hardly surprising considering the commercial importance of these porcelains at the time of the introduction of blue printing on earthenwares. Furthermore, this was a local Staffordshire based porcelain manufactory with many earthenware potters nearby. When comparing a relatively common early pattern on earthenware with the porcelain version of the original, details in the design will vary, especially when the pattern is used by several earthenware manufactories. Take, for example, the New Hall 'Trench Mortar' pattern which was copied from the Chinese. There is a bamboo to the left of the building in the porcelain examples which may or may not be present when the design appears on blue printed earthenwares. The willow tree is replaced with a bamboo on Spode pieces and the design is known as 'Malayan Hut' (Cat. Ref. Case 22/2; Copeland 1980). The use of two or more names for the same pattern on different ceramic bodies is an unfortunate state of affairs and should be avoided unless a different name is used for the design at the factory.

The number of blue printed chinoiserie designs on earthenware at the end of the 18th century may run into hundreds. Some of them were very popular and were used by many potters into the 19th century. Unfortunately, it is outside the scope of this article to consider the intricacies and differences in the patterns which make possible the identification or grouping of the wares, nor can real attention be given to the border patterns, which underwent several evolutions during

the first quarter of a century of blue printed earthenware production.

A useful yardstick for identifying which blue printed earthenware patterns were in use in the 18th century is provided by those potters who ceased potting at the turn of the century. Unusually, one of these potters marked his wares. Ralph Wedgwood used the mark Wedgwood & Co. (in lower and upper case) while he was potting in the last decade of the 18th century, first in Burslem and then in Ferrybridge, Yorkshire. He stopped potting on 1st January 1801. Amongst the variety of chinoiserie patterns he used are 'Trench Mortar'/'Malayan Hut' and 'Pagoda'/'Mandarin' patterns. In addition, like a number of potters of his day he was inspired by classical sources from antiquity. His 'Classical Figures' (Cat. Ref. Case 34/16) are taken from the splendid tomes of Hamilton's *Collection of Etruscan, Greek and Roman Antiquities* (Holdaway 1986); that is, he was using the same sources as Josiah Wedgwood.

Geometric patterns appeared just before the end of the century and a useful dateline concerning one of these comes from the sherds of Bradley and Co., who potted in Coalport for a brief period between 1796 and 1800. Amongst the earthenware sherds from the site are items which match the plate (Cat. Ref. Case 34/14), which is decorated with 'Violin' pattern (Edmundson 1981). With this pattern, which was used by several potters, we turn our attention to the shapes of some early blue printed wares.

In keeping with the copying of porcelain designs, the shapes which were used at the beginning of the manufacture of blue printed earthenware reflect the shapes in use for other ceramic bodies. So it is not only the patterns that were copied on to tea wares but the shapes as well. Another early globular teapot, similar to the 'W. Tonill 1789' teapot (Plate 29), is illustrated with

38. Globular teapot and creamer about 1790. Teapot Height 16 cms. Jug Height 10 cms.

37. Covered butter dish with 'Fence' pattern. Length 14 cms. Width 10 cms. Height 10 cms.

39. Teapot of Leeds creamware shape with strap handles and flower knop. Height 13 cms.

an en suite sparrow-beak creamer in Figure 38; they look remarkably like porcelain. Another teapot (Figure 39) has strap handles and a flower knop and could have been made at Leeds, where this shape and handles were used for creamware. It is always tempting to use this kind of argument in identifying ceramics and perhaps it provides a useful idea at the start of identification with the hope of confirmation from excavated material, or a marked example, in due course.

The earthenware teapot shape and the moulding of the handle and spout shown in Plate 2 were also used at Caughley. The earthenware spout has three pairs of moulded scrolls and the handle has a raised bead-like spine with feather-like moulding to the outside along its length. These features were copied by Caughley from Chinese export wares.

It is not only the shape of the earthenware teapot in Plate 2 that resembles Caughley porcelain, but the remainder of the tea service as well. Both services have teapot stands, spoon trays, covered canisters and covered sugar boxes which are of very similar shape including the knops. It is thought that once there was a cover on the earthenware creamer, now missing. The cover of the tea canister fits the creamer very well so that these covers would have been interchangeable and, when it was made, the earthenware tea service was a very close copy of a Caughley porcelain tea service. The similarity is enhanced by the earthenware pieces being heavily gilded and, it is difficult to distinguish between the Caughley porcelain and the earthenware services when viewed at a short distance.

This earthenware tea service, which would have graced any tea table, has tea bowls and saucers. The solitary matching cup also has a moulded handle after the Chinese. Each piece of the tea service has a large blue printed mark consisting of three leaves on a twiggy branch. The identity of the maker is uncertain but it was probably made between 1785 and 1790. Drakard (1988) describes a different shape of teapot and covered sugar box which, with the remainder of the service which includes a slopbowl, tea bowls and saucers, are believed to have been made by Spode. These fluted wares decorated with 'Mandarin' pattern were probably made during the closing years of the 18th century when fluted and plain wares were popular.

Turning to early earthenware table wares, the finely potted soup tureen (Figure 40) is a splendid piece with a carefully moulded knop like Josiah Wedgwood's flower or plume knop of about 1775 complete with a circle of moulded leaves immediately below. The handles of this soup tureen are splayed at the top so that they are attached to the body over a width of 16 cm (more than 6 inches), and the moulding, together with the elevated centre to the known stand, all feature in cream-coloured earthenwares such as Queen's Ware, made by Josiah Wedgwood and appear in the '1790' Catalogue (Reilly 1989). Here, then, is an example where attribution on the basis of shape is not possible for it is well known that Josiah

Wedgwood did not begin to decorate his earthenwares with underglaze blue printed designs before 1805–1806, and this tureen belongs to the 18th century. However, whoever made the dinner service of which this soup tureen is a part must have been a very good potter of discerning taste and the ladle has an elaborately moulded handle. The tureen is decorated with 'Willow Mandarin I' pattern illustrated in Figure 32 (Cat. Ref. Case 4/4) on the mug which has 'W. Morshall, 1790', printed on the base (Plate 29). The pattern features a large willow tree and large birds overhead, and once again one wonders whether this was the first willow pattern, i.e. the 'Old Willow' mentioned by Shaw in 1829. Shaw stated that the first table wares had a border of 'Willow and Dagger' and certainly this soup tureen has 'Daggers' along the border edge.

There is the possibility that the pattern 'Old Willow' mentioned by Shaw (1829) did not have a willow tree in it at all and that the term was one which was loosely applied to another, or indeed any, design found on Chinese export wares of the mid 18th century. After all, by the time he was writing in 1829, early blue printed designs had undergone several transformations, with many new patterns from a great variety of sources. For the most part, the new patterns of the 19th century can be divided into two groups; those which are distinctly European and those which are chinoiseries. Many of the chinoiseries of the early 19th century gradually became more European and soon prints from Botanical and Zoological texts and travelogues, as well as other sources, were being copied onto blue and white printed earthenware.

However, chinoiseries continued to be popular, and some patterns such as 'Broseley' (Cat. Ref. Case 1/21) and 'Three Man Willow' continued for decades unchanged. It is possible that Shaw saw the European designs as new in contrast to the 'Old Willow', that is, those patterns derived from the painted decoration on Chinese export porcelain. Perhaps we shall never know but it is worth noting that the first blue printed earthenware for teawares was described by Shaw as 'Broseley', that is, a pattern said to have been named after a town in Shropshire, England. Perhaps, and it is no more than a thought, Shaw was contrasting English porcelain and Chinese export designs in some way when referring to the earliest patterns used on blue printed earthenware tea and tablewares.

40. Soup tureen and ladle of 'Willow Mandarin I'. Tureen Width 44 cms. Height 27 cms. Ladle Length 32 cms.

The Useful Wares

by Doreen Otto, Vice-Chair of Friends of Blue

The vintage years for blue and white transfer printing were from 1800 to 1835, and although the process had been invented earlier it was not until towards the end of the Napoleonic Wars that public demand, spurred on by the extra spending power of the masses brought about by the Industrial Revolution, engendered a boom market. This in turn, enabled prices to be lowered still further and placed simple blue and white ware within the reach of most levels of society. This surge in demand was probably a symptom of the natural urge of a class of people to better themselves who had previously been without hope or ambition, the slow spread of education leading to a desire to emulate the moneyed and aristocratic classes. Blue and white earthenware looked at a casual glance very much like the Chinese and European wares which had been imported for many years but had been far too expensive for the average person.

In order to survive in business, the manufacturers had to sell, and to sell they had to produce goods which were basically useful, as most of their potential customers could not afford to spend hard-earned money on luxuries. A very high proportion of blue and white printed pottery was therefore useful as opposed to purely ornamental, but the process of decorating wares with striking designs enabled the public to combine utility with ornament. There was great scope for elegant and unusual shapes among, for instance, dessert services, and some remarkable pieces have been produced over the years.

All the larger factories made table services. Spodes were particularly notable, especially those in their 'Indian Sporting' and 'Caramanian' series of patterns, but landscape and other pictorial designs did not lend themselves for use on teawares or other relatively small items. Spode maintained the high quality of their potting and printing as well as the shapes, sometimes the designs of their dinner and dessert services did not vary very much over many years. Perhaps this was a factor in the factory's survival until the present day despite the usual financial crises which have constantly beset the industry.

The shapes of tureens and covered dishes were frequently distinctive; the handles and knops can be very ornate – for instance the 'Antique Scenery' services from an unknown maker. Often, too, these shapes were unique to a particular manufacturer and have enabled educated guesses to be made as to the probable origin of unmarked pieces. Particularly impressive handles appear on items in the 'Beemaster' pattern, by a still unidentified maker (Cat. Ref. Case 6/1), and there are fine knops in the shape of swans, pineapples, lions and other natural objects. The serving dishes came in a variety of sizes, for soup, vegetables, sauces, and many of the tureens had their own ladles; these and ordinary spoons have not survived in quantity.

The dinner services included also several large dishes or platters, sometimes up to at least 70 cms long, and often four or more different sizes of plates. The shapes displayed a certain ingenuity in their appropriateness for their particular use. Drainers were flat trays made to fit in standard sizes of serving dish and were pierced to allow juices to drain away from the meat or fish placed on the dish. Later, the drainer was rendered superfluous by the introduction of 'well and tree' dishes, grooved to channel the juices into a well at one end of the dish.

In dessert services the designer's imagination ran riot, producing an amazing variety of shapes although the basic functional pieces were relatively few. Plates were somewhat smaller than dinner plates, whilst the serving dishes, usually open, were made in a variety of forms including cushion, lobed or shell-like shapes. Dessert services also included comports on low or high pedestal stands and sometimes openwork baskets on stands, intended for fruit, chestnuts or perhaps sweetmeats. The handles of the dishes and comports were most elaborate, and sometimes the rims of plates and stands were pierced or 'arcaded', like the baskets, giving an attractive openwork appearance.

Full tea services (Plate 2) were among the earliest productions in blue and white earthenware, and usually consisted of teapot and stand, cream jug, sugar box or basin (lidded or open), slop bowl, plates and cups and saucers. The early services often included a tea canister. Coffee sets were of much the same composition, with the pot taller and thinner than the teapots, but usually did not include plates. Before long, the manufacturers followed the sales gimmick, used by the porcelain manufacturers, amalgamating the two types of service by providing 'trios', a teacup, coffee cup and a single saucer for use with either cup. The coffee cups, like the pots, tended to be taller and slimmer than those used for tea. Less common were chocolate pots, which were similar in shape to coffeepots but were not usually accompanied by their own set of cups and saucers.

Notable among the breakfast tablewares were the egg-stands, which carried a variable number (usually between three and six) of egg cups. Marmalade or jam jars still surface occasionally, but time has taken its toll of the lids. Toast racks (Plate 31) were not uncommon, though the shape was not ideal for the display of a large pattern and geometric or 'sheet' (all-over) patterns were often used. Jugs for toast-water were quite common, this was simply an infusion of toast in water, perhaps drunk for medicinal purposes. These jugs usually incorporated a strainer inside the pouring lip.

For the other meals of the day, many pieces were available to complement the main services. Small pickle dishes, pickle sets on stands, divided dishes, salts and pepper pots (these were usually set at each individual place), mustard pots, knife rests, plate lifters, table candlesticks, ice pails, monteiths for cooling wine glasses (a rare item in blue and white), hot plates designed to hold hot water to keep food warm, and argyles (Plate 3) and spouted vessels to fulfil the same function for gravy and other liquids. This list is far from complete, but gives some idea of the many different shapes in use 150 years or more ago.

For the last meal of the day there were supper sets, normally with covered dishes so shaped as to fit into a wooden tray (usually oval or circular) (Cat. Ref. Case Dining Room/32) and leaving a space in the middle which might hold a pickle dish or possibly a taller and more elaborate container. Possibly the huge cheese stands, either bases with domed covers, or cradles in which a whole circular cheese could rest, were used at supper as well as at earlier meals.

Once the satisfaction of the inner man had been catered for, the manufacturers turned to other essentials, especially to the kitchen in which the food and drink were prepared. Cooking pans, patty pans, storage vessels such as gooseberry jars (Plate 11), sauce bottles, strainers for milk and eggs, dairy items such as skimmers for curds and occasionally larger items such as pails – these are just a few examples, new shapes are still found and sometimes defy identification of their original use. Jugs, of course, were made in all shapes and sizes and for many different specific uses. The size ranged from the massive harvest or bellringers' jug (Plates 8 & 9), sometimes up to three feet tall and needing an extra lifting handle below the spout, to tiny jugs with pointed sparrowbeak lips only a couple of inches high. Their uses ran from ale or cider (the harvest jugs) to cream vessels for individual place settings. Kitchen items frequently came to be used for advertising purposes as trade competition increased.

Jugs and mugs (in sizes up to two quarts) were in common use in the home and also in the taverns, and frequently doubled as commemorative pieces covering family events, local history or happenings on a national scale. Some of the pieces made especially for tavern use illustrate the rather basic sense of humour of the day, with puzzle jugs which would pour beer over the unfortunate drinker if he did not know the secret of covering a small hole located on the underside of the handle, and mugs containing lifelike frogs, toads and newts which, if they did not spit liquid over the user's face, probably put him at risk of a heart attack when they suddenly surfaced as the mug was drained (Cat. Ref. Case 4/6; 5/4 and 21/12). At the other end of the scale came the two-handled loving cups (Cat. Ref. Case 16/8; 19/13; 23/15 and 36/10).

Another area in which blue and white was popular was toiletries, especially the services intended for use with the old-fashioned wash-stands. These might consist of wash basin, ewer, slop pail, soap dish, toothbrush holder, chamberpot, perhaps a beaker and even a hair tidy. Few complete ornamental blue and white dressing table sets seem to survive, however, some little pots for powders and potions, lotions and

liniments and all the intricacies of the female toilet still exist. Patch-pots were used around the turn of the 18th/19th centuries, when artificial moles were very much the fashion perhaps in an attempt to cover up the ravages of disease or dissipation.

Large footbaths were common, and fixed washbasins and lavatory bowls, as well as commode fittings are also known. Shaving mugs were particularly popular in the second half of the 19th century and many are known with flow blue decoration. Much sought after today are personal and medical items such as ladies' coach-pots (known as bourdalous), gentlemen's urinals (Plate 14), spitting and vomit pots, invalid feeding jugs and sucking pots, posset pots for medicinal foods and various other shapes right through to the ubiquitous bedpan and chamberpot.

Practically every room in the house attracted blue and white items with specific uses. In the drawing room stood garnitures of vases, usually in the Chinese style, and furniture was sometimes lifted off the carpet on furniture blocks (Cat. Ref. Case 32/10). In the library or the study, writing or desk sets (Plate 25) and inkwells were quite usual, and if there was no separate smoking room one might also have found such items as snuff-boxes or the magnificent and complicated smokers' sets (Plate 26) which contained every item needed by a smoker, all within a single tall column of blue and white earthenware. Portable and pillar candlesticks were quite common. Outside in the hallway there would probably have been a large umbrella stand, and a few manufacturers, notably Masons, made complete fireplaces and even tables in earthenware. Rare are the blue and white equivalents of the superb ornamental semi-circular bough-pots made by so many of the top porcelain manufacturers.

The nursery was not forgotten, with baby requirements such as pap boats and various shapes of feeding bottle, and for growing children right through to their teens the useful wares of their parents were duplicated in miniature, with a profusion of tiny tea and dinner services (Plate 24) and many other items.

Blue and white found its way outside too, with garden seats in the Chinese fashion, flower pots and other items for conservatories, bird feeders, dog bowls and even water bottles or pilgrim flasks for use on journeys.

Just as the decoration on blue and white earthenware can tell us the social and fashion history of the day, so the useful wares over a period of 150 years can relate the changes which took place in the day-to-day life of the average middle-class family and show us how our grandparents and great-grandparents moved towards 20th century living. The luxuries becoming necessities and new inventions constantly presenting fresh possibilities for the improvement of domestic life. Yet, at the same time, we are presented with a forceful picture of the drive and ingenuity of past generations and may well go away with the sobering thought that many things which we regard as new are in fact adapted from the experience of 200 years.

Changing Styles 1840–1870
by Rosalind Pulver

British collectors and researchers have, in the past, concentrated their interests on wares up to 1835 at the latest, so the period from 1840– 1870 can be seen as virtually new territory. Wares from this latter period have often been considered 'too late' or of inferior quality. It has been suggested that with younger collectors now taking an interest in blue printed wares, this could be a new and less expensive field of collecting. However, there are two areas of collecting which are exceptions – children's plates, which are often unmarked and, especially if printed in blue, are much sought after, and commemorative items, which have always been more desirable than other wares of this period.

This essay is restricted, as far as possible, to the investigation of designs produced from about 1840 to 1870, although it must be stressed that popular patterns, especially from large firms such as Wedgwood (e.g. 'Botanical' pattern; Cat. Ref. Case 24/1) and Copeland (e.g. 'Italian'; see Cat. Ref. Case 22/8) were produced throughout this period and in some cases beyond. Smaller firms also continued to produce patterns such as 'Nuneham Courtenay' ('Wild Rose'; see Cat. Ref. Case 23/18), and copies of Spode's 'Italian' pattern, without keeping up the previously high standards or even renewing copperplates when they became too worn. As a result, there are many low-quality pieces around today bearing pale fuzzy designs which have given later blue printed wares such a bad name. This essay will include printed patterns which may not necessarily have so far been found in blue. As many successful designs were produced in a range of colours such as black, green, slate grey and pink as well as blue, prints found in these colours have been included in the eventuality of a blue piece turning up, which has sometimes been the case.

Historical and Social Background

Queen Victoria came to the throne in 1837 and with her came the dawning of a new age of prosperity for the British Isles and the future British Empire. As people became more prosperous they could afford bone china for their dinner-tables and consequently there was a decline in demand for blue printed wares. This resulted in a downward spiral – a lowering in price and therefore quality, as the wares were made mainly for the cheaper end of the market. Copperplates would be used for a much longer time or else sold off when they were very worn to other less successful factories for further use. Evidence of this is the discovery of a large service of very pale, inferior quality 'Asiatic Pheasants' pattern (see Cat. Ref. Case 23/1) in a London Almshouse some years ago.

Blue coloured wares generally had a very good innings, through Chinese Ming porcelain, Delft wares,

British porcelains of the 18th century and, from the 1780's, blue printed pottery. However, in the 1830's, with improvements in firing and chemistry enabling new colours to be produced, members of the public who wanted wares for everyday use were able to purchase them printed in a range of colours. The transfer of 'popularity' from blue to green printed wares took place in the late Spode and Copeland & Garrett period of the early 1830's. A good example of this change in fashion can be drawn from Spode's 'Aesop's Fables' series, which was originally produced in blue, then slightly later in green; by the time of the succeeding Copeland & Garrett partnership (1833–1847) this pattern was produced in both colours, as was the 'Byron Views' series made by the same firm (Cat. Ref. Case 33/12).

From around 1840, blue transfer prints were generally not only paler in colour but revealed a much larger surface area left in the white. This resulted in the central transfer print being considerably smaller, because it did not have to cover the entire well of a plate and extend to the border, as was generally the case in earlier wares. These smaller designs had an advantage in economic terms, in that the same transfer could be used for more shapes, since it was no longer necessary to prepare separate copperplates for each individual shape and size. A good example of this can be seen in a jug illustrating 'Napoleon's Victories', by W. Smith & Co. The engraving around the body of the jug is of mediocre quality, probably due to wear in the copperplate, whereas the border decoration around the pouring lip is much clearer, possibly from a copperplate which had been subjected to much less use.

Factories of the period

Current information on factory output and dating of designs depends, for the most part, on easily accessible factory records or on published material which is the result of the interests of individual collectors who have made their research information available to the world at large. The registration of pattern designs is also of great help in determining the dates of different styles, but it does not always indicate colour.

Searches of various sources reveal that the most prolific factories include J.M.P. Bell who produced over 32 patterns; W.T. Copeland (over 36 patterns); Davenport (over 20); William Adams & Sons, and Wedgwood (over 30). Other, lesser-known partnerships active in the period under review include John & George Alcock, Edward Challinor, Joseph Clementson, Robert Cochran, Cork Edge & Malkin, Thomas Godwin, Joseph Heath, James Jamieson, T.J. & J. Mayer, Podmore Walker, John Ridgway & Co., William Ridgway Son & Co., Anthony Shaw, John Wedge Wood, and Wood & Challinor. There were, of course, many other manufacturers who operated within and overlapping the period, and to date there is a record of around 185 firms who produced printed wares. As interest and research continue, many more patterns will certainly come to light.

Changes in copperplate engraving techniques

As demand for blue printed wares decreased, cheaper methods of producing the copperplates had to be found. Time-consuming stipple engraving over large areas was replaced either by a return to line engraving or by the use of the acid etching technique. The line engraving was made coarser and thicker, with the lines further apart, giving rise to less tonal variation and a paler overall effect. Thus, savings were achieved in engravers' salaries, wear on copperplates and inking time. However, top quality engravers were still in demand, as is shown by the following extract from a bill sent to Wedgwood in 1846 by Thomas Allen for his work on the high-quality 'Trent' pattern, which shows a horse-drawn goods' wagon crossing a river, taken from a low viewpoint and with Italianate buildings in the background:

Bill: from his address at Shelton, dated September 30th, 1846

Table Plate	£5.5.0.
London Cup	£2.12.6.
Saucer	"
Twiffler	£4.4.0.
Round Dish	£9.9.0.
Broad Straight Borders	£4.10.0.
Narrow Borders	£3.0.0.
Middle Borders	£3.15.0.

2 narrow borders and 2 beads on straight border plate – 18 shillings.

The above forms part of a total invoice for £122.14.0. for work carried out on that date.

THE WARES

This section deals with changes in style during the period 1840 to 1870, covering the general appearance of patterns, especially the changing emphasis on areas left in the white, as well as new developments in central patterns, borders and backstamps. In general, new designs of the 1840's saw a continued interest in views; in the 1850's many plant and flower designs were drawn in a more naturalistic way and in the 1860's centres were in small roundels or in some cases just disappeared altogether, the only decoration being broad bands of border stringing. These roundels were particularly associated with Moorish or Persian border designs such as Copeland's 'Sardinia' (registered 17th December 1858), and the later 'Turco' and 'Venetia' patterns. Sometimes the central motifs were reduced to a star or similar geometric shape.

The obvious difference between the earlier wares and those of this period lies in the change from the complete coverage of the surface, found especially in the dark blue American export wares, in which the only visible areas of white surface might have been

clouds or the sails of shipping, to the contrasting appearance of thirty years later, when the entire centre of a plate might be left white. The demand for all-over decoration was obviously a fashion, as it can be seen also on bone china such as the Spode pattern 1166, which features a dark royal-blue background with gilt overpainting. This contrasts completely with the change in style evidenced by such pieces as a washbasin made by the Bristol based partnership of Pountney & Goldney (1836–1849) and printed in the 'Bouquet' pattern of sprays of flowers scattered over the white surface.

CENTRAL DESIGNS
Landscapes

Views were still popular in the 1840's, reflecting the contemporary fascination with travel to far distant places not yet accessible by the railway. The archaeological and historical scenes found on the earlier wares reflected the antique interests of the wealthy to whom the Grand Tour was considered an essential part of their education, and are illustrated ideally in the 'Named Italian Views' series made by the Don Pottery (Cat. Ref. Case 11/3). As the world became smaller these interests were available to a much wider audience, but the popular conception of the rest of the world changed and invested the designs used on ceramics with a romanticism which resulted in idealised panoramic scenes taken from a high viewpoint which, within the surrounding area of white, appeared to recede even further into the distance, giving an impression of unreality. Some of the later views copied loosely the style of the 17th century French painter Claude Lorraine, who depicted buildings in deep recession on either side of a central waterway flowing directly back into the picture plane, rather than winding away through the scenery as in earlier scenes such as Spode's 'Italian' pattern. Claude Lorraine had also been copied in the earlier period (Cat. Ref. Case 24/8).

Classical

The strictly classical themes of the earlier period were replaced by romantic scenes including sculpture or large urns, for example 'Claremont' by Joseph Clementson (design registered in 1856), which illustrates two classical urns set amid flowers on a terrace. The more typical sculptural scenes show statues, usually female, in the foreground of a distant view, such as 'Pomona' by Anthony Shaw (about 1850). Scenes from antiquity were not totally forgotten; the 'Classical Antiquities' series by Joseph Clementson illustrates episodes from the lives of the ancient Greeks.

The majority of these scenes were fictional, or at best heavily idealised or romanticised versions of reality. Copeland's 'Ruins', or 'Melrose' series, registered on 15th September 1848, retains some reality, illustrating idealised ruins set in central transfers with surrounding large white areas.

Flowers and Fruit

In the 1840's and 1850's large sprays of flowers were used as central designs, drawn naturistically rather than stylised. 'Lobelia' was registered on 19th June 1845 by George Phillips, but the copperplate was later purchased by Copeland. In 1849, Copeland registered similar patterns such as 'Garland' and 'Mock Orange'. William Ridgway and Son contributed 'Apple Blossom', with a large spray in the centre and six smaller sprays as a border.

Plain Centres

These may have been considered 'tasteful' by some High Victorian home-makers and although these rarely occurred earlier, in the 1860's Copeland produced at least three ('Osborne', 'Shamrock' and 'Violet') out of a possible 10 designs. 'Marguerite' by Wedgwood has the flower with bead border. With leading firms like Wedgwood and Copeland supplying similar designs, these could not have been made for reasons of economy – perhaps they were intended eventually to accommodate a crest.

Commemoratives

The period under review provided many landmarks worthy of commemoration, and the manufacturers did not let these pass, though the ephemeral nature of such occasions is often shown by the print quality, which suffered because of the necessary speed of production. However, the quality of engraving was frequently above the normal standard.

Royal events started with the accession of Queen Victoria in 1837 and progressed through her marriage to Prince Albert in 1840 and the birth of the Prince of Wales (the future Edward VII) in 1841. With many other occasions in between, the Golden Jubilee in 1887 was a great occasion, and one small commemorative mug illustrates the Queen in her pony cart.

The Great Exhibition of 1851 naturally attracted a huge amount of interest, and various views of the Crystal Palace were produced (Cat. Ref. Case 5/2). See Plate 7.

The firm of Anthony Shaw made several series aimed at the American market in the 1850's; this market is discussed in more detail elsewhere in this book, but it is worth mentioning two of his titles – 'Texan Campaign' and 'Peruvian Horse Hunt' (1853), the latter presumably destined for South America.

'California' was a popular name, possibly associated with the gold rush of 1849, and was used by Podmore Walker and Francis Morley, among others. These titles frequently had no apparent connection with the engravings; the former was a Swiss scene and the latter a floral and scroll design.

Borders

Before the 1830's, the most common style of border had been variations of those used on Chinese porcelain and adapted by English potters, or narrow and closely packed floral patterns. Occasionally these floral borders would be interspersed with other motifs such as fruit or medallions containing miniature scenes, all confined by inner and outer bands of geometric stringing or beading.

During the 1830's the floral borders became less tight, giving the appearance of a lacy, almost Rococo style. Typical also was the inner border which acted as a frame to the inner pattern. At this time also there started the gradual departure of the blue coloured background. A good example of this is in the Davenport 'Scott's Illustrations' series, which at a quick glance resembles a lacy doyley. Perhaps the movement towards the more pale blues was a reflection of fashion changes resulting in the contrast between the new teenage Queen and the rule of the older male monarchs George IV and William IV.

By the 1840's borders tended to lose their inner stringing and consisted mainly of the following principal design variations:-

1. Large plants or flowers interspersed with Rococo scrolls and overflowing towards the centre of a dish. A border of vines features in 'Lobelia' (George Phillips), while naturalistic strawberries appear in Copeland's 'Strawberry', registered in 1852. The Copeland & Garrett 'Louis Quatorze' border, registered in 1844 contains scrolls.

2. Geometric designs, such as the 'Ermine' pattern seen on Joseph Clementson's 'Eglintoun' (1839–1840).

3. Wide bands of geometric or floral design, alternating with large cartouches containing several different patterns, sometimes with ribbons or garlands. This of course must have added considerably to the engraving costs. Examples of this style include the Elkin, Knight & Co. 'Hannibal Passing the Alps', and 'Habana', registered by William Adams & Sons in 1845, which included portraits of members of the Spanish Royal Family (presumably a Cuban connection).

4. Trellis-type framing for cartouches – a refreshing change from interminable scrolls as seen in 'Marmora', by William Ridgway & Co.

5. Broad stringing near the outer rim, which began to appear in the 1860's, sometimes with a small central motif. Copeland's 'Shamrock' pattern, registered on 17th September 1861, has no central design and heralds a somewhat uneventful era for the collector.

Registered designs

As far as dating is concerned, we are particularly fortunate that some firms registered their designs at the Patent Office and marked their wares with a diamond registration lozenge which was in use from 1842 until 1883, after which the system continued with a simple series of 'Regd. No. 1234'. This did not necessarily mean that a particular object with such a mark was made in the year of registration, but the original copperplate was probably produced at that time. This registration gave protection of the design for three years.

In Appendix 'C' of this book there is a list of designs registered in the period 1842 to 1870, but these do not specify colours used. The diamond registration mark gives the classification of the object, year, month, date and parcel number, and from this information it is possible to identify the maker of the item. John Cushion's *Handbook of Pottery and Porcelain Marks* (Appendix B, page 173), contains a list of such firms. Makers can be easily identified from the above information, but further information such as pattern name or process registered would require a personal visit to the Public Record Office archives at Kew, Surrey.

Marks

Although many pieces dating from before the 1830's were impressed and/or printed with the name of the maker, and sometimes also the name of the pattern, an even greater number were not marked at all, so that attribution can be an interesting though taxing and frustrating pastime.

By the 1840's, it was becoming customary, probably for commercial reasons, to give more information in these marks or backstamps, for example the name and location of maker, type or trade name of the particular earthenware used, and sometimes a year mark indicating date of manufacture. Some of these marks are in themselves decorative and interesting, with their framed cartouches, scrolls and miniature pictures. One of the most handsome is the 'draped curtain' mark used by Copeland & Garrett for their 'Seasons' series (Cat. Ref. Case 16/3).

Shapes

The Victorian era was a time of eclecticism when styles from many preceding periods were embraced. Through the influence of A.W.N. Pugin, the Gothic style became popular and this is reflected in the perpendicular style of many jugs, moulded and otherwise, made in the mid-century, and replacing the long running Neo-classical fashion. This change reflected the religious feelings of customers for whom the Neo-classical taste represented the paganism of the Greeks and Romans, whereas the Gothic style represented the Church. Other shapes, including plates and bowls, were also moulded decoratively in keeping with this taste.

Collecting later wares

The period 1840–1870 can open up a large field to the new collector. Most items are clearly marked with useful information concerning origin, so that there is not so much need for attribution or guesswork. To an extent, too, the younger the piece the better the condition. Nonetheless, this was inexpensive ware, and as such a great deal was broken or discarded, thus creating the rarities of today. Collectors may specialise in such areas as shapes, registration marks, whole services or the output of a single factory, helped in the latter instance by the fact that some manufacturers like Wedgwood and Spode still have their archives. Unfortunately, this is not generally the case.

Summary

The following is a general aid to identifying later blue printed wares. By combining some of the evidence listed below, it should be possible to determine which pieces were made in the period under discussion, particularly as there are factory marks which ran for many years on either side of the period.

1. Pale blue colour and lower quality printing than pre-1840's.
2. White background. The central pattern is smaller than previous designs and is often set within a surrounding band of white undecorated areas.
3. Broad line engraving and less stippling.
4. Almost no inner stringing.
5. Borders with loosely packed and more naturalistic flowers, often overlapping into the wells of plates, and the presence of Rococo-style scrolls.
6. Geometric line engraved borders.
7. Prominent cartouches integrated into borders.
8. Heavier body, often accompanied by moulding to rims.
9. No background colour in borders. Stipple engraving gradually moves to the rim in the 1830's and disappears by the 1840's.
10. Views are seen from a high viewpoint and are depicted in deep recession.

CATALOGUE

NOTES TO CATALOGUE SECTION

All the objects included in the exhibition, unless otherwise stated, are made of earthenware.
All the pieces are transfer printed in underglaze blue cobalt.
Where no mark is indicated in the text the item is unmarked.
All measurements are given in centimetres.
The measurements are always given in the order: Length; Width; Height.

Abbreviations used in the Catalogue
Mark: the mark on the item is indicated by a number, for example A1. This refers to the photographs of the individual marks illustrated in Appendix B.

Manuscript References
Where documents are quoted in the footnotes these have been left with the original spelling and punctuation.

Illustrations in Catalogue
Because many of the pieces in this exhibition have not been illustrated before in generally available publications a photograph of every item has been included at the end of the catalogue section. In order to achieve this objective many of the pictures have been provided by the respective owners and this has, of necessity, led to some variations in quality. As far as possible each individual design and shape has been portrayed clearly for identification.

Lenders to the exhibition
Where no lender's name appears it should be assumed that either a general acknowledgement only or complete anonymity has been requested.

DINING ROOM

1 to 26.
Six-place setting **Dinner Service** (see plate 1) consisting of plates (25.3, 21.5 and 16.5 cms), two serving dishes (38.2 and 35.6 cms), soup tureen with stand, cover and ladle, sauce boat, sauce tureen with stand and cover, vegetable dish and cover.
Mark: Various – mainly an impressed factory mark (including W19, W20 and W21) and a ribbon cartouche, printed in blue giving the title of the view (W24).
Enoch Wood & Sons, Burslem. About 1825–1830.
'Grapevine Border' series of named British views with over sixty-five different scenes which is probably the largest of this type of series. The main source from which the views were taken appears to have been John Preston Neale's *Views of the Seats of Noblemen and Gentlemen in England and Wales, Scotland and Ireland* (Six volumes 1818–1823).
Loaned by John and Sally Storton.

Views on the individual objects:
Dinner Plates (25.3 cms)
Esholt House, Yorkshire; Holyrood House, Edinburgh; Taymouth Castle, Perthshire; Wardour Castle, Wiltshire; Warwick Castle; Wellcombe, Warwickshire

Dessert Plates (21 cms)
Barlborough Hall, Derbyshire; Cashiobury, Hertfordshire; Cave Castle, Yorkshire; Compton Verney, Warwickshire; Maxstoke Castle, Warwickshire;
(19.2 cms) Belvoir Castle

Side Plates (16.5 cms)
Castle Forbes, Aberdeenshire; Cathedral at York; Dunraven, Glamorgan; Hagley, Worcestershire; Shirley House, Surrey; Luscombe, Devon

Platters (38.2 cms)
View of Greenwich
(35.6 cms) Harewood House, Yorkshire

Soup Tureen (33.7 × 23 × 19.5 cms) on one side
Hollywell Cottage, Cavan

Stand (38 × 25.6 cms)
Wellcombe, Warwickshire

Vegetable Dish (24.5 cms square) inside, view of
City of Canterbury

Sauce Boat (19 × 9 cms)
Sproughton Chantry
and *Stand* (20 × 15.5 cms)
Gubbins, Hertfordshire

Sauce Tureen (18.5 × 12 × 13.5 cms) on cover
Rivenhall Place, Essex

The **Cutlery** included on the table is 18th century in origin with ivory pistol-grip handles. The silver centrepiece bears an inscription 'Presented to James Meakin Esq. by the united work people in his employ. April 13 1868'.

27. Pair of **Knife Rests** (see plate 1) (exhibited on the dining table) 8 × 3 cms.
Attributed to *James Keeling, Hanley.* About 1820–1830.
Border from 'Grazing Rabbits' pattern, attributed on the grounds of sherds found on site of factory.

28. **Salt** on a diamond shaped foot (exhibited on the dining table) 7.6 × 10.1 cms.
Possibly *Leeds.* About 1795–1800.
As often happened on smaller items, the border pattern from a larger design has been adapted in order that the piece should match a full dinner service.
Footnote: Salt was always considered indispensable to human well-being, and this gave rise to the ceremony of the salt, (the taking of salt in strict hierarchical order from the single salt placed on the table). By the 17th century the concept of the small salt had been adopted, a practice which has remained. It became increasingly popular to have matching salts to the dinner service.
Loaned by Flora Rabinovitch.

29. Pair of footed **Salts** (see plate 1) (exhibited on the dining table) 7.1 cms diameter.
Maker Unknown. About 1800–1810.
An unidentified chinoiserie pattern (see footnote to Cat. Ref. Case Dining room 28).

30. **Pepper Pot** (see plate 1) (exhibited on the dining table) 5.5 × 12.2 cms.
Maker Unknown. About 1810–1815.
Chinoiserie derived with some European influences. The space available seems to have been filled with odd pieces of the design, one being repeated twice. This seems to have been standard practice on small or difficult shapes. At a casual glance the overall blue and white effect was maintained.

Footnote: Several different types of pepper pot are known, including those with a domed lid as shown here and ones with a flatter lid and fewer holes. From the late 16th century onwards pepper was dispersed over food through a caster. These casters frequently came in sets of three; one large for sugar, and a smaller pair for pepper and cayenne. It soon became apparent that the fierce pungency of the cayenne greatly restricted its use and it was replaced eventually by the mustard pot. The 'Kitchen pepper' for culinary purposes was larger and usually cylindrical with a single practical handle.

31. **Mustard Pot** and Cover (see plate 1) (exhibited on the dining table) 8 × 5.6 cms.
Davenport, Longport. About 1820.
'The Villagers', a popular rural scene including a boy blowing bubbles. Other makers used this title.
Footnote: Mustard is made from the brown and white seeds of cruciferous plants of the Brassica family. In classical times it was prepared by mixing the pounded seed with 'mustum' – unfermented wine. The suffix 'ard' is derived from the Teutonic '-hart' meaning hard or strong and denoted the intensity. Mustard has always been used for culinary purposes often in the past in the genuine need to disguise bad tastes. The commercial manufacture of mustard is thought to have originated with a Mrs. Clements at 73, Saddler Street, Durham about 1720. By 1742 Messrs Keens had established a mustard-making factory at Garlick Hill, London (this probably gave rise to the expression 'keen as mustard'). Initially dry mustard powder was sprinkled over the food from a caster. As prepared mustard made its appearance the caster with a pierced lid became superfluous, though the form remained with a solid lid (Cat. Ref. Case 1/18 and 2/11), the condiment being lifted out on a spoon; these shapes however were gradually replaced with squat mustard pots.

32. **Supper Set**, with Egg Stand and Cruet Centre (Egg hoops and cruet missing) 55 × 45 × 20 cms.
Mark: Covers (various) S4 and S6, Bases (various) S4 and S5.
Spode, Stoke. About 1810–1815.
'Caramanian' series (see Cat. Ref. Case 15/13). The views on this set are:
Segments and lids: 'Colossal Sarcophagus near Castle Rosso'
Centrepiece lid: 'Citadel near Corinth'
Centrepiece interior: 'Caramanian Castle'
Footnote: In the edited version of *Passages from the diaries of Mrs Philip Lybbe-Powys* by Emily J. Climenson (1899) she records her visit to Wedgwood's London showroom at York Street on 31st August 1789: 'In the morning we went to London a-shopping, and at Wedgwood's, as usual, we were highly entertained as I think no other shop affords so great a variety. I have amongst other things purchas'd one of the newly invented *petit soupes*, which I think equally clever, elegant and convenient when alone or a small party, as so much less trouble to ourselves and servants'.

33. **Wine Cooler** (see plate 20) 21.1 × 18.4 cms.
Maker Unknown. About 1815–1835.
'Standard Willow' pattern.

34. **Pickle Set** on Stand with Central Salt (see plate 12) 18 cms square × 11 cms high.
Mark: X10.
Series attributed to *J & W Ridgway* on the basis of comparison of shapes. About 1820–1830.
'Cashiobury, Hertfordshire' from a 'British Scenery' series which contains at least twelve different views. No single source seems to have been used for the scenes in this series. This view may have been taken from a print by John Preston Neale (Cat. Ref. Case Dining room/1).

35. **Chestnut Basket** and stand.
Basket 27.5 × 18.8 × 9.4 cms, Stand 23.9 × 19.1 cms.
Mark: W19.
Enoch Wood & Sons, Burslem. About 1825–1830.
'Dorney Court' from 'Grapevine Border' series (Cat. Ref. Case Dining room/1).
Loaned by John and Sally Storton.

TEA ROOM

Although not taken as seriously as the Chinese tea ceremony, tea-drinking in England around the turn of the 18th/19th centuries was a serious business among the upper and middle classes. Services were produced in various materials. Transfer printed earthenware gave a strong and consistent decoration to every piece. Many contemporary prints show tea-drinking in progress.

1. **Part Tea Set** (see plate 2) comprising: teapot, cover and stand (15 cms), tea canister with cover, sugar box with cover, creamer, slop bowl, saucer dish, eight tea bowls and seven saucers and a spoon tray.
Mark: Most printed with a leaf spray in blue (X34).
Maker Unknown. About 1790.
A typical chinoiserie scene including a boat with a canopy and an unusual domed pagoda with a geometric and floral border.

2. **Baluster Vase** and Cover with a widow knop 29.2 cms high.
Maker Unknown. About 1790–1800.
A standard chinoiserie landscape view, a version of the 'Two Figures' pattern. The decoration is divided into four shaped reserves, two with the main scene and the other of landscape vignettes divided by flowers and leaves.
Footnote: The seated widow finial rests her arm on a barrel. The knop represents the widow of Zarephath who, in the Bible (1 Kings 17, 9–24), shares her last meal with a beggar who subsequently reveals himself to be the prophet Elijah. He rewards her by promising that her barrel of meal and cruse of oil will not run out while famine remains in the land.

3. Two **Pouch Vases** with mouldings towards the foot.
16.3 cms high.
Maker Unknown, possibly Swansea. About 1795–1805.
The pieces are decorated with an unusual chinoiserie design of a large palm and banana tree.

4. **Candlestick** 10.5 cms diameter × 11 cms high.
Maker Unknown. About 1820–1840.
'Village Church', a design used by several potters. The only identified piece bears the mark of J & R Clews, Cobridge, though a somewhat similar view appears on a cream jug from the Castleford pottery. Pieces with two sheep (as on this candlestick) are known with the impressed mark 'WEDGWOOD' but this version of the pattern is not recorded by the Wedgwood Museum. Possibly these were sold as blanks and decorated elsewhere or made by one of the other factories, such as William Smith and John Wedge Wood, who are known to have used a Wedgwood mark.

5. Two **Vases** (part of a garniture).
These two vases would probably have had covers with the spaniel knop 17.7 cms high.
Attributed to *Spode* (via workmen's mark). About 1795–1805.
'Boy on a Buffalo' (or 'Buffalo', for short). This pattern is copied directly from a Chinese painted original design which itself had several versions. Most of the early English makers of blue printed earthenwares used the pattern. The rider could perhaps represent the Chinese philosopher, Lao-Tzu, the founder of Taoism, on his way to the 'regions beyond'.

6. **Baluster Vase** 8.2 cms (at base) × 22 cms high.
Maker Unknown. About 1790.
'Two Figures' pattern with floral borders.
Loaned by Mervyn Gibbs.

7. **Garden Seat** 47 × 32.9 cms.
Mark: S6.
Spode. About 1815–1825. 'Gothic Castle' (see Cat. Ref. Case 22/14).
Loaned by Dorothy Mugleston.

8. **Umbrella Stand** 53.5 × 25.5 cms.
Maker Unknown. Probably made between 1860–1890.
The entire surface has been covered with dark blue printing,
mainly a repetition of two designs in the romantic style, with
groups of people and ornate buildings.
Loaned by City Museum and Art Gallery, Stoke-on-Trent.

TECHNIQUES (Wall mounted)

1. **Copper Engraving Plate** and a **Tissue Pull** of the design
(see plate 6).
T & J Bevington, Cambrian Pottery, Swansea. About 1817–1825.
'Monopteros' (see Cat. Ref. Case 12/13).
Loaned by Dorothy Mugleston.

2. **Framed Pull** from a copper plate.
About 1820. 'A View of Oxford' from '*Views of Picturesque Scenery
in the Environs of London*'. '*Drawn from nature and on stone*' by
T.M. Baines. Published in six parts. This view was used in the
Herculaneum 'Cherub Medallion' border series.
Loaned by Dorothy Mugleston.

3. **Well and Tree Platter** 51.7 × 40.2 cms.
3A. Framed Pull from the Copper Plate.
Attributed to *Robert Hamilton, Stoke.* About 1815–1820.
'Gothic Ruins'. A comparison of the finished article with the
transfer pull, and reference to the copper plate in (Cat. Ref. Case
Techniques/1), demonstrates quite clearly the process from the
image on the plate through a mirror image on the tissue and
back to the original design on the finished item.
Loaned by Dorothy Mugleston.

Case 1. EARLY DESIGNS WITH DIRECT CHINESE INFLUENCE

When production of blue printed earthenwares commenced
in Staffordshire, the market was such that chinoiserie patterns
attracted most interest. Consequently the early designs were, with
few exceptions, either direct copies of Chinese export porcelain or
based closely on the decoration of these wares. This situation lasted
for some twenty years, right up to the end of the 18th century.

1. **Octagonal Oblong Dish** 29.2 × 21.6 cms.
Possibly *Joshua Heath, Hanley.* About 1795–1800.
'Conversation' pattern (Two men talking on the bridge).

2. **Jug** 25.3 cms high.
Maker Unknown. About 1795–1800.
'Chinese Tea Drinker' an unrecorded pattern.
Loaned by Renard Broughton.

3. **Coffee Pot** 26.9 cms high.
Mark: X34.
Maker Unknown. About 1800–1810.
A version of the 'Mandarin' pattern.
Loaned by Ian Graham.

4. **Lobed Oval Dish** 17 × 11.2 cms.
Attributed to *Job Ridgway, Shelton.* About 1800–1810.
'Curling Palm' pattern. Other versions are known, mostly
unmarked, though J. & G. Rogers (Burslem) made a similar variant.

5. **Octagonal Soup Plate** 22.9 cms.
Maker Unknown. About 1790–1795.
'Full Nankin', a pattern used by the Caughley porcelain factory
and following very closely a Chinese original.

6. **Leaf-Moulded Jug** 22 cms high.
Possibly *Joshua Heath, Hanley.* About 1790–1800.
A version of the 'Two Figures' pattern.

7. **Octagonal Oblong Dish** 23 × 19 × 4.2 cms.
Mark: X34.
Maker Unknown. About 1790–1800.
A version of the 'Two Figures' pattern. The leafy spray mark
on the base may possibly indicate a particular maker but has not,
so far, been identified. The larger sprays on the reverse copy a
practice often used on Oriental pieces.

8. **Coffee Pot** with domed lid and acorn knop 25 cms high.
Maker Unknown. About 1795–1800.
A typical chinoiserie pattern, apparently pieced together from
different transfers, and with an acanthus-style leaf border. Great
trouble has been taken with the decoration, for example, the
boat added at the base of the spout.
Loaned by Margaret Ironside.

9. **Dish** Shell-shape 19.7 cms diameter.
Mark: X19 (not yet attributed to a particular maker).
Maker Unknown. About 1800–1810.
'Fitzhugh', a pattern introduced at the end of the 18th century,
probably at first as replacements for a large Chinese service
owned by the Fitzhugh family, long-time servants of the East
India Company. The design is based on some of the many
Chinese symbols, in this case the 'flowers of the seasons' and the
'four treasures' (or cultural accomplishments). The pattern was
produced by several makers including Joshua Heath, G. Harrison,
Ralph Wedgwood and the Cambrian Pottery, Swansea.
Loaned by Flora Rabinovitch.

10. **Saucer Dish** 18.3 cms.
Maker Unknown. About 1800–1810.
An unusual Oriental pattern with central panel enclosing a
figure in elaborate robes holding a parasol and attended by a boy.

11. **Silver-topped Vase** 6.7 × 20.9 cms.
Mark: H19 (an extremely rare mark).
T & J Hollins, Shelton. About 1795–1805.
An unnamed design including a man fishing from steps and a
large butterfly.

12. **Bowl** Cushion-shape 24.3 × 23.9 × 8.8 cms.
Maker Unknown. About 1800–1805.
'Long Bridge' pattern made by several potters with a large
number of variations in detail. An unmarked example is very
difficult to attribute with confidence.
Loaned by Mervyn Gibbs.

13. **Mug** with floral moulding
9.0 cms diameter × 12.0 cms high.
Maker Unknown. About 1790–1800.
An unusual design featuring a tall pagoda with curved roof ends.

14. **Plate** 23.5 cms.
Maker Unknown. About 1800–1810.
An unusual design incorporating a domed temple and a tall

pagoda at the right hand edge.
Loaned by P.L. and A.E. Maclean-Eltham.

15. **Arcaded Plate** 18.8 cms.
Maker Unknown. About 1810–1815.
A version of the 'Mandarin' pattern.
Loaned by Ian Graham.

16. **Oval Arcaded Dish or Stand** 21 × 17 cms.
Mark: T6.
W & J Turner, Lane End. About 1800.
A version of the 'Mandarin' pattern, on the same lines as the 'Willow' but without bridge and birds.
Loaned by Mervyn Gibbs.

17. **Square Dish** 20.7 cms square.
Maker Unknown. About 1800–1815.
A version of the 'Mandarin' Pattern.
Loaned by Ian Graham.

18. **Dry Mustard Pot** 6 × 12 cms.
Possibly *Spode, Stoke*. About 1795–1800.
'Tall Door' pattern (see Cat. Ref. Case 22/1).
Footnote: (See Cat. Ref. Case Dining room/31) and for a similar form (Cat. Ref. Case 2/11). This type of mustard pot or jar frequently has a screw top, sometimes with holes for sprinkling the mustard powder.

19. **Argyll** and Cover (see plate 3) 21.6 cms.
Maker Unknown. About 1795–1805.
'Two Figures' with a geometric border.
Footnote: Argyll, sometimes incorrectly called an argyle, is a gravy warmer which has a handle and spout. The gravy is kept warm by hot water which is contained in a separate compartment created by a double wall, a false bottom or a central vertical tube. The shape is also designed to pour the gravy without spilling the water. This peculiarly English utensil is said to have been invented by the 3rd Duke of Argyll about 1750 and was originally manufactured in silver.
Loaned by Ian Graham.

20. **Tertial Flower Vase** 14.6 × 15.3 × 16.7 cms.
Maker Unknown. About 1800–1810.
An unrecorded design featuring a temple, some prominent trees and shrubs, swans and two chinamen with a fishing rod. The name 'Malayan Long House' has been suggested for this pattern. The shape name given to this vase derives from the three separate flower spouts. These forms were popular as they kept the blooms separate and distinct.

21. **Jug** (see figure 7) 19.8 cms high.
Maker Unknown. About 1790–1800.
A version of the 'Broseley' pattern with the unusual addition of a bunch of flowers under the spout.

22. **Fluted Cup** 6 × 6.5 cms.
Maker Unknown. About 1790–1795.
The same chinoiserie pattern as on the coffee pot (see Cat. Ref. Case 1/8).
Loaned by Margaret Ironside.

23. **Tea Canister** (cover missing) 8.3 × 11.4 cms.
Possibly *Joshua Heath, Hanley*. About 1795–1800.
'Conversation' pattern – two men conversing on a bridge.
Footnote: Tea canisters are also referred to as tea jars and would have been an essential part of a tea equipage, designed to hold the different teas such as black tea or green tea, ready to be mixed by the lady of the house.

24. **Jug** 10.8 cms high.
Maker Unknown. About 1790–1800.
'Fisherman' pattern, sometimes known as 'Caughley Fisherman' because of its use on Caughley porcelains, where it was also known under the names of 'Cormorant' and 'Pleasure Boat'.
Loaned by Margaret Ironside.

25. **Platter** 36.5 × 27.0 cms.
Mark: H7.
G. Harrison, Lane Delph. About 1795.
A 'Bridgeless Willow' pattern, with the addition of two figures in the left foreground.

26. **Tile** 13.3 cms square.
Marks: C13 and C16.
Copeland and Garrett. About 1833–1847.
'Lanje Lijsen', also known as 'Jumping boy'. The name comes from a Dutch term for the elongated Chinese figures – translated as 'Long Elizas' – and the design was copied originally from Chinese wares of the K'ang Hsi (Kangxi) period (1662–1722). This is an example of the continued use of a pattern introduced early in the 19th century.
Loaned by Flora Rabinovitch.

27. **Large Bowl** 26 cms diameter × 11.5 cms high.
Possibly *Turner, Lane End*. About 1800–1810.
A chinoiserie pattern with an unusual border, recorded under the name 'Chinaman with Rocket', though the object being carried over the bridge may just be a parasol.

28. **Asparagus Dish** 28.2 × 12.8 cms.
Maker Unknown. About 1800–1805.
'Chinese House on Bridge', a pattern whose maker has still not been identified. 'Fisherman' has been excluded from the title to avoid confusion with other patterns.

29. **Mug** 12.4 cms high.
Maker Unknown. About 1790–1800.
A most unusual pattern depicting a Chinese woman choosing accessories at a shop or market stall.

30. **Stand** for a sauce boat 16.2 × 11.4 cms.
Maker Unknown. About 1805–1810.
'Two Temples' (Broseley) pattern.
Loaned by Flora Rabinovitch.

31. **Plate** 20.3 cms.
Mark: H7.
G. Harrison, Lane Delph. About 1795.
'Fitzhugh' pattern (see Cat. Ref. Case 1/9).

32. **Fluted Beaker**, possibly for syllabub.
Decorated with an ochre rim 6.5 × 7.0 cms.
Attributed to *Swansea*. About 1790–1800.
A typical chinoiserie landscape, including a rock formation which looks like an elephant, from which the attribution has been made.

Case 2. EUROPEAN INTERPRETATIONS OF THE CHINESE.

As Europeans began to adapt Chinese sources and create fresh designs based only loosely on Oriental originals, a wealth of striking, unusual and fanciful patterns emerged. This phase served as a stepping stone to the point where pure European influences began first to merge with and later to oust altogether the Chinese style.

1. **Plate** 24 cms.
Maker Unknown. About 1805–1810.
'Chinese Gardener', a pattern attributed to the partnership of Wood and Brettel, Tunstall (1818–1823) from an example impressed 'W&B'. However, the transitional style of the design favours an earlier date so that the attribution cannot be considered other than tentative.

2. **Plate** 24.9 cms.
Mark: H6.
Robert Hamilton, Stoke. About 1812–1820.
'Sampan', sometimes called 'Canton River Scene'. The design is a composite scene taken from at least two prints in Thomas and William Daniell's *Picturesque Voyage to India by the way of China* (1810).

3. **Teapot** 9.5 × 10 cms.
G.M. & C.J. Mason, Lane Delph. About 1815.
'Veranda' pattern (see Cat. Ref. Case 2/24).

4. **Jug** 18 cms high.
Mark: M13.
Minton, Stoke. About 1835–1845.
A view from the 'Chinese Marine' series of several different Chinese scenes. This is taken from a William Alexander drawing of 'The Audience Hall of Yuan-Ming Yuan', published around 1800–1805 in Staunton's *Authentic Account of an Embassy to the Emperor of China*. The Embassy (under Lord Macartney) took place in 1793–1794.

5. **Jug** 11.0 × 6.8 × 6.9 cms.
Maker Unknown. About 1805–1810.
An unnamed scene featuring two figures under a parasol beneath a tree with large banana-like leaves (see Cat. Ref. Case 2/7).

6. **Arcaded Plate** 18 cms.
Maker Unknown. About 1810–1815.
An unusual all-over pattern recorded as 'Dragons and Snakes', but possibly derived from the Chinese 'Dog of Fo'.
Footnote: 'Dog of Fo' is also known as 'Lion of Fo'. Chinese lions, a pair of which were originally temple guardians, were often miscalled 'dogs'. The male is represented playing with a ball and the female with a cub. Fo means Buddha.

7. **Plate** 21 cms.
Mark: impressed cross in a circle.
Maker Unknown. About 1805–1810.
'Feathered Hat', a pattern of which several examples are known, none of them marked. The very distinctive tree is similar to that on Cat. Ref. Case 2/5. *Ralph Stevenson, Cobridge* has been suggested as the maker.

8. **Plate** 25 cms.
Maker Unknown. About 1800–1810.
'Swans and Peacocks' pattern, depicting an elaborate village built over water, including a causeway and an ornate bridge.

9. **Plate** 12.7 cms.
Mark: R1.
Rainforth & Co., Leeds. About 1805–1815.
'Rainforth's Willow', an elaborate chinoiserie landscape not really related to the standard 'Willow' pattern.
Loaned by Margaret Ironside.

10. **Two-handled Goblet** or Loving cup 11.5 × 12 cms.
Maker Unknown. About 1810–1820.
An unnamed Chinese landscape featuring a summer-house with a chequered floor.
Footnote: A loving cup was a large drinking vessel with two or more handles to be passed round at a banquet or similar gathering.

11. **Dry Mustard Pot** with domed lid 5.5 × 10.5 cms.
Maker Unknown. About 1800–1810.
Unidentified part of a larger pattern, depicting two Chinese ladies with a parasol, beside a long fence (see Cat. Ref. Case Dining room/31 and Cat. Ref. Case 1/18)

12. **Mug** 12 × 13.9 cms.
Maker Unknown. About 1805–1810.
A typical chinoiserie landscape showing figures outside a temple or pavilion. Not so far named.

13. **Pierced Dish or Stand** 25.5 × 19.3 cms.
Maker Unknown. About 1800–1810.
'Chinese Fisher Boys', an unusual scene depicting a fishing boat with a net across a stream and a strange long-necked animal in the background.

14. **Plate** 25.3 cms.
Mark: A1.
William Adams, Stoke. About 1810–1820.
'Birds and Basket Chinoiserie' pattern. The factory name is now known to have been 'Chinese Bird'.
Loaned by Dr. and Mrs. David Furniss.

15. **Handled Oval Dish** 27.7 × 20.2 cms.
Mark: D1.
Davenport, Longport. About 1805–1815.
'Chinoiserie High Bridge' (see Cat. Ref. Case 11/9).
Loaned by Mervyn Gibbs.

16. **Footed Bowl** 20.9 × 9.5 cms.
Maker Unknown. About 1805–1815.
Group of four people, two apparently European, with dog and two Chinese gardeners, and a castle-like mansion in the background. Unnamed and unidentified so far.

17. **Tea Canister** (Cover missing) 9.6 cms high.
Attributed to *Spode* on the basis of excavation on the factory site. No pieces in this pattern marked 'Spode' have yet been found. About 1800–1810. 'Oriental Birds' pattern.

18. **Cream Jug** 12.7 cms long.
Attributed to *Spode* (see Cat. Ref. Case 2/17). About 1800–1810. 'Oriental Birds' pattern painted with an ochre rim.

19. **Slop Bowl** 13.3 × 6.3 cms.
Maker Unknown. About 1810–1815.
'Chinese Picnic' (see Cat. Ref. Case 2/21).

20. **Pickle Dish** 15.2 × 12.7 cms.
Maker Unknown. About 1810–1815.
'Chinese Family'.
Loaned by The Strong Collection.

21. **Cup and Saucer** Bute-shape.
Cup 8.2 × 5.7 cms. Saucer 13.3 cms.
Maker Unknown. About 1810–1815.
Recorded as 'Chinese Picnic'.
The technique of printing the background in blue and leaving the design in white was used by several makers.

22. **Cup and Saucer** Porringer-shape.
Cup 5.1 cms high. Saucer 12.0 cms.
Maker Unknown. About 1820–1825.
An all-over design of fanciful Chinese dragon motifs, recorded under the title of 'Dragon's Claws'.

23. **Deep dish,** oblong octagonal 37.0 × 27.0 cms.
Mark: 'SPODE'S NEW STONE' impressed.

Spode, Stoke. About 1820–1825.
'Peplow' central pattern with borders from two other designs, presumably to avoid the need for a larger than standard engraving of the usual border.
Loaned by Dorothy Mugleston.

24. **Tea Bowl and Saucer.** Tea Bowl 8.8 cms. Saucer 13.6 cms.
G.M. & C.J. Mason, Lane Delph. About 1815.
'Veranda' or 'Chinese Veranda' pattern, produced on porcelain by Miles Mason from about 1810. It seems likely that the same engraved plates were used for the decoration of earthenwares (see Cat. Ref. Case 2/3).

25. **Lobed Dessert Dish** 20.7 cms diameter.
Maker Unknown. About 1805–1815.
An elaborate and fanciful scene in a Chinese garden, with a border of continuous landscape. So far unnamed and unidentified.

26. Low oval-footed **Comport** with pewter rim.
25.7 × 16.5 × 8.0 cms.
Maker Unknown. About 1800–1810.
'Fisherman and Castle' pattern, a design with Gothic buildings and an Oriental temple or summer house. This design tends towards the transitional with European and Chinese images intermingled.
Footnote: The pewter rim is possibly a later 19th century addition to strengthen the edge or disguise some damage.

27. **Saucer Dish** painted with an ochre rim 19.3 cms.
Richard Dudson, Hanley – attributed on the basis of sherds found on the factory site.
About 1810–1815.
'Galloping Horse' pattern.
Footnote: This pattern has some similarities with a Chinese K'ang Hsi (Kangxi) (1662–1722) original now referred to as 'The Eight Horses of Mu Wang'. This pattern was used by the English Delftware potters and at the porcelain factories of Worcester, Derby and Vauxhall.

28. **Segment from a Supper Set** 37.4 × 17.8 cms.
Maker Unknown. About 1810–1820.
An interesting design showing Oriental children at various forms of play, recorded under the name 'Chinese Boy's Games'. The maker has not been identified though a similar pattern on bone china is known to have been made by Minton.

Case 3. THE TRANSITIONAL PERIOD AND LATER REVIVED CHINOISERIE

Between the period of full chinoiserie and the change over to totally European designs there came an era in which the two styles intermingled. After the original Chinese style had faded out, it enjoyed a minor revival in a more elaborate and fanciful fashion, surprisingly quickly, starting towards the end of the 1830's.

1. **Platter** 35.5 × 25.9 cms.
Mark: A10.
William Adams & Sons, Stoke. About 1845–1855.
'Jeddo' pattern in flow blue. Patterns in this style and with similar Oriental names were very much in vogue between about 1850 and 1870.
Loaned by Dr. and Mrs. David Furniss.

2. **Pair of Jugs** 8.2 × 13.9 cms.
Mark: W12.
Whitehaven Pottery, Cumbria (John Wilkinson). About 1835–1850.
'Nanking' pattern. The only recorded marked example of this design.
Loaned by Wendy Mitton, Carlisle.

3. **Mug** 11.0 cms high.
Maker Unknown. A Dudson origin has been suggested for one of these designs (see Cat. Ref. Case 2/27).
About 1810–1820.
'Ethiopian Horn Player' one of two designs featuring this musician, who also appears on a pattern known as 'Hunting with Cheetahs' (see Cat. Ref. Case 3/7).

4. **Tea Pot**, London-shape 24.7 cms long × 13.7 cms high.
Joseph Twigg, Swinton, Yorkshire. Attributed on the basis of a marked saucer with a matching design. About 1820–1830.
A simple outline pattern of 'Temple and Flower', very similar to a design recorded as 'Figure, Vase and Fence' and known to have been made by J. & G. Rogers, Longport. The attribution of this piece can only be tentative.

5. **Tea Pot** 12 cms diameter × 12 cms high.
Maker Unknown. About 1805–1812.
A pattern showing white horses being fed before a church and a house with a 'Christmas Tree' in front. The border and the general layout of the scene are in a chinoiserie style.

6. **Jug** 20.3 cms high.
Maker Unknown. About 1810.
An unnamed pattern depicting a landscape in the chinoiserie style but including European buildings.

7. **Plate or Stand** painted with an ochre rim 14.2 cms.
Mark: '2' painted in blue. This may possibly indicate a Castleford Pottery origin.
Maker Unknown. About 1810–1820.
'Hunting with Cheetahs'. The African figure playing a horn appears in another pattern known as 'Ethiopian Horn Player' (see Cat. Ref. Case 3/3).

8. **Saucer** 13.8 cms.
Maker Unknown. About 1805–1815.
An unnamed design depicting a Chinese garden scene with three figures, a tall summer house and a brick wall with large circular opening.

9. **Plate** 25 cms.
Probably *J & R Riley, Burslem.* About 1815–1825.
'Eastern Street Scene', based on two different prints from T. & W. Daniell's 'Oriental Scenery' (1795–1808).
It is thought that, after the Riley factory closed in 1828 the copper plates of the pattern continued to be used by Samuel Alcock.

10. **Plate** 25.4 cms.
Mark: B impressed. This impressed mark could have been used by several potters.
Maker Unknown. About 1810–1820.
'Octagonal Chinoiserie'. A pattern depicting Chinese figures with European buildings. The central pattern, in an octagonal frame, is surrounded by landscape vignettes.
Loaned by Mervyn Gibbs.

11. **Mug** painted with an ochre rim 11 × 12.2 cms.
Cambrian Pottery, Swansea. About 1810–1820.
'Boy with Whip' pattern, showing Chinese figures in a European landscape.

12. **Segment from a Supper Set** (see figure 35) 32 cms long.
Mark: W7.
Wedgwood and Co., Ferrybridge, Yorkshire. About 1800.
'Elephant' pattern. One of many designs featuring this animal. The figures and buildings are more Oriental Indian than pure Chinese.

13. **Stand** for a Sauce Boat or Tureen 20.5 × 13.5 cms.
Maker Unknown. About 1835–1845.
An Oriental river scene very similar to 'Chinese Marine' –
several series or individual designs known to have been made
by various makers including Minton, Bellevue Pottery (Hull)
and Thomas Fell, Newcastle-on-Tyne. From the border, this is
not the Minton version. The distinctive handles may eventually
assist us in identification.

14. **Platter** 52.9 × 41.8 cms.
Maker Unknown. About 1805–1815.
'Queen of Sheba' pattern, sometimes called 'Indian Procession'
in which European figures and buildings are set out in a
chinoiserie style.
Footnote: It would appear that very similar figures to this design
were used as shop signs in London in the 18th century, from
about 1722 to 1800. They went under various titles of 'Indian
Queen', 'Old Indian Queen' and the 'Indian Queen and Star'.
These signs covered a whole range of trades including Chinamen,
dyers, scourers and silk dyers, feathermakers, engravers, linen
drapers, Mercers, playing card makers and staymakers. A male
version the 'Indian King' was also used as a shop sign.
Loaned by Christopher Fiorini.

KITCHEN

The kitchen was an area in which transfer printed
decoration found considerable scope. The decoration '*en masse*'
went well with the polished copper pans which were normally
used and earthenware itself was a most useful material for food
preparation. Contemporary prints give a good idea of the
striking appearance of a large country-house kitchen and of the
variety of shapes made to serve in all aspects of the task of
feeding large numbers of people. Fortunately for posterity, many
kitchens and a few dairies are preserved in the stately homes
now open to the public.

1. **Treacle Pot** and lid 15.7 cms high.
Maker Unknown. About 1810–1820.
'Swans, Deer and Horses'. The swans and bridge are repeated on
the screwed lid, and unusually the border with its repetition of
some of the central design features appears again at the base, but
upside down.
Loaned by Flora Rabinovitch.

2. **Gooseberry Jar** (see plate 11) 10.1 × 25.4 cms.
Maker Unknown. About 1820–1835.
Two horses, one with a rider, drink from a stream beside a
wooden fence or gate, in front of a large abbey ruin.
Footnote: A recipe dated 1756 gives the following instructions:
'To preserve Goose-berries:
  Take the largest gooseberries before they change colour, and
  are at full growth, then make a split in their sides, and with
  a small quill take out their seeds, and to a pound of
  gooseberries before they are stoned put a pound of double
  refined sugar pounded and sifted, and as you stone them
  strew some sugar over them, to keep their colour, then take
  almost a pint of water, and the remainder of the liquid,
  boyle it and clarify it, boyle it til it spatters, then put in the
  gooseberries, and boyle them up quickly, and take them
  often off the fire, to see if they look clear, and if they do
  take them out, and put them in the glasses very carefully,
  and strain the liquid they were boyled in, thru' a piece of
  muslin, but don't squeeze it, then set it by, and in the mean
  time, pound some gooseberries in a mortar and strain them,
  but don't squeeze them hard, and put in about the bigness
  of a nut of rock allum to a pint of juice, then take a pound
  of double refined sugar, and clarifie it in a little water, and

boyle it to a candy height, then strain in the juice, and keep
out the allum, and boyle it til it will jelly, then put in the
gooseberries by degrees, not all at once for fear they should
rize at the top, and when the glasses are half full, let them
cool a little and then fill up your glasses, and set them in
your store, and paper them up.'
Loaned by Flora Rabinovitch.

3. **Gooseberry Jar** (see Cat. Ref. Case Kitchen/2)
11 × 17.8 cms.
Maker Unknown. About 1825–1840.
An unidentified rural scene featuring a large ruined abbey.

4. **Pilgrim Flask** (Water Bottle) 14 cms diameter.
Maker Unknown. About 1840–1860.
A border of holly printed in pale blue. This example has lugs for
the attachment of a carrying strap.
Footnote: A pilgrim flask was usually of a flattened, gourd shape,
with one or two pairs of lugs at each side through which passed
a strap whereby it was slung from the shoulder. They are thought
to be of Roman origin but the form is also found in Chinese
porcelain, where it was termed, 'pien hu'. As the name suggests it
was used by pilgrims to carry drinking water. Also see Glossary
of Terms.
Loaned by City Museum and Art Gallery, Stoke-on-Trent.

5. **Pilgrim Flask** (Water Bottle) 15.2 cms diameter.
Maker Unknown. About 1830–1845.
A rural scene with a white horse and cattle (see footnote to
Cat. Ref. Case Kitchen/4)
Loaned by City Museum and Art Gallery, Stoke-on-Trent.

6. **Potting Pan** (for making potted meats) 18 × 14.5 × 7.5 cms.
Maker Unknown. About 1820–1830.
Rural scene with distant church. A horseman converses with a
man on a wooden bridge over a stream.

7. **Pair of Toast Racks** (see plate 31) 21 × 10.2 × 8 cms.
Mark: H1 (on one piece).
Possibly *William Hackwood, Hanley*. About 1825–1840.
House fronts, ascending and descending in height, a simple but
effective decoration on a shape totally unsuited to a normal
sheet pattern.

8. **Stand with Four Egg Cups** 23 × 20 × 18 cms.
Mark: D3.
Davenport, Longport. About 1812.
'By the River' ('Fisherman' series of ten different fishing scenes,
each incorporating a large, ruined church). The egg cups show
various portions of different views from the series. The factory
name for this series is now known, from an invoice found in the
USA, to have been 'Gothic Ruins'.

9. **Muffin Dish** and cover 20.3 × 22.3 cms.
J & W Ridgway, Shelton. About 1815–1820.
Unidentified view (possibly Lacy House, Middlesex) from the
'Angus Seats' series of at least fifteen views (see Cat. Ref. Case
Kitchen/38).

10. **Bowl Divider** 26 cms.
Maker Unknown. About 1800–1810.
A typical geometric chinoiserie border on a rare shape, known
also in creamware.

11. **Patent Mustard Pot** with metal lid and plunger 4.7 × 7.4 cms.
Mark: X23 (a London retailer's mark).
Maker Unknown. About 1896.
Romantic pattern of a Continental style castle in lake and
mountain scenery.

12. **Jug** 13.9 × 15.2 cms.
Maker Unknown. About 1820–1830.
'Lady of the Lake' sometimes referred to as 'Lord Ullen's Daughter'. This version differs very slightly from that known marked 'Dixon, Austin & Co.' (Sunderland) and may have been made by Gordon's Pottery, Prestonpans. A ship's bowl and dish is known, impressed 'R & R Gordon' in a scroll below a crown. A similar design in which a man is playing a harp was made by T. & J. Carey (Lane End).
Footnote: This design appears to be based on engravings by F. Engleheart and Charles Heath of drawings by Richard Westall RA which were used as illustrations for the first edition of Sir Walter Scott's, *Lady of the Lake* published by John Sharpe of Piccadilly, London in 1810.

13. **Jug** 16 × 17.8 cms.
Maker Unknown. About 1810–1820.
View of lake scenery with tall château in foreground (probably fictitious) within a chinoiserie border. The landscape has a European, possibly Scottish, appearance.

14. **Jug** 16.6 × 16 cms.
Maker Unknown. About 1815–1820.
Fishermen hanging nets in a tree.
Possibly derived from a pattern made by Robert Hamilton, Stoke, and known as 'Fishermen with Nets'.

15. **Pair of Jugs** 22.8 × 17.8 × 15.3 cms.
Series attributed to *J & W Ridgway* on the basis of comparison with sherds. About 1820–1830.
a) 'Palladian Mansion', now identified as a view of 'Wanstead House, Essex' taken from a print in Grey's *The Excursions through Essex*.
b) 'Gleaners II'. ('British Scenery' series; see Cat. Ref. Case Dining room/9)

16. **Pie Dish** 26.5 × 21 cms.
Mark: as H11.
Henshall & Co., Longport. About 1820–1825.
'Langley Park'.
'Fruit and Flower Border' series (see Cat. Ref. Case Kitchen/33) Originally thought to be Langley Park, near Beckenham, Kent, which was destroyed by fire in 1913. It now seems possible that the correct location was in Buckinghamshire.
Loaned by John and Sally Storton.

17. **Pie Dish** 31 × 24.7 cms.
Mark: H10.
Henshall and Co., Longport. About 1820–1825.
'Moditmonham' (*sic*).
'Fruit and Flower Border' series (see Cat. Ref. Case Kitchen/33) This view is of Moditonham House, near Saltash, Cornwall, which also features in the 'Grapevine Border' series made by Enoch Wood & Sons.
Loaned by John and Sally Storton.

18. **Soup Tureen** and cover, with stand. Tureen 33 × 35 cms high, Stand 32.6 cms diameter.
Mark: S12.
Ralph Stevenson, Cobridge. About 1820–1830.
'Milking the Goats', one of at least seven rural scenes in a series known (from the mark) as 'Semi-China Warranted'.
Loaned by John and Sally Storton.

19. **Cake or Cheese Stand** 27.3 × 6.4 cms.
John Meir, Tunstall. About 1820–1830.
'River Fishing'.

20. **Drainer** 41.5 × 26.6 cms.
Maker Unknown. About 1810–1815.
'Durham Ox', from the series of that name (see Cat. Ref. Case 31/8).
Loaned by Terry Sheppard.

21. **Small Platter** 26 × 20.8 cms.
Mark: M9.
Attributed to *John Meir, Tunstall. About 1825–1830.*
St Joseph's Chapel, Glastonbury, Somersetshire, from the 'Pineapple Border' series of at least sixteen views, mainly of abbeys, churches and castles.
No apparent source publication for this series has yet been identified.
Loaned by John and Sally Storton.

22. **Small Platter** 24.5 × 19.6 cms.
Mark: M7.
John Meir, Tunstall. About 1820–1830.
'Tewin Water, Hertfordshire' from the 'Crown, Acorn and Oak Leaf Border' series of about eighteen named views.
Loaned by John and Sally Storton.

23. **Platter** 44.3 × 34.4 cms.
Mark: R14 (Printed mark only – used by both Rogers and the Pountney partnership).
Pountney & Goldney, Bristol. About 1835–1840.
'King Henry 6, act 2, scene 4'. From the 'Drama' series of at least twenty-four scenes from plays. Produced, initially, by Rogers and later copied by Pountney & Goldney, Bristol, using a different border. This is the Pountney version.

24. **Plate** 26.1 cms.
Mark: C9 & C12.
J & R Clews, Cobridge. About 1825–1830.
'Winter View of Pittsfield, Mass'. From the 'American Views' (Scroll Border) series of at least seventeen scenes. The woman in the foreground is reputed to have been a local character named 'Crazy Sue'. The Meeting House was the scene of a happening during the American revolution, when the preacher led his congregation out to join the rebels. The Pittsfield Elm, which fell in the 1860's, was not fenced around until 1825, which helps to date the pattern.

25. **Platter** 48.1 × 35.4 cms.
Attributed to *Wood & Brettel* (Item marked 'W&B' known).
About 1815–1820.
Bird's nest in a fruit tree, with bird feeding young, with a border of fruit and flowers. Recorded as 'Bird's Nest II' pattern.
Loaned by Mr. and Mrs. M. Houlden.

26. **Platter** 30.5 × 23.4 cms.
Mark: as W24.
Enoch Wood & Sons, Burslem. About 1825–1830.
'Lismore Castle, Waterford'. From the 'Grapevine Border' series (see Cat. Ref. Case Dining room/1).
Loaned by John and Sally Storton.

27. **Platter** 36 × 31 cms.
Mark: W13.
Whitehaven Pottery, Cumbria (John Wilkinson). About 1835–1850.
'Marseilleise'. A romantic seascape including a group of gentry on the shore, one of whom is watching the shipping through a telescope.
Loaned by Mr. and Mrs. D.T. Sibson.

28. **Platter** 51.5 × 42 cms.
Herculaneum Pottery, Liverpool. About 1815–1825.
'View in the Fort, Madura'. A composite scene derived from at

least four aquatints taken from engravings by Thomas Daniell in the six-volume work *Oriental Scenery*, published between 1795 and 1808. William Daniell, Thomas' nephew, was also involved in the last four volumes.
Loaned by Mr. and Mrs. Maclean-Eltham.

29. **Platter** 47 × 36.8 cms.
Mark: H15 and H17.
Herculaneum Pottery, Bristol. About 1815–1825.
'Lancaster', the second of two views of this town in the 'Cherub Medallion Border' series (see Cat. Ref. Case 32/3).

30. **Plate** 25.3 cms.
Mark: A2 and A8.
William Adams, Stoke. About 1827–1830.
'Villa in the Regents Park, the Residence of G.B. Greenough, Esq.'. From the 'Regents Park' series (see Cat. Ref. Case 26/4). The house was designed by Decimus Burton. Greenough was the first President of the Geological Society of London.
Loaned by Dr. and Mrs. David Furniss.

31. **Platter** 38 × 29 cms.
Mark: A2 and A4.
William Adams, Stoke. About 1810–1820.
'Fleurs, Roxburgheshire' (*sic*). 'Flowers and Leaves Border' series of at least twenty-eight British views, usually named. No specific source for the scenes has yet been identified.
Loaned by John and Sally Storton.

32. **Platter** 48 × 37.6 cms.
Mark: A2 and as A4.
William Adams, Stoke. About 1810–1820.
'Tixall, Staffordshire'. 'Flowers and Leaves Border' series (see Cat. Ref. Case Kitchen/31).
Loaned by John and Sally Storton.

33. **Platter** 42 × 33.7 cms.
Mark: as H11.
Henshall & Co., Longport. About 1815–1820.
'Kimberley Hall'. From the 'Fruit and Flower Border' series of at least thirty-one European and American views, mostly named. Some pieces bear the mark 'British Views'.
Loaned by John and Sally Storton.

34. **Platter** 52 × 41 cms.
Mark: as S14
Andrew Stevenson, Cobridge. About 1820–1825.
'Mereworth House'. From the 'Rose Border' series of at least twenty-five named views, nearly all in East Anglia. As many of the views are of south-east England, it is possible that the series was based on a publication about this particular region. Mereworth House is near Tonbridge in Kent. This platter is printed in the dark 'American Export' blue.
Loaned by John and Sally Storton.

35. **Platter** 37 × 27.6 cms.
Mark: S13 and as S14.
Andrew Stevenson, Cobridge. About 1820–1825.
'Tunbridge Castle, Surrey' (*sic*). From the 'Rose Border' series (see Cat. Ref. Case Kitchen/34).
Loaned by John and Sally Storton

36. **Platter** 38.2 × 29.2 cms.
Mark: E1.
Elkins & Co., Lane End. About 1825–1830.
'Brownsea Castle, Dorsetshire'. 'Irish Scenery' series of about six views, mainly named and mostly in England. This series, like the 'Grapevine Border' series, seems to have been taken from John Preston Neale's *Views of the seats of noblemen and gentlemen in*

England and Wales and Scotland and Ireland.
Loaned by John and Sally Storton.

37. **Platter** 33 × 26 cms.
Mark: H4.
Ralph Hall & Co., Tunstall. About 1825–1830.
'Boughton House, Northamptonshire'. From the 'Select Views' series of at least seventeen British and continental views, made largely for export and printed in dark 'Export Blue'. A possible source publication for this series has not yet been identified.
Loaned by John and Sally Storton.

38. **Large Platter with Drainer**.
Platter 53.2 × 42.3 cms. Drainer 38.8 × 27.5 cms.
J & W Ridgway, Shelton. There is a body of opinion in favour of re-attribution to the factory of George Ridgway, also at Shelton. About 1815–1820.
Platter 'Lee, Kent', Drainer 'View of Newnham Court'. Both from the 'Angus Seats' series of at least fifteen views, mostly based on *Seats of the nobility and gentry in Great Britain and Wales* (Short title) by W. Angus (1797). The print of 'Lee, Kent' is Plate XLIII in that volume. Engraved by W. Angus and first published in 1797.
Loaned by Anne and Graham Aylett.

39. **Soup Tureen** and cover with stand (see plate 5).
Tureen 39 × 21.5 × 31.8 cms, Stand 37.1 × 30 cms.
Mark: as R4.
J & W Ridgway, Shelton. About 1825–1830.
Tureen 'Alms House, Boston'. Cover 'Cambridge College, Massachusetts'. Stand 'Deaf and Dumb Asylum, Hartford, Connecticut'. From the 'Beauties of America' series (see Cat. Ref. Case 35/16).
Loaned by David and Linda Arman.

40. **Platter and Drainer**.
Platter 56 × 46 cms. Drainer 36.2 × 27 cms.
Mark: X4.
This has been tentatively attributed to *Thomas Godwin, Burslem*. About 1830–1840.
A composite scene taken from two prints in Parry's *Journal of a Voyage for the Discovery of a North-west Passage* (1821) (Short title of the journal of his first voyage). The ships, 'Hecla' and 'Griper' are shown among ice floes. From the 'Arctic Scenery' series (see Cat. Ref. Case 21/1).

41. **Platter** 46.5 × 36.7 cms.
Maker Unknown. About 1815–1825.
'Monk's Rock, Tenby'. An identified scene after which a series of unnamed rural views has been called. It was considered improper to walk across a beach in bathing costume so, to preserve propriety, a covered changing hut was towed into the water.

42. **Platter** 46.5 × 34.2 cms.
Maker Unknown. About 1795–1810.
'Fisherman Willow' a transitional chinoiserie pattern.

43. **Platter** 38.3 × 29.8 cms.
Maker Unknown. About 1840.
A striking pattern known as 'Floral Horse', denoting three Chinese figures in front of a villa with gate and fences.
Two girls stand with a man and a spotted horse, with a small dog at their feet. One example is known with a printed retailer's mark of D. Davis, Commercial Road, London. Daniel Davis did not start in business until 1839, so the style of the pattern is in keeping with the chinoiserie revival which took place in the late 1830's.

44. **Platter** 45 × 35.4 cms.
Mark: X27.

Maker Unknown. About 1830–1840.
A romantic garden scene in an elaborate border with vignettes of a castle. Unidentified, but in a similar style to a pattern (or series) known as 'Spanish Beauties' and possibly produced by the Deakin partnerships at Longton.

45. **Drainer** 40.8 × 36 cms.
Maker Unknown. About 1820–1830.
'Leopard and Antelope' or 'Crouching Leopard' pattern. Taken from a tail piece woodcut in Thomas Bewick's *General History of Quadrupeds* (1790).

46. **Platter** 49.5 × 38.5 cms.
Mark: X6.
Maker Unknown. About 1820–1830.
'Brecknock Castle and Bridge'. From 'Beauties of England and Wales', a small series of unnamed views of which only one has so far been identified. This is a hitherto unrecorded pattern. Between 1801 and 1808, a series of twenty-six volumes of engravings was published under the title *Beauties of England and Wales, or delineations topographical, historical and descriptive* by John Britton and Howard Brayley. No connection between the two has been established.
Loaned by John and Sally Storton.

47. **Cheese Cradle** 42 × 16 × 18.6 cms.
Maker Unknown. About 1860–1880.
Standard 'Willow' pattern.
Footnote: This shape holds a wheel of cheese on end, as opposed to the more traditional covered stands for Stilton Cheese.

48. **Basin** (with plug outlet) 40 cms diameter.
Maker Unknown. About 1860–1880.
A design duplicated to cover the entire interior of the basin and comprising various standard romantic elements – classical buildings, a gondola and a massive urn featuring various figures probably Mythological.
Loaned by the City Museum and Art Gallery, Stoke-on-Trent.

Case 4. NAMED AND DATED PIECES

From an early date ceramic pieces have been used as a reminder of important personal occasions, personalised gifts and as patriotic symbols. This range of production ran from specially designed pieces to the addition of an appropriate hand painted inscription to a standard commercial item. The collection and study of these pieces opens the way to a better understanding of family life in the period concerned.

1. **Jug** (see plate 29) 20.3 cms.
Maker Unknown. Dated 1794.
Chinoiserie pattern and border, a version of the 'Precarious Chinaman' – often attributed to Swansea.
Inscription (painted in blue): 'Mrs. Addis – 1794'
Loaned by Chenda Clark.

2. **Jug** 16 cms.
Swansea. Dated 1798.
Printed with one of several chinoiserie patterns featuring a Chinese figure with a large umbrella and usually referred to as 'Precarious Chinaman'. These are probably taken from Thomas Rothwell engravings of Jean Pillement's *The Ladies' Amusement* (1762)
Inscribed 'George Johns, Polmesk, 1798'.
Loaned by Jonathan Gray.

3. **Tea Pot** and cover (see plate 29) 17 cms.
Maker Unknown. Dated 1789.
A chinoiserie pattern of the 'Buddleia' type.
Inscribed: 'S. Tonill, 1789'.

4. **Mug** (see plate 29 and figure 32) 9 cms.
Maker Unknown. Dated 1790.
A design of the 'Buddleia' type. Willow Mandarin I.
Inscribed (on the base): 'W. Morshall. Sedbergh 1790'.

5. **Piggin** (see plate 13).
10.7 cms diameter × 9.5 cms high excluding handle.
Maker Unknown. About 1820–1830.
All-over floral pattern. Inscribed: 'Mr John Squers Junr' in ochre enamel.

6. **Frog Mug** Two handled (see plate 29) 14.5 × 18 cms.
Mark: large incised 'W'.
Maker Unknown. Dated 1848.
A chinoiserie design featuring temple, towers and two Chinese figures with an umbrella at the foot of a staircase.
Inscribed: 'William. Gool, 1848'.

7. **Tankard** 12 cms.
Maker Unknown, possibly Swansea. About 1793.
The Duke of York on horseback, with a battle scene in the background.
Inscribed (round bottom rim): 'His Royal Highness Frederick Duke of York'.
Footnote: King George III insisted that the British military expedition to Flanders (1793–1794), to co-operate with the Austrian Army under the direction of the Prince of Coburg, should be commanded by his second son, Prince Frederick, The Duke of York and Albany. The Prince had shown considerable aptitude and liking for the army. The combined forces drove the French out of Belgium, defeating them at Tournai and Farmars, before capturing the northern French town of Valenciennes on 26th July, 1793. These British successes were greeted with considerable enthusiasm by the British public and with the expectation of a ready market the potters brought out a range of commemoratives decorated both in underglaze blue and overglaze black enamel. Despite mixed success on the battlefield Prince Frederick repaired army discipline, stamped out abuse and improved the administration, which greatly benefitted the army and the Nation.

8. **Mug** (see figure 34) 9 cms.
Possibly *Swansea.* About 1793.
A view of the 'Guillotine' with victim and executioner, and two male figures in period dress. Four floral sprays fill up the vacant spaces.
Inscription: 'View of LA GUILLOTINE or the modern beheading machine at PARIS by which LOUIS XVI late King of France suffered on the Scaffold Jan 21 1793'
Footnote: The view of the guillotine on this mug would appear to have been taken from an illustration on a broadsheet entitled *Massacre of the French King* published by William Lane early in 1793. Lane's illustration was an adaptation of a slightly earlier print issued prior to the King's death. (For further detail see *English Printed Pottery* by David Drakard 1992.)

9. **Tea Pot** (cover missing) (see plate 29) 15.2 cms.
Maker Unknown. Dated 1829.
'Queen of the May', showing the Queen being led by her attendants to the maypole. Another similar pattern is known entitled 'May Queen'. Overpainted in black: 'Thompson & Ann Gowland 1829'.

Case 5. COMMEMORATIVE WARES

The idea of issuing mementoes or keepsakes to commemorate events of national, or sometimes merely local importance, has established, over many years, a very lucrative market from which manufacturers in many fields have drawn benefit. Pieces bought at the time, perhaps, for reasons of personal interest, soon change into collectors' items and the area of commemorative ware is now very important in that respect, having expanded over the years to encompass a great diversity of occasions and a wide range of quality.

1. **Plate** 22.5 cms.
Mark: X25.
John Thomson, Annfield Pottery, Glasgow. Dated 1842.
A romantic pattern showing a cowherd before a fanciful castle set in lake and mountain scenery. A cartouche has been superimposed at the top of the design, with the inscription: 'As a small tribute of respect to the memory of the late Mr Samuel Coulters of this city, this service is presented to the surviving members of his family by John Thomson, Annfield Pottery, Glasgow, 1842.'
Coulters was a local tile maker. It is thought that John Thomson and Samuel Coulters were connected in business.

2. **Jug** (see plate 7) 21.5 × 17.8 cms.
Maker Unknown. About 1851.
View of the 'Crystal Palace' with a memorial apparently incorporating naval and agricultural elements.
Footnote: The Great Exhibition of 1851 was primarily a showcase for Industrial Britain, exhibiting what was thought to be the best of British craftsmanship and technology. The idea of such an exhibition was the brainchild of Prince Albert and Sir Henry Cole who were assisted by an organising committee. The Crystal Palace was designed by Joseph Paxton and was a huge steel and glass construction which enclosed 19 square acres of Hyde Park, London. The display was considered to be a huge success and when it closed on 11th October 1851 the building was dismantled and removed to Sydenham Hill. A considerable number of commemorative items were produced, in all mediums especially ceramics, to mark the Great Exhibition.
Loaned by Ian Graham.

3. **Mug** 5.8 cms.
Maker Unknown. About 1825–1840.
A cartouche containing the inscription: 'A present for my Dear Boy', superimposed on a rural industrial scene.

4. **Frog Mug** 10.5 × 10.5 cms.
Probably *Whitehaven Pottery, Cumberland* (by reference to the border). About 1835–1845.
Two child's patterns, one on either side:
'Keeping School' (Girl at a table with her dolls).
'The Romp' (Girl with skipping rope playing with a dog).
Loaned by Mr. and Mrs. D.T. Sibson.

5. **Segment from a Supper Set** (no cover) 33.5 × 16 cms.
Mark: D3.
Davenport, Longport. About 1810–1815.
Portrait bust of George III within a wide border.
Footnote: The cornucopia and agricultural implements comprising the border of this design are probably an allusion to King George III's nickname of 'Farmer George', earned by his keen and often comical love of country pursuits. It is difficult to date the introduction of this pattern as George III ascended the throne in 1760 so that 1810 was his Golden Jubilee year, but it is equally possible that the piece commemorated the Peace of 1815, as the King is depicted wearing a wreath of laurels (for Victory) and the border of farming implements could be interpreted as denoting Peace.

6. **Tall Mug** (see plate 27) 7.0 × 12.0 cms.
Maker Unknown. About 1805.
Commemorative of the Battle of Trafalgar decorated with two prints:

a) 'The Victory off Trafalgar, Oct. 21 1805'
b) The much quoted signal, 'England expects every man this day will do his duty', surrounding a portrait of 'ADM. Ld. Nelson'.
Footnote: Horatio Nelson (1758–1805). The Peace Treaty of 1802 signed at Amiens between England, France, Spain and Holland only lasted 18 months. On 21st October 1805 Nelson fought the Battle of Trafalgar, vanquishing the combined fleet of the French and Spanish of 33 ships, taking 20,000 prisoners in the process. The Battle confirmed British naval supremacy with Nelson becoming a National hero. His death was commemorated in a vast range of wares.

7. **Plate** 26.2 cms.
Mark: R13.
J. Rogers & Son, Longport. About 1832.
'Britannia', with a kneeling figure, ships and flags, within a 'Union Border' (Rose, Thistle and Shamrock).
Issued to commemorate the Reform Bill of 1832.

8. **Bowl** 25.4 cms.
Maker Unknown. About 1800–1810.
Chinoiserie border and rose sprays surrounding a portrait medallion of a King and Queen with the inscriptions: 'A King Revered. A Queen Beloved', and 'Long May They Live'. Possibly to commemorate the Golden Jubilee, in 1810, of George III and Queen Charlotte.

9. **Saucer** 15.2 cms.
Maker Unknown. About 1817.
Seated female figure in a classical landscape with a large urn of flowers. The border includes Prince of Wales' feathers and sprays of privet (a symbol of mourning). Rim and central pattern are banded in deep ochre. This is possibly a piece produced after the death, in 1817, of Charlotte, the only child of the future George IV.

10. **Vegetable Dish** and cover 22.8 cms square.
Maker Unknown. About 1810–1820.
Inside the dish is an unidentified scene from the 'Kirk' series of classical patterns (see Cat. Ref. Case 34/2). Close examination shows that the shield at the top of the central design appears to incorporate a Masonic emblem. This same emblem also appears in one of the two scenes used twice each on the lid.
Loaned by Flora Rabinovitch.

Case 6. SINGLE PATTERNS

In addition to the thousands of designs which were produced in series based on special themes many more thousands of one-off patterns were made, some very ordinary but others of artistic merit or at least eye-catching. Sometimes an entire service would carry the same pattern, while on others a particular design was used for one specific shape. Some examples of striking patterns are included in this section.

1. **Comport** 35.4 × 22.8 × 10.2 cms.
Maker Unknown. About 1815–1825.
'The Beemaster' pattern (see Cat. Ref. Case 6/6).

2. **Footed sugar bowl** (missing lid) of goblet shape 10.1 cms.
Patterson & Co., Tyneside. About 1837.
'Bacchanalian Cherubs', an apt and self-explanatory title.

3. **Hot Water Plate** 25 cms.
Maker Unknown. About 1815–1825.
'The Winemakers', a pattern known on both table and toilet wares. In the sale of the factory of John Denton Bagster (1823–1828), a design called 'Wine Press' was included.
Footnote: Hot water plates were double-walled plates with a

hollow space between the upper and lower surfaces to contain hot water, to keep the food warm. The water was poured in through a small hole in the rim.

4. **Sauce Tureen** with cover and stand.
All have added gilding on handles.
Tureen 22.0 × 11.5 × 14.5 cms, Stand 19.0 × 14.0 cms.
Maker Unknown. About 1820–1825.
'The Winemakers' pattern (see Cat. Ref. Case 6/3).

5. **Slop Bowl** 14.6 × 8.9 cms.
Maker Unknown. About 1815–1825.
'The Beemaster' pattern (see Cat. Ref. Case 6/6).
Loaned by Terry Sheppard.

6. **Sauce Tureen**, cover, stand and ladle.
Tureen 19.7 × 10.4 cms, Stand 21.3 × 13.2 cms and Ladle 12 cms long.
Maker Unknown. About 1815–1825.
'The Beemaster' – a pattern, found on dinner and tea wares, and recently on a garden seat, which has consistently defied attempts to attribute it to any particular maker.
Footnote: The scene is based on a water-colour by George Robertson (d. 1788) called 'Swarm of Bees, Autumn', now in the Cecil Higgins Art Gallery, Bedford.

7. **Cup and Saucer**.
Cup 6.0 cms high, Saucer 13.4 cms diameter.
Maker Unknown. About 1810–1820.
'Bee-Catcher', showing a large hive and a man trying to catch a bee in his hat.

8. **Cake or Cheese Stand** 26.5 cms.
Maker Unknown. About 1815–1825.
'Hop Pickers', a particularly striking rural scene.

9. **Jug** 21.0 cms high.
Maker Unknown. About 1820–1830.
'Sheep Shearer'. Several different patterns have been given this name. The design first recorded (Sheep Shearer I) is a mirror image of that on this jug – the figures all face in the opposite direction, but the border is the same.

Case 7. ARMORIAL PATTERNS

The manufacture of ceramics for use by Royalty, aristocracy, societies, and companies amongst others is almost as old as ceramics themselves. A great deal of the early production of Chinese porcelain was designed for the Imperial palaces. Transfer printed earthenware was an eminently suitable and relatively inexpensive medium for this type of ware and enabled its use to expand into a much broader market.

1. **Platter** 41.8 × 32.9 cms.
Mark: S8.
Spode, Stoke. About 1815–1820.
The border from the 'Greek' series (see Cat. Ref. Case 34/5) surrounding the arms of the City of Newcastle-upon-Tyne, confirmed in 1575. Motto: 'Fortiter Defendit Triumphans' ((She) Bravely Defends and Triumphs).
Loaned by Terry Sheppard.

2. Two Small **Bowls** (Mess Bowls) 15.8 × 8.9 cms.
Possibly *Bovey (Tracey) Pottery Co., Bovey Tracey, Devon.*
About 1845–1860.
Alternating cartouches of Sailors and 'Mess' numbers. The first with 'No. 3' and the second with 'No. 29'. These bowls were in common use in ships' messes, probably because they helped to avoid spillage.
Loaned by Flora Rabinovitch.

3. **Pierced Stand** (see illustration on back cover) 27.9 × 20.9 cms.
Mark: L2.
Thomas Lakin, Stoke. About 1812–1817.
Prince of Wales' feathers in a coronet, surrounded by the Royal Lion on a crown, all within a border of thistles and roses. A plate is known with the same blue decoration and a painted red background and is reputed to have come from a service in the collection of the late Queen Mary. The design does not match the arms, crest or badge of any British regiment, current or disbanded.
Loaned by Terry Sheppard.

4. Footed, Diamond-shaped **Dish** 29.1 × 24 × 10.1 cms.
Probably *Pountney and Allies, Bristol.* About 1820–1830.
Floral border surrounding the arms of the City of Bristol. These were confirmed in 1569. Motto: 'Virtute et Industria' (By Virtue and Industry). One commentator (W.J. Brown in *Old Bristol Potteries,* 1920) states that the copper plates of a dinner service made by Pountney for the City of Bristol were engraved by a workman from Burslem, named Wildblood. The border on this dish is a direct copy of that used with the 'Elephant' pattern, made by the Burslem firm of John Rogers & Son.
Loaned by Terry Sheppard.

5. **Dessert Dish** 25.5 × 18.0 × 4.0 cms.
Mark: S6 and S7.
Spode, Stoke. About 1820–1830.
'Dresden' border surrounding the badge of the 43rd Regiment, Bengal Native Infantry. The use of the same border on a contemporary service made for General Fagan, CB, may indicate a connection between the two (see Cat. Ref. Case 7/6), or simply that Spode habitually used the border on Mess china.

6. **Hot Water Plate** 25.3 cms.
Mark: S6 and S7.
Spode, Stoke. About 1820–1830.
'Dresden' border surrounding the arms of General Fagan, CB.
Motto: 'Deo Patrique Fidelis' (Faithful to God and Country).
Footnote: Major General Fagan joined the Indian Army in 1799 and became Colonel of the 37th Regiment of Bengal Native Infantry. He served in many of the Indian campaigns between 1803 and 1837, rising to command a field force, until ill health forced him to retire. He died at Devizes, Wiltshire, in May, 1843 (also see Cat. Ref. Case 6/3).
Loaned by Terry Sheppard.

7. **Platter** 48.2 × 36.1 cms.
Possibly *Minton, Stoke.* About 1815–1825.
'Bamboo and Flowers', with coat of arms having camels as supports. The arms and the motto 'Concordia Parle Res Crescunt' have not so far been identified.
Pieces in this pattern are known with the 'Semi-China' seal mark (see mark X29) used by Minton, among other makers.
Loaned by Flora Rabinovitch.

Case 8. BOY ON A BUFFALO

This pattern, sometimes called simply 'Buffalo', is a direct copy from Chinese export porcelain and was among the earliest designs to become popular with English earthenware manufacturers in the late 18th century. Its appeal lasted for nearly 50 years. There were several minor variations used by the Chinese, and these were faithfully copied by British potters. It was not until fairly recently that other variations have come to light, for instance 'Buffalo on the Bridge' and a version in which a figure appears on each side of the animal.

1. **Dinner Service** made by *Enoch Wood & Sons, Burslem.* About 1825–1830.
Cat. Ref. Case Dining room/1.

2. **Tea Service** with typical chinoiserie pattern. *Maker Unknown.* About 1790.
Cat. Ref. Case Tea room/1.

3. **Argyll and Cover**. *Maker Unknown*.
About 1795–1805. Cat. Ref. Case 1/19.

4. **Dessert Dish** attributed to *Edward & George Phillips, Longport*. About 1830.
Cat. Ref. Case 19/15.
Egg Cup. *Maker Unknown*. About 1815–1830.
Cat. Ref. Case 19/14.

5. **Soup Tureen, Cover and Stand** showing the Alms House, Boston, by *J & W Ridgway, Shelton*.
About 1825–1830. Cat. Ref. Case Kitchen/39.

6. **Engraved Copper Plate and Tissue Pull** of the 'Monopteros' design of *T & J Bevington, Cambrian Pottery, Swansea.* Cat. Ref. Case Techniques/1.

7. Left: **Jug** showing 'Tam O'Shanter' by *Thomas Godwin, Burslem*. About 1835–1845.
Cat. Ref. Case 33/17.
Middle: **Jug** with a view of the Crystal Palace. *Maker Unknown*. About 1851. Cat. Ref. Case 5/2.
Right: **Ewer** with the 'Armorial' pattern by *William Smith & Co., Stockton-on-Tees*.
About 1825–1830. Cat. Ref. Case 13/10.

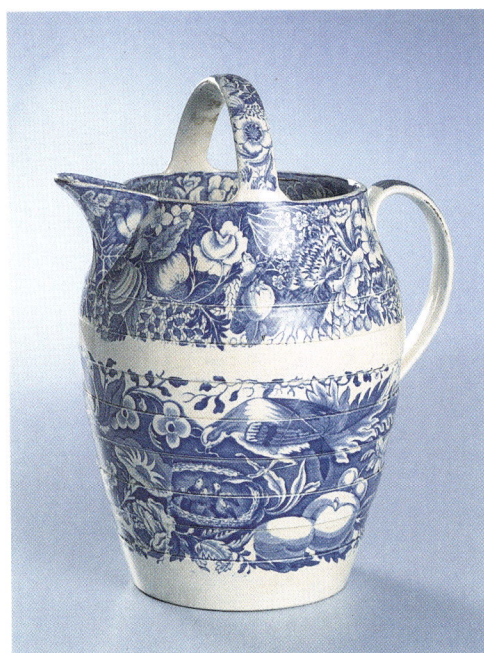

8. **Harvest Jug** attributed to *Wood & Brettell, Tunstall*. About 1820. Cat. Ref. Case 39.

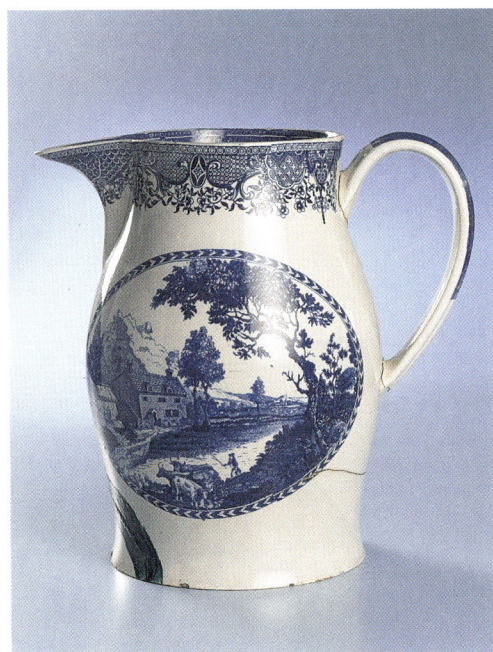

9. **Large Milk or Water Jug**. *Maker Unknown*. About 1795–1800. Cat. Ref. Case 38.

10. Left: **Teapot** attributed to *Sewell & Donkin* or *Fell & Co.* About 1820–1825. Cat. Ref. Case 13/7. Right: **Teapot** 'Violin' pattern. *Maker Unknown.* About 1800–1815. Cat. Ref. Case 34/15.

11. Left: **Pair of Preserve Pots** made by *Wedgwood, Etruria.* About 1830–1840. Cat. Ref. Case 24/28. Right: **Gooseberry Jar.** *Maker Unknown.* About 1820–1835. Cat. Ref. Case Kitchen/2.

12. **Pickle Set** made by *J & W Ridgway*.
About 1820–1830.
Cat. Ref. Case Dining room/34.

13. **Piggin**. *Maker Unknown*.
About 1820–1830. Cat. Ref. Case 4/5.

14. **Group of Medical Wares** by various manufacturers. Cat. Ref. Case (clockwise from the top)
27/9, 27/17, 27/8, 27/2, 27/3 & 27/12.

15. **Basket** showing the 'Landing of Lafayette' made by *J & R Clews, Cobridge*. About 1825–1830. Cat. Ref. Case 35/12.

16. **Cake or Cheese Stand** with the 'Giraffe and Obelisk' pattern. *Maker Unknown*. About 1810–1820. Cat. Ref. Case 21/11.

17. **Two plates**, made for the American Market, by *Henshall & Co., Longport*. About 1820–1828. Cat. Ref. Case 35/10.

18. **Vegetable Tureen, Lid and Cover** made by *Wedgwood, Etruria*. About 1825–1835. Cat. Ref. Case 24/25.

19. **Basket and Stand** made by *J & R Riley, Burslem*. About 1820–1828. Cat. Ref. Case 10/6.

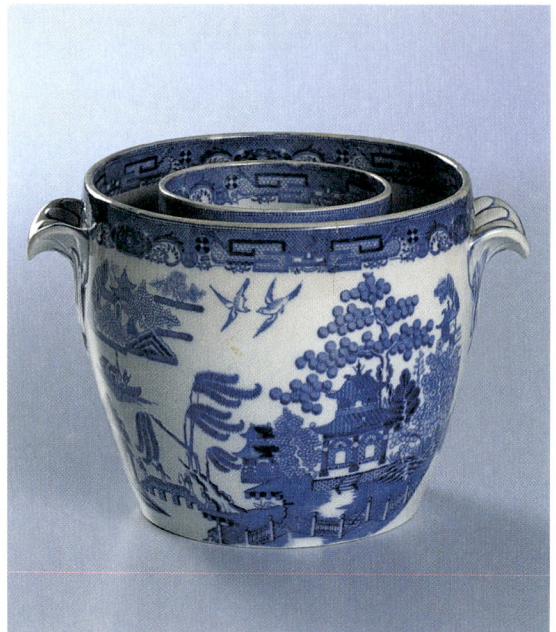

20. **Wine Cooler** with the 'Willow' pattern. *Maker Unknown*. About 1815–1835. Cat. Ref. Case Dining room/33.

21. Three pieces depicting different versions of the pattern 'Boy on a Buffalo'. All by unidentified makers dating between 1790–1805.
Jug Cat. Ref. Case 8/4; **Bowl** Cat. Ref. Case 8/6; **Vase** Cat. Ref. Case 8/2.

22. **Soup Tureen, Lid and Stand** with the 'Peony' pattern made by *Wedgwood, Etruria*. About 1815–1825. Cat. Ref. Case 24/14.

23. **Pair of Shoes or Slippers** in the 'Shepherd' pattern made by the *Glamorgan Pottery, Swansea*. About 1825-1835. Cat. Ref. Case 12/11.

24. **Selection of Miniature pieces** by various manufacturers dating from 1800-1825.
Cat. Ref. Case (clockwise from the top) 17/28, 17/16, 17/19, 17/15, 17/16, 17/33, 17/32, 17/17, 17/24, 17/25, 17/29; (in the centre) a tea bowl and saucer Cat. Ref. Case 8/3.

25. **Desk Set** in the 'Ferrara' pattern. *Wedgwood, Etruria.* About 1910. Cat. Ref. Case 34/12.

26. **Two Smokers' Sets** (at the back) attributed to *Shorthose*. About 1815–1825. Cat. Ref. Case 9/1; (at the front) to show all the component parts. *Maker Unknown*. About 1815–1830. Cat. Ref. Case 9/5.

27. **Mug** commemorating the Battle of Trafalgar and Lord Nelson. *Maker Unknown.* About 1805. Cat. Ref. Case 5/6.

28. **Plate** showing George Washington made by *Joshua Heath of Hanley* for the American Market. About 1790. Cat. Ref. Case 35/5.

29. Selection of inscribed and dated pieces by various manufacturers.
Cat. Ref. Case (clockwise from the top) 4/6, 4/3, 4/9, 4/4 & 4/1.

30. **Cow Creamer** decorated with the 'Willow' pattern. *Maker Unknown.* About 1840–1860. Cat. Ref. Case 23/12.

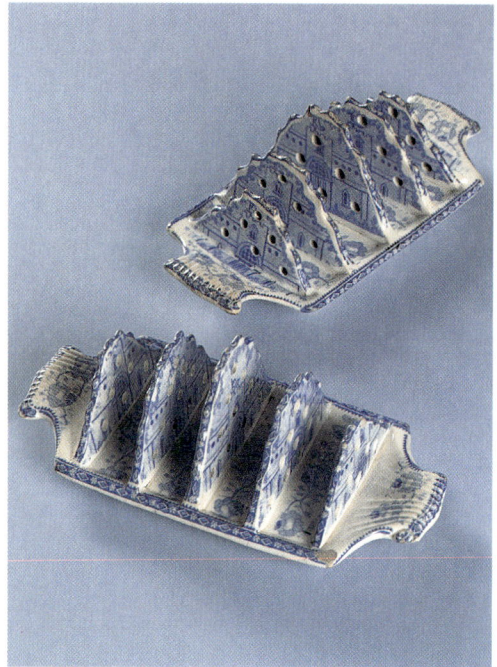

31. **Pair of Toast Racks** probably made by *William Hackwood of Hanley.* About 1825–1840. Cat. Ref. Case Kitchen/7.

32. **Veilleuse**, attributed to *Minton, Stoke.* About 1830–1840. Cat. Ref. Case 27/1.

33. **Handled Bowl** with the 'Whampoa' pattern attributed to *Dillwyn & Co., Cambrian Pottery, Swansea.* About 1840–1850. Cat. Ref. Case 12/15.

Case 8. BOY ON A BUFFALO

1. Pair of **Bough Pots** (covers missing) 17.8 × 10.5 × 7.0 cms.
Maker Unknown. About 1795–1805.
'Buffalo' (see Case Tea room/5). The narrow rectangular shape is not found as often as the semi-circular design. Bough Pots were used to display small sprays of flowering shrubs.

2. **Pouch Vase** on diamond-shaped foot (see plate 21).
Overall length 9.5 × 14.5 cms high.
Maker Unknown. About 1800–1805.
'Buffalo' (see Cat. Ref. Case Tea room/5). This version is extremely rare, having one standing figure on each side of the Buffalo whereas the other known variations show two figures to the left. A similar pattern has been noted on porcelain of the 1810–1820 period.

3. **Miniature Tea Bowl and Saucer** (see plate 24).
Bowl 5.7 × 3.8 cms.
Saucer 10.1 cms.
Probably *Spode.* About 1800–1805.
'Buffalo' (see Cat. Ref. Case Tea room/5).

4. **Jug** (see plate 21) 16.3 cms.
Maker Unknown. About 1795–1800.
'Buffalo' (see Cat. Ref. Case Tea room/5)
Loaned by P.L. and A.E. Maclean-Eltham.

5. **Sauce Boat** 17.2 × 7.7 cms.
Maker Unknown. About 1795–1805.
'Buffalo' (see Cat. Ref. Case Tea room/5).

6. **Bowl** (see plate 21) 22.3 × 10.1 cms.
Maker Unknown. About 1790–1800.
A rare variation of the 'Buffalo' pattern, to be called 'Buffalo on the Bridge'. The border has been noted on a piece bearing a retailer's mark 'Hilcock'.
Loaned by Anne and Graham Aylett.

Case 9. SMOKING

A backwater, though a substantial one, of the 'useful wares' category. The ornate 'Smoker's Sets' contained various combinations of accessories, augmented by such items as writing sets and goblets. Many individual tobacco pots and snuff boxes were also made, but the manufacture of pipe bowls appears to have been limited to porcelain and pipe-clay. The smokers themselves are depicted in several well-known designs.

1. **Smoker's Set** (see plate 26), consisting of: Reversible stand, tobacco jar with reversible cover, snuff container with weight and cover, wine goblet and candlestick. 34 cms overall height.
Attributed to the *Shorthose* partnerships of Hanley and Shelton.
About 1815–1825.
'Birds' pattern, a group of domestic fowl.
Loaned by Anna Wolsey.

2. **Snuff Box** and lid 4.5 × 4.5 cms.
Maker Unknown. About 1815–1825.
'Auriculas', with a border of scrolls and spearpoints. The lid decorated with a rose and lily.

3. **Pickle Dish** Shell-shape 10.6 cms.
Maker Unknown. About 1820–1840.
A man smoking a long-stemmed pipe and a kneeling woman holding a basket of flowers, both beside a trellis garden pavilion.

4. **Snuff Box** (with pewter back) 8.2 × 4.0 × 2.6 cms.
Maker Unknown. About 1820–1840.
A simple landscape with foreground trees, in a circular cartouche with blue dots. Prunus-like twigs outside cartouche. This is a rare shape in blue printed earthenware.

5. **Smoker's Set** comprising tobacco jar and cover, wine goblet and a base including tray and cover, two ink wells, sander, seal (a crown), and water pot. A candlestick would probably have rested on top of the goblet.
Total diameter 22.8 cms, total height 40.5 cms.
Maker Unknown. About 1815–1830.
Seaweed scrolls/fronds all over.
Loaned by Terry Sheppard.

Case 10. RILEY, ROGERS AND WOOD.

A trio of famous Burslem earthenware potters operating during the first quarter of the 19th century. See Appendix A on 'Manufacturers' for further details.

1. **Soup Tureen**, cover and ladle. Tureen 38 × 21.5 × 29.5 cms.
Ladle 31.5 cms long.
Mark: as W24.
Enoch Wood, Burslem. About 1825–1830.
Tureen: 'Holywell Cottage, Cavan' from the 'Grapevine Border' series (see Cat. Ref. Dining room/1).
Cover: repeated view of a church, not identified.
Ladle: An unidentified country house.
Loaned by John and Sally Storton.

2. **Plate** 23.4 cms.
Mark: W26.
Enoch Wood & Sons, Burslem. About 1825–1840.
A previously unrecorded view in the 'European Scenery' series in which about three designs have been identified so far.

3. **Jug** 19 × 22.5 cms.
Mark: as W24.
Enoch Wood & Sons, Burslem. About 1825–1830.
'Orielton, Pembrokeshire', from the 'Grapevine Border' series (see Cat. Ref. Case Dining room/1)
Loaned by John and Sally Storton.

4. **Tea Pot** and cover London-shape 24.1 × 14.0 cms.
Tentatively attributed to *Enoch Wood & Sons, Burslem.* About 1820–1830.
A lady and gentleman seated at a table, not unlike the various 'Tea Party' patterns (see Cat. Ref. Case 13/5). The mansion in the background may be Petworth House.

5. Pair of **Syllabub Cups** 7.6 × 9.0 cms.
Enoch Wood & Sons, Burslem. About 1825–1830.
Unidentified Views from the 'Grapevine Border' series (see Cat. Ref. Case Dining room/1 for other examples of this design).
Footnote: Professional city confectioners advertised in the 18th century, 'jellies, creams and syllabubs to be eaten on the premises, or ordered in quantity for such social events as a ball supper'. 'Whipt' syllabub was floated on sweetened wine in little glasses or cups with a belled top, which helped support the delicate froth and stop it sinking into the wine. Syllabub was made by whipping together wine, lemon juice, sugar and cream with a chocolate mill and laboriously skimming the bubbles off as they rose to the surface. After draining on a sieve for a number of hours, the froth was transformed into a light fluffy spume which was then transferred to the glasses or cups of wine.

6. **Basket** and stand (see plate 19) 28 × 27 cms.
J & R Riley, Burslem. About 1820–1828.
Basket: 'Bretton Hall', Stand: 'Dalguise' (Perthshire), from the 'Large Scroll Border' series of nearly twenty patterns. 'Dalguise' is hitherto unrecorded in this series.
The source of both designs is John Preston Neale's *Views of the Seats of Noblemen and Gentlemen in England and Wales, Scotland and Ireland* (Six volumes 1818–1823).
Loaned by John and Sally Storton.

7. **Helmet Jug** 21.4 cms.
Mark: R13.
John Rogers & Son, Dale Hall, Burslem. About 1815–1825.
'Galleon at Anchor', one of the 'Rogers' Views' series of at least twelve scenes, some identified and mostly English (see Cat. Ref. Case 34/6).
Loaned by Mr. and Mrs. M. Houlden.

8. **Plate** 22.3 cms.
Mark: R11A.
J & R Riley, Burslem. About 1820–1828.
One of a series of six rural views with a 'Union Border' of Rose, Shamrock and Thistle.
Footnote: It is possible that this pattern derived its name from the general acceptance of the 'Acts of Union'. The first which merged England with Scotland occurred in 1707 but a second act to form a single United Kingdom, including Ireland, was made effective from 1st January 1801.

9. **Saucer** 14.0 cms.
Mark: R12 and R12A. The impressed hand is a rare mark, not previously recorded by the Friends of Blue.
J & R Riley, Burslem. About 1820–1828.
'Girl Gardeners' – two girls, one kneeling with a watering can.

10. Individual **Butter Boat** for Asparagus 7.8 cms.
Attributed to *J & R Riley, Burslem.* About 1820.
Part of the floral border of the 'Europa' pattern from which the attribution has been made.

11. **Tea Pot** Oval-shape 25.3 × 15.1 cms.
Mark: R12.
J & R Riley, Burslem. About 1810–1815.
A fishing boat in the foreground with a house and a windmill behind. A pattern not previously recorded.

Case 11. DON AND DAVENPORT

Two more major manufacturers of blue printed earthenware – The Don Pottery, near Rotherham, Yorkshire and the Davenport factory which lasted from 1794 to 1887, remaining for the entire period in family control and at the same site at Longport, near Burslem. Some parts of the original buildings still stand.

1. **Plate** 24.8 cms.
Mark: D4.
Davenport, Longport. About 1795–1810.
'Chinese Fishermen'.

2. **Square Dish** 19.1 cms square.
Davenport, Longport. About 1800–1810.
'Chinese Flagbearers' – two figures carrying large pennants, crossing a bridge similar to that in the Willow pattern.

3. **Cake or Cheese Stand** 28.5 × 9.5 cms.
Unmarked but pattern name incorporated in main design.
Don Pottery. About 1820–1830.

'Tomb of Theron, Aggrigentum', from the 'Named Italian Views' series of nearly forty views, taken from *Voyages Pittoresque ou Description des Royaumes de Naples et de Sicile* by the Abbé Jean Claude Richard de St. Non (Paris 1781–1786).
Loaned by P.L. and A.E. Maclean-Eltham.

4. **Kitchen Jug**, unusual shape. Diameter of base 15.7 × 13.5 cms.
Davenport, Longport. About 1815–1825.
'The Villagers', this name has also been used for different designs by other potters.

5. **Pepper Pot** with domed lid 12.7 cms.
Davenport, Longport. About 1820–1840.
'Muleteer', a popular pattern used extensively on toilet wares as well as on table wares. There seem to be several different versions, all centred on a mounted muleteer and an attendant pedestrian (see footnote Cat. Ref. Case Dining room/30).

6. **Shaped Dish** 27.3 × 21.5 cms.
Mark: D3.
Davenport, Longport. About 1810–1820.
Originally known as 'Tudor Mansion', this pattern was first identified as 'Oxburgh Hall, Norfolk' and later as 'Bisham Abbey, near Henley-on-Thames'. Because alterations have taken place over the years, no closely matching pictures of the rival claimants have been found and there is still some controversy as to whether the pattern represents either or neither of the named buildings.

7. **Plate** 22.3 cms.
Mark: D2.
Davenport, Longport. About 1805–1815.
'Chinoiserie High Bridge' (see Cat. Ref. Case 11/9).

8. **Basket** and Stand 26 × 18.4 × 10.8 cms.
Mark: D3.
Davenport, Longport. About 1805–1815.
'Chinoiserie Ruins', a transitional pattern made also by other factories including Ridgway and Rogers.

9. **Arcaded Plate** 18.4 cms.
Mark: D1.
Davenport, Longport. About 1805–1815.
'Chinoiserie High Bridge', a scene showing a straight bridge crossing high above a river, between two temples; three Chinese figures appear on a terrace in the foreground.

10. **Saucer** 13.5 cms.
Davenport, Longport. About 1810–1815.
'Eskimo on Snow Shoes', this and a similar design are known as 'Snow Scenes' and appear to have been taken from Thomas Bankes' *A Modern Authentic and Complete Geography*. The views may be Siberian rather than Canadian as Bankes' description is 'The Ostiak's Method of Travelling in Winter'.

11. **Drainer** 24.2 × 17.4 cms.
Attributed to *Don Pottery.* About 1820–1930.
Probably a view from the 'Landscape' series of three or more scenes.

12. **Ewer** 21.5 cms.
Possibly *Don Pottery.* About 1820–1830.
An Italianate view with a statue on a column and a building like the Leaning Tower of Pisa, with a border of flowers and leaves.

13. **Tea Pot** 24.6 × 12.7 cms.
Don Pottery. About 1810–1820.
A rural scene in an oval reserve surrounded by random ribbon-like lines. One of a series of at least six views known as the 'Vermicelli Border' series.

14. **Segment from a Supper Set** (without cover)
27 × 18.8 cms.
Unmarked but pattern name incorporated in main design.
Don Pottery. About 1820–1830.
'Port of Tarentum', from the 'Named Italian Views' series (see Cat. Ref. Case 11/3).
Loaned by P.L. and A.E. Maclean-Eltham.

15. **Leaf Pickle Dish**, moulded leaf exterior 17.4 × 14 cms.
Unmarked but pattern name incorporated in main design.
Don Pottery. About 1820–1830.
'Ruins of the Castle of Canna', from the 'Named Italian Views' series (see Cat. Ref. Case 11/3).
Loaned by Celia Lowe.

Case 12. SCOTTISH AND WELSH POTTERIES

Both the output and the reputation of the Staffordshire manufacturers has always over-shadowed the other pottery centres of the United Kingdom, but both Scotland and Wales can boast of factories almost as old as, and certainly comparable in quality to their Staffordshire counterparts. Particularly notable as a centre was Swansea in south Wales and the factory of J. & M.P. Bell & Co. in Glasgow which lasted for nearly a hundred years and enjoyed an excellent reputation, borne out by the size of its output.

1. **Plate** 25.5 cms.
Mark: G2.
John Geddes (& Son), Verreville Pottery, Glasgow. About 1820–1825.
The design was originally known as 'Country Mansion', but is now believed to be a view of 'Daylesford House, Worcestershire', the home of Warren Hastings, taken from a print in John Preston Neale's *Views of the Seats of Noblemen and Gentlemen in England and Wales, Scotland and Ireland* (1818–1823).
Loaned by John and Sally Storton.

2. **Bourdalou** (see Glossary) 28 × 8.5 cms.
Mark: B3.
J. & M.P. Bell & Co., Glasgow. About 1840–1850.
'Triumphal Car', a pattern known in at least eleven variations, mostly by Scottish potters. The maker of a similar pattern known as 'Arcadian Chariots' has not so far been identified (see Cat. Ref. Case 27/8 and 34/1).

3. **Jug** 9.5 × 9.5 cms.
Mark: G3.
Glamorgan Pottery, Swansea. About 1820–1830.
'Cottage Girl', a very popular pattern at this factory, showing a girl with a hoop and a dog, beside two wooden pails.

4. **Soup Plate** 26 cms.
J. & M.P. Bell & Co., Glasgow Factory and pattern names printed in fox's head design. About 1845–1865.
'Hunting Subjects', possibly one of a series. The mark includes a hunting whip, a horn and a fox's head.

5. **Fluted Custard or Syllabub Cup** 6.2 cms.
Possibly *Swansea (Cambrian Pottery).* About 1795–1800.
Part of a chinoiserie landscape, with one figure on a long bridge (see Cat. Ref. Case 10/5).

6. **Circular Pot** with cover, probably for kitchen or toilet use
14.5 × 8.5 cms.
Attributed to *Glamorgan Pottery, Swansea.* About 1820–1830.
'Cowherd', a man leaning against one of a pair of cows, conversing with another man seated on the ground.

7. **Miniature Pot** with cover probably for kitchen or toilet use
7.4 × 5.3 cms.
Attributed to *Glamorgan Pottery, Swansea.* About 1820–1830.
A man in a horse and cart on a road leading from a farm house.
Footnote: Note the similarity in shape to Cat. Ref. Case 12/6 which appears to be closely based on an Oriental form.

8. **Butter Tub** with cover 11.3 × 10.8 cms.
Mark: Pattern name printed in a small floral cartouche.
Attributed to *David Methven & Sons, Kirkcaldy Pottery, Fife.*
About 1840–1850.
'Imperial', a design of flowers and scrolls.

9. **Tea Bowl** 8.8 cms diameter.
Attributed to *Thomas Rathbone & Co., Portobello.*
About 1815–1825.
Deer grazing. Various designs similar to this, showing a range of barns and other farm buildings, sometimes under snow, are known by different makers.

10. **Plate** 24.5 cms.
Maker Unknown but sometimes attributed to *Swansea.* About 1800–1810.
Variously known as 'Chinese Birds' or 'Banana Tree Chinoiserie'.

11. **A pair of Shoes or Slippers** (see plate 23)
17.1 × 5.1 × 4.4 cms.
Glamorgan Pottery, Swansea. About 1825–1835.
'Shepherd' pattern.
Footnote: A model pair of shoes, containing a lump of sugar in one and a lump of coal in the other, was a customary Welsh wedding gift. These represented a life of sweetness and warmth or harmony. This is the first record of a pair of shoes in blue transfer printed earthenware. Shoes have been manufactured in every ceramic body from Chinese porcelain, where they were referred to as 'hsai', through Persian tin glazed earthenware, to European porcelain.

12. **Soup Ladle** 27.9 × 8.8 cms.
Baker, Bevans and Irwin, Glamorgan Pottery, Swansea.
About 1820–1830.
Part of the 'Ladies of Llangollen' pattern.
Footnote: In 1778 two independent minded Irish aristocrats, Lady Eleanor Butler and Miss Sarah Ponsonby, moved to Llangollen, North Wales, with their maid Mary Carryl where they settled at a house known locally as Plas Newydd. Their mannish clothes attracted a good deal of attention, but their reputation for hospitality and humour was widespread. They received many distinguished visitors including The Duke of Wellington and William Wordsworth. The Ladies were depicted in various mediums including ceramics.

13. **Ladle** 17.7 × 5.7 cms.
T & J Bevington (& Co.), Cambrian Pottery, Swansea. About 1817–1824.
'Monopteros', a pattern produced also by John Rogers & Son. The design is taken from a print 'Remains of an Ancient Building near Firoz Shah's Cotilla, Delhi' in Thomas Daniell's *Oriental Scenery* (1795).
Footnote: For the full design see copper plate and tissue pull (see Cat. Ref. Case Techniques/1).

14. Probably a **Watercress Dish** (One handle missing) 17.8 cms.
Attributed to *Swansea* on the basis of the pattern and the arrangement of the draining holes (Prince of Wales' feathers).
About 1795–1805.
'Two Figures' pattern, made by many of the early makers of blue and white.

15. **Handled Bowl** (see plate 33) 25.7 × 7.3 cms.
Mark: S17.
Attributed to *Dillwyn & Co., Cambrian Pottery, Swansea*. About 1840–1850.
'Whampoa', a popular name for later patterns. Whampoa is a sea port on an island off the coast of China.
This piece is an early example of the 'Flow (or Flown) Blue' printing technique.

Case 13. YORKSHIRE AND THE NORTH EASTERN POTTERIES

The pottery producing regions of the British Isles, outside Staffordshire, have a great deal to offer to collectors of blue and white earthenware. In each of them can be found factories which lasted for many years and often competed with Staffordshire in terms of quality, yet tended to retain their own characteristic differences which today are recognisable to the trained eye. East of the Pennines, the classic example is the Leeds Pottery, but there are many smaller firms between the 1780's and the present day.

1. **Platter** 39 × 29 cms.
Mark: L3.
Leeds Pottery. About 1800–1810.
'Great Wall of China' pattern (see Cat. Ref. Case 13/2).
Loaned by P.L. and A.E. Maclean-Eltham.

2. **Plate** 18 cms.
Mark: L3.
Leeds Pottery. About 1800–1810.
'Great Wall of China', this small plate has a completely different border to that on the platter (see Cat. Ref. Case 13/1), probably for reasons of size.

3. **Tea Bowl and Saucer**
Tea Bowl 5.3 cms high, Saucer 12.3 cms diameter.
Attributed to *Ralph Wedgwood, Ferrybridge Pottery*, on the basis of the pattern which is found in the 'W & Co Ferrybridge Shape and Pattern Book' in the Wedgwood Archives, Barlaston. About 1800.
'Elephant and Castle' or 'Elephant and Howdah'. The design is very similar to the standard 'Buffalo' pattern, apart from the substitution of animals.

4. **Small Plate** 11.6 cms.
Mark: D9.
Davies, Cookson & Wilson, Tyneside Pottery, Newcastle-upon-Tyne. About 1824–1829.
A version of the 'Broseley' or 'Two Temples' pattern.

5. **Coffee Pot** 25.4 cms high (including lid).
William Smith & Co., Stockton-on-Tees. About 1825–1830.
'Tea Party', one of several versions produced by various potters from the North East and Staffordshire.
Loaned by Dr. David Greenbaum.

6. **Pot Pourri Jar** 13.8 cms.
J.Dawson & Co., Sunderland. About 1815–1830.
'Bird's Nest' – a boy showing a bird's nest to a girl with a dog.

7. **Globular Tea Pot** with cover and high prow (see plate 10) 13.7 cms high.
Probably of north-eastern manufacture, perhaps by *Sewell and Donkin* or *Fell & Co.* About 1820–1825.
Man smoking a long clay pipe, woman seated at a tea table. Sometimes termed 'Smoking Party' (see Cat. Ref. Case 13/8).

8. **Tea Bowl** 7.8 × 5.0 cms.
Attributed to *T. Fell & Co., Newcastle-on-Tyne.* About 1820–1830. (Pattern similar to Cat. Ref. Case 13/7.)

9. **Small Platter** 25.3 × 20.3 cms.
Mark: M11.
Middlesbrough Pottery. About 1835–1850.
A romantic river view with a large château on cliffs and a column surmounted by a globe in the foreground.

10. **Ewer** (see plate 7) 19.5 cms high.
Mark: S21.
William Smith & Co., Stockton-on-Tees. About 1825–1830.
'Armorial', an equestrian statue seen through an archway across a fountain court.

11. **Tea Bowl and Saucer** Saucer 14 cms diameter.
Mark: V1. The mark 'Vedgwood', which was obviously intended to indicate quality by a minor deception, does not appear to have attracted litigation from Wedgwood as did the use of this name by William Smith & Co.
Carr & Patton, North Shields. About 1845–1848.
'Musk Deer', a girl feeding a small deer in a romantic landscape (see Cat. Ref. Case 13/17).

12. **Miniature Cup and Saucer**.
Cup 4.8 cms high, Saucer 6.8 cms diameter.
Brameld & Co., Rockingham Works, Swinton. About 1825–1830.
'Flower Groups', a pattern of flowers and butterflies.

13. **Saucer** 12.7 cms.
Attributed tentatively to *Swinton Pottery, Yorkshire.*
About 1795–1805.
A typical chinoiserie design including a gazebo with a pennant and an angled bridge.

14. **Saucer** 13.2 cms.
Attributed to *Robert Maling, Ouseburn Pottery, Newcastle-upon-Tyne* on the basis of a marked piece in the same pattern.
About 1820–1825.
'Pillar with Urn' pattern.

15. Covered **Sugar Box** 10 × 13.6 cms.
Mark: D13.
David Dunderdale & Co., Castleford. About 1810–1820.
'Violin' or 'Chinoiserie Wheel' pattern, made by several different factories including Bradley of Coalport and Joshua Heath of Hanley (see Cat. Ref. Case 34/15).

16. **Tea Bowl and Saucer**
Bowl 8.4 cms diameter; Saucer 12.9 cms diameter.
Mark: S19 and 'Wedgewood' impressed.
William Smith & Co., Stockton-on-Tees. About 1825–1830.
'Lion Antique'. This is one of many patterns known to have been exported to Belgium. Pieces are known with the mark of J. & B. Cappellemans the Elder, a Brussels retailer.

17. **Tea Bowl and Saucer.** Bowl 7.7 cms; Saucer 12.7 cms.
Mark: S20 and 'Wedgewood' impressed.
William Smith & Co., Stockton-on-Tees. About 1825–1840.
'Girl with Pitcher' pattern.

Case 14. INDIAN SPORTING

An extension to the fashion of transferring to earthenware prints published by travellers returning from Europe, the Middle East and the Orient. Hunting of any sort was always a popular subject at all levels of society and the exotic nature of Indian field sports created an excellent market for ceramics decorated in this way.

1. **Charger** 36.7 cms.
Mark: C3.
E. Challinor, Tunstall. About 1845.
'Driving a Bear out of Sugar Canes' from the 'Oriental Sports' series. Derived either from Spode's 'Indian Sporting' series or from the source of that series (see Cat. Ref. Case 14/6). At least six designs are known to have been made by this manufacturer.
Loaned by Terry Sheppard.

2. **Comport** and cover, canoe-shaped 26.0 × 17.5 × 20.0 cms.
Mark: C3 (Tureen only).
E. Challinor, Tunstall. About 1845.
a) 'Hunting a Civet Cat' b) 'The Hog at Bay' from the 'Oriental Sports' series (see Cat. Ref. Case 14/1).

3. **Plate** 24.8 cms.
Mark: S6, S7 and as S9.
Spode, Stoke. About 1820–1830.
'Death of the Bear', from the 'Indian Sporting' series (see Cat. Ref. Case 14/6).
Loaned by City Museum and Art Gallery, Stoke-on-Trent.

4. **Set of three graduated Baking Dishes**
a) 29.2 × 20.2 cms, b) 24 × 17.2 cms and c) 20.6 × 15.9 cms.
Mark: S6, S7 and as S9.
Spode, Stoke. About 1820–1830.
a) 'Hunting a Buffalo', b) 'Hunting a Civet Cat' and c) 'Battle between a Buffalo and a Tiger', from the 'Indian Sporting' series (see Cat. Ref. Case 14/6).

5. **Oval Dish** 27.5 × 19.0 cms.
Mark: S6, S7 and as S9.
Spode, Stoke. About 1820–1830.
a) 'Hunting a Civet Cat', from the 'Indian Sporting' series (see Cat. Ref. Case 14/6).

6. **Soup Tureen** and cover 35.5 × 22.5 × 25.3 cms.
Mark: Tureen S6, S7 and as S9, Cover S6 and S7.
Spode, Stoke. About 1820–1830.
Tureen: 'The Hog at Bay', Cover: 'Hunting a Buffalo', from the 'Indian Sporting' series of at least nineteen designs taken from engravings of drawings by Samuel Howitt in Capt. Thomas Williamson's *Oriental Field Sports, Wild Sports of the East* (1807). The series was copied in part by two other makers – J. & R. Clews and Edward Challinor (see Cat. Ref. Case 14/1 & 2 and 37/3 & 3A).
Loaned by Terry Sheppard.

7. **Platter** (Well and Tree) 51.9 × 39.3 cms.
Mark: S6, S7 and as S9.
Spode, Stoke. About 1820–1825.
'Shooting a Leopard' from the 'Indian Sporting' series (see Cat. Ref. Case 14/6).
Loaned by Terry Sheppard.

8. **Platter** 26.7 × 19.2 cms.
Mark: S6, S7 and as S9.
Spode, Stoke. About 1820–1825.
'Hunting a Civet Cat', from the 'Indian Sporting' series (see Cat. Ref. Case 14/6).
Loaned by Mervyn Gibbs.

9. **Arcaded Plate** 18.4 cms
Possibly *James and Ralph Clews.* About 1820–1830
'Common Wolf Trap' which matches closely the view in Spode's 'Indian Sporting' series (see Cat. Ref. Case 14/6).
Footnote: The lack of any marks suggests that this could have been made by Spode.

10. **Plate and Source Print of Pattern** Plate 20.9 cms.
Mark: S6, S7 and as S9.
Spode, Stoke. About 1820–1825.
'Common Wolf Trap' from the 'Indian Sporting' series (see Cat. Ref. Case 14/6).
The source print shows an engraving of this pattern from a drawing by Samuel Howitt in Capt. Thomas Williamson's *Oriental Field Sports, Wild Sports of the East* (1807).

11. **Plate** 15.5 cms.
Mark: S6, S7 and as S10.
Spode, Stoke. About 1820–1825.
'Groom (or Syce) Leading out a Horse' from the 'Indian Sporting' series (see Cat. Ref. Case 14/6).

12. **Jug** 19.0 × 20.5 cms.
Maker Unknown. About 1820–1830.
A scene of a tiger attacked by dogs, probably taken from a source similar to those used for Spode's 'Indian Sporting' series (see Cat. Ref. Case 14/6).
Brown monogram 'RCH' below lip. Top and bottom rims picked out in white enamel.
Loaned by City Museum and Art Gallery, Stoke-on-Trent.

13. **Platter** 51.5 × 40.8 cms.
Maker Unknown. About 1820–1830.
'Tiger Hunt' from an 'Indian Sporting' series

14. **Sauce Tureen** with lion head handles
19.0 × 10.6 × 11.9 cms.
Maker Unknown. About 1820–1825.
'Returning from the Hunt' from an 'Indian Sporting' series copying the series by Spode (see Cat. Ref. Case 14/6).
The border of scrolls and petals is completely different to any other known versions.

15. **Small Plate** with moulded rim 21.7 cms.
Maker Unknown. About 1840–1850.
Probably derived from 'Hunting a Civet Cat' (see Cat. Ref. Case 14/8). This is a somewhat later re-creation of a pattern used in Spode's 'Indian Sporting' series.

Case 15. MIDDLE EASTERN VIEWS

The popularity of the Middle East was brought about by the publication in the 1790's and onwards of volumes of travel books illustrated by prints from drawings made on the spot by professional travellers. The Napoleonic Wars widened the horizon of the Middle East and the fashion never really disappeared, fuelled by the romantic adventures of such travellers as Lady Hester Stanhope.

1. **Quart Mug** 12.6 × 12.6 cms.
Maker Unknown. About 1815–1820.
A European traveller confronting two men in Middle-Eastern dress outside a walled town with minarets and towers.
Loaned by Christopher Fiorini.

2. **Plate** 25.8 cms.
Mark: S4.
Spode, Stoke. About 1820–1825.
'Sarcophagi and Sepulchres at the Head of the Harbour at Cacamo', from the 'Caramanian' series (see Cat. Ref. Case 15/13).
Loaned by Mervyn Gibbs.

3. **Plate** 21.5 cms.
Mark: S4.
Spode, Stoke. About 1820–1825.

'Necropolis or Cemetery of Cacamo', from the 'Caramanian' series (see Cat. Ref. Case 15/13).
Loaned by Mervyn Gibbs.

4. **Platter** 53 × 45 cms.
Mark: R6.
J & W Ridgway, Shelton. About 1820–1825.
'Triumphal Arch at Latachia', from the 'Ottoman Empire' series of at least fifteen views with a distinctive incense burner in the border and taken mainly from Luigi Mayer's *Views in the Ottoman Dominions, in Europe, in Asia, and some of the Mediterranean Islands* (1810) (Short title).
Loaned by John and Sally Storton.

5. **Ewer** 12 × 17 cms.
Probably *Elkin, Knight and Bridgwood, Fenton.* About 1830–1840.
'Indian Temple', a romantic scene of minarets and towers beside a river bridge.
Loaned by Mervyn Gibbs.

6. **Bowl** 21.6 × 10.1 cms.
Possibly *Herculaneum Pottery, Liverpool.* About 1815–1825.
Believed to be 'Tomb of Prince Khusrau/Mausoleum of Sultan Chuero, near Allahabad', a hitherto unrecorded pattern.
Loaned by Flora Rabinovitch.

7. **Plate** 25.3 cms.
Mark: K1.
James Keeling & Co., Hanley. About 1828–1830.
'The Tomb of Zobeida, the wife of Haroun al Rashid, the Caliph of Baghdad', from 'Views in Mesopotamia' series. The source of this series is J.L. Buckingham's *Travels in Mesopotamia* (1828).
Loaned by City Museum and Art Gallery, Stoke-on-Trent.

8. **Plate** 18.2 cms.
Mark: G5.
Thomas & Benjamin Godwin, Burslem. About 1825–1835.
'Sicre Gully Pass, Bengal', from the 'Indian Scenery' series of at least ten views. The series was subsequently copied by other makers.

9. **Comport** 30.5 × 22.5 × 11.0 cms.
Mark: R7.
J & W Ridgway, Shelton. About 1820–1825.
'Caravansary at Kustchiuk Czenege', from the 'Ottoman Empire' series (see Cat. Ref. Case 15/4).
Loaned by Celia Lowe.

10. **Pickle Tray**, probably part of a Supper Set 14.8 × 11.6 cms.
John Rogers & Son, Longport, Burslem. About 1815–1825.
The 'Camel' pattern (on this dish the camel appears on the outside of the dish instead of being part of an integral scene). The view is based on an aquatint by Thomas Daniell, in his *Oriental Scenery* (1795–1808), and shows, 'Gate leading to a Musjed, at Chunar Ghur'. The camel is taken from another print in the same series.

11. **Soup Tureen** 35.5 × 21.6 × 25.3 cms.
Mark: S8.
Spode, Stoke. About 1815–1820.
Tureen: 'Colossal Sarcophagus near Castle Rosso'.
Cover: a) 'A Colossal Sarcophagus at Cacamo in Caramania'.
b) 'A Colossal Vase near Limisso in Cyprus'.
From the 'Caramanian' series (see Cat. Ref. Case 15/13).
Loaned by Terry Sheppard.

12. **Pickle Dish** Diamond-shape, probably from a set 12.2 × 8.6 cms.
Mark: S5.

Spode, Stoke. About 1820–1825.
Taken from a larger scene, probably 'Sarcophagi and Sepulchres at the Head of the Harbour at Cacamo', from the 'Caramanian' series (see Cat. Ref. Case 15/13).

13. (Wall mounted) Four framed and glazed **Prints** from Luigi Mayer's *Views in Egypt, Palestine and the Ottoman Empire,* mainly from Volume II, *Views in the Ottoman Empire, chiefly in Caramania* (1803) (short title).
a) 'Principal Entrance of the Harbour at Cacamo'.
b) 'An Ancient Bath at Cacamo in Caramania'.
c) 'Ancient Granary at Cacamo'.
d) Castle of Boudron in the Gulf of Stancio'.
All views used in Spode's 'Caramanian' series of at least seventeen scenes, based mainly on three volumes of prints, Luigi Mayer's *Views in Egypt* (1801), *Views in the Ottoman Empire, chiefly in Caramania, a part of Asia Minor hitherto unexplored* (1803), and *Views in Palestine* (1804). The animals in the border come from Capt. T. Williamson's *Oriental Field sports, Wild sports of the East* (1807).
Loaned by Terry Sheppard.

Case 16. EUROPEAN VIEWS

The 'Grand Tour' – the essential finishing school for gentlemen of the 18th century aristocracy, opened up the rest of Europe to the English eye, and, as more people became able to travel, and as travel itself became easier and safer, documentary works about the continent of Europe became popular and soon graduated from publications to reproductions on ceramics.

1. **Plate** 21.5 cms.
Mark: B6.
Brameld & Co., Swinton, near Rotherham. About 1830–1835.
'Castle of Rochefort, South of France', a pattern known to have been used for complete dinner services. Rochefort was a fortified town on the Bay of Biscay.
Loaned by City Museum and Art Gallery, Stoke-on-Trent.

2. **Plate** 26.0 cms.
Mark: A2 and A5.
William Adams, Stoke. About 1820–1830.
'Gracefield, Queen's County, Ireland', from the 'Flowers and Leaves' border series (see Cat. Ref. Case Kitchen/31)
Loaned by Dr. and Mrs. David Furniss.

3. **Platter** 37.6 × 28.3 cms.
Mark: C13 and draped curtains surrounding a plaque containing 'Copeland and Garrett, Stoke upon Trent and London. The Kremlin, China Glaze' (printed).
Copeland and Garrett, Stoke. About 1833–1847.
'Winter' from the 'Seasons' series of scenes which show a large vase of flowers bearing the name of a month or season, with a landscape scene in the background. Presumably all twelve months and all four seasons were represented, though examples of them all have not yet come to light. As the mark indicates this view is of 'The Kremlin', Moscow.

4. **Tea Bowl and Saucer** Bowl 7.7 cms. Saucer 12.1 cms.
Mark: S2 (Saucer only).
John Shorthose, Hanley. About 1815–1820.
'Wellington Hotel, Waterloo', a building which was Napoleon's Headquarters during the Battle of Waterloo. It is clearly identifiable from an engraving by George Cruickshank in his *Historical Account of the Battle of Waterloo* (1817) with the name over the door, 'A LA BELLE ALLIANCE/ WELLINGTON HOTEL'.

5. and 5a **Soup Plate and Source Print** of its pattern.
Plate 25.2 cms.
Mark: L5.
Lockett & Hulme, Lane End. About 1822–1826.

'Ponte Rotto', a view taken from a print published in 1796 in Merigot's *Views and Ruins in Rome and its Vicinity*.
Loaned by Celia Lowe.

6. **Sauce Tureen**, with stand and cover 18.4 × 11.4 × 12.7 cms.
Mark: D12 (on stand only).
Don Pottery, Swinton, Yorkshire. About 1815–1825.
Tureen: 'View in Alicata'. Cover: 'Unidentified view'.
Stand: 'View of the Ruins of the Temple of Juno at Agrigento' (A partial view).
All from the 'Named Italian Views' series (see Cat. Ref. Case 11/3).

7. **Vegetable Dish** and cover 22.5 cms square.
Don Pottery, Swinton, Yorkshire. About 1815–1825.
Dish: 'Ruins near Agrigenti' from the 'Named Italian Views' series (see Cat. Ref. Case 11/3).
Cover: Details from a) 'View of Stromboli from the part facing the North-East'. b) 'View of the Rocks or Cape of Scarletta'.
Loaned by Celia Lowe.

8. **Two-handled Mug** (Loving Cup)
11.5 cms diameter × 12.1 cms high.
William Adams & Sons, Stoke. About 1830–1840.
'Huntsmen with Pennants', from the small 'Andalusia' series of hunting scenes featuring whippets. Andalusia is the region around Granada and Seville in Southern Spain.

9. **Dish** Shell-shape 21 × 19 × 4.0 cms.
Mark: Impressed asterisk *.
Don Pottery, Swinton, Yorkshire. About 1815–1825.
'View of the Town of Cava near Salerno', from the 'Named Italian Views' series (see Cat. Ref. Case 11/3).
Loaned by Celia Lowe.

10. **Pierced Stand** 23.6 × 19.0 cms.
Enoch Wood & Sons, Burslem. About 1820–1830.
An unidentified view from the 'French Views' series of about twenty-three scenes in France.
Loaned by David and Linda Arman.

11. **Pierced Stand** 25.4 × 20.5 cms.
Mark: Impressed 'B'.
Enoch Wood & Sons, Burslem. About 1820–1830.
'Chateau de Chillon', from the 'Italian Scenery' series, of twenty-seven views in Italy.
Loaned by David and Linda Arman.

12. **Platter** 49 × 38.8 cms.
Mark: T1 and T5.
Tams, Anderson & Tams, Longton. About 1820–1830.
'Four Courts, Dublin', from the 'Tams Foliage Border' series (see Cat. Ref. Case 26/9).
Loaned by John and Sally Storton.

Case 17. MINIATURES

There is still some uncertainty as to whether the many miniature ceramic pieces which were produced in the 18th and 19th centuries were intended as toys, or ornaments for dolls houses or one of several other suggested possibilities. Probably all of these explanations are partially correct. Today they have left us with a fascinating field of specialist collecting, about which several books have been written.

1. **Miniature Mug or Coffee Can** 7.7 cms.
Maker Unknown. About 1820–1830.
An unidentified pattern showing a boy and girl dancing while another boy plays a violin.

2. **Miniature Tea Bowl and Saucer** 12.7 × 5.1 cms.
Mark: D10.
Dawson & Co., Sunderland. About 1825–1835.
A stylised floral design, not unlike some of the patterns produced by Continental potteries.

3. **Miniature Tea Bowl and Saucer.**
Bowl 6.9 × 4.4 cms. Saucer 11.5 cms.
Attributed to *Leeds Pottery* on the basis of an example of the same design with an inscription which may relate to an employee of the pottery. About 1815–1820.
A fisherman in a small boat, in front of a castellated mansion.
Pattern recorded as 'Castellated Manor House'.

4. **Miniature Cup and Saucer** London-shape
11.4 × 5.1 cms.
Mark: S7.
Spode, Stoke. About 1820–1830.
'Geranium', a design first produced in 1818 and the pattern is still produced today.

5. **Miniature Cup and Saucer** Bute-shape
Cup 6.2 cms diameter. Saucer 10.1 cms.
Attributed to either the *Cambrian* or the *Glamorgan Pottery, Swansea*. About 1820–1830.
'The Carter'. The two potteries often duplicated each other's patterns.

6. **Miniature Cup and Saucer** Porringer shape
Cup 6.4 × 4 cms. Saucer 9.5 cms.
Dixon, Austin & Co., Sunderland. About 1820–1825.
'Milkmaid with Pail on Head', so-called to distinguish it from several other 'Milkmaid' patterns (see Cat. Ref. Case 18/2).

7. **Miniature Cup and Saucer.** Cup 4.7 cms. Saucer 9.8 cms.
Maker Unknown. About 1815–1825.
An unidentified rural scene with a thatched cottage beside a river.

8. **Miniature Cup and Saucer.** Cup 6.8 cms. Saucer 10.7 cms.
Mark: R9A.
W. Ridgway & Co., Shelton. About 1835–1845.
'Beehive' pattern.

9. **Miniature Cup and Saucer.** Cup 7.2 cms. Saucer 11.3 cms.
Mark: G1. The 'G' could indicate one of several different makers.
Maker Unknown. About 1840–1850.
'Cottage', a romantic landscape featuring a Swiss chalet.

10. **Miniature Cup and Saucer.** Cup 7.3 cms.
Saucer 11.3 cms.
Mark: G8.
J & R Godwin, Cobridge. About 1835–1845.
'Goat', a girl grooming a goat.

11. **Miniature Cup and Saucer.** Cup 7 cms. Saucer 8.4 cms.
Mark: G6.
Benjamin Godwin, Cobridge. About 1835–1840.
'Peacock', a pair of peacocks in a geometric border.

12. **Miniature Cup and Saucer.** Cup 6.8 cms.
Saucer 10.3 cms.
Maker Unknown. About 1830–1845.
Cup: Scenes of children playing, one with a dog and two with a bird cage. Saucer: A boy riding a large dog.
Both pieces are printed in pale blue and have a narrow border of stylised flowers.

13. **Miniature Cup and Saucer.**
Cup 7.6 cms. Saucer 11.2 cms.

Mark: C4.
Edward Challinor, Tunstall. About 1845–1850.
'Ardennes', a romantic pattern with a large monument in the foreground.

14. **Miniature Cup and Saucer**.
Cup 7.2 cms. Saucer 11.5 cms.
Mark S22.
South Wales Pottery, Llanelly. About 1840–1850.
A 'Fern' pattern, printed all over.

15. Part of a **Miniature Tea Service** (see plate 24)
comprising Cup 6 cms and Saucer 10 cms,
Jug 7 cms and Sucrier 6.5 cms.
Probably *Spode, Stoke.* About 1815–1830.
'Daisy and Bead' pattern (see Cat. Ref. Case 17/34).

16. Part of a **Miniature Tea Service** (see plate 24) comprising
Tea Pot 8.9 cms. Covered Sucrier 8.5 cms, Jug 7 cms and Tea
Bowl 5.5 cms.
Attributed to *Spode* (on the basis of a workman's mark).
About 1800–1810.
'Gloucester' pattern.

17. **Miniature Tea Pot and Cream Jug** (see plate 24)**.**
Pot 13.3 × 11.4 cms. Jug 7.0 × 3.8 cms.
Davenport, Longport. About 1815–1825.
Probably a cut-down version of a pattern in the 'Rustic Scenes' series.

18. **Miniature Tea Pot**, prow-shape 11.4 cms.
Mark: R13.
J. Rogers & Son. About 1820–1830.
A version of the 'Broseley' or 'Two Temples' pattern.

19. **Miniature Jug** (see plate 24) 3.5 × 6.3 cms.
Maker Unknown. About 1800–1810.
A version of the 'Curling Palm' pattern, known to have been
produced by Job Ridgway. The barrel shape and the 'Sparrow
beak' lip both point to an early date.

20. **Miniature Jug** 8.0 × 6.0 × 6.5 cms.
Mark: M14.
Minton, Stoke. About 1825–1835.
'Dresden Flowers', a pattern of floral sprays and a scroll border
found on miniature services.

21. **Miniature Cream Jug** 8.6 × 4.2 × 7.0 cms.
Mark: a small blue printed mock-Chinese seal mark.
Maker Unknown. About 1820–1830.
'Broseley' or 'Two Temples' pattern.

22. **Miniature Jug** 9.2 × 5.8 × 9.0 cms.
Mark: Impressed 'D'.
Maker Unknown, possibly *Wood & Brownfield, Cobridge.*
About 1840–1845.
A girl feeding two rabbits beside a wooden fence.

23. **Miniature Jug** 7.0 cms high.
Maker Unknown. About 1825–1830.
White horse (with rider) drinking at a waterfall. Riderless black
horse behind.
Transfer appears to have been cut lengthways and applied one
half inside the jug rim and the other outside.

24. **Miniature Tureen** (see plate 24) 6.7 × 4.5 × 5.7 cms.
Maker Unknown. About 1805–1810.
'Chinoiserie Bridgeless', a design used by Davenport (Longport),
Andrew Stevenson and several other manufacturers.

25. **Miniature Tureen** and cover (see plate 24)
9.5 × 6.0 × 8.2 cms.
J. Rogers & Son, Longport. About 1815–1825.
'Monopteros' (see Cat. Ref. Case 12/13 and Techniques/1).

26. **Miniature Soup Ladle** 10.8 × 4.5 cms.
Minton, Stoke. About 1820–1830.
An unidentified partial view from the 'Minton Miniatures' series
(see Cat. Ref. Case 17/28).

27. **Miniature Platter** 10.6 × 8.0 cms.
J. Rogers & Son, Longport.
About 1820–1830.
'Monopteros' pattern (see Cat. Ref. Case 12/13 and 17/25).

28. **Miniature Platter** (see plate 24) 13.4 × 10.2 cms.
Minton, Stoke. About 1820–1830.
'Tewkesbury Church', from the 'Minton Miniatures' series of
about fourteen different views of churches and castles. This view
is taken from Storer and Greig's *The Antiquarian and Topographical
Cabinet* (1807–1811).

29. **Miniature Platter** (see plate 24) 11.4 × 8.9 cms.
Possibly *Rainforth & Co., Leeds.* About 1800–1810.
'Parasol and Birds', a chinoiserie pattern featuring two Chinese
ladies apparently feeding some crane-like birds. A jug marked
'Rainforth & Co.' and bearing this pattern is known, but the
border is not exactly the same, perhaps because of the difference
in size of the piece.

30. **Miniature Platter** 13.9 × 11.4 cms.
Maker Unknown. About 1820–1840.
A typical English rural scene.
Loaned by The Strong Collection.

31. **Miniature Pie Dish** 9.8 × 7.6 cms.
C. Heathcote & Co., Lane End. About 1820.
'Cattle and River', featuring an unidentified stately home.

32. **Miniature Sauce Boat** (see plate 24)
8.8 × 3.2 cms.
Probably *J. Rogers & Son, Dale Hall, Longport.* About 1820–1825.
'Net, Trellis and Flowers' pattern.

33. Pair of **Miniature Sauce Boats** (see plate 24)
6.6 × 2.9 × 3.8 cms.
Maker Unknown. About 1810–1820.
A typical chinoiserie pattern with European-style buildings.

34. **Miniature Plate** 7.6 cms.
Mark: S6 and S7.
Spode. About 1815–1830.
'Daisy and Bead' pattern (see Cat. Ref. Case 17/15).

35. **Child's Plate** 10.7 cms.
Mark: S6 and S7.
Spode. About 1820–1830.
'French Birds' pattern.

36. **Miniature Plate** 10.1 cms.
Maker Unknown. About 1815–1830.
'Batalha, Portugal'. Part of a larger design which includes
monastery buildings. This pattern depicts a British infantryman
in conversation with a girl who has beside her a baby in a
basket. Batalha is to the north of Lisbon, between Coimbra and
Santarem, an area in which some of the battles of the
Peninsular War were fought. The invasion of Portugal was over
by 1811.

37. Miniature Plate 11.4 cms.
Possibly *Don Pottery, Yorkshire*. About 1820–1830.
'Turkeys Two by Two', pattern known on other unmarked pieces.

38. Miniature Plate with moulded floral border 12.0 cms.
Maker Unknown. About 1825–1845.
The bridge from a 'Standard Willow' pattern.

39. Child's Plate with moulded rim 12.0 cms.
Mark: MEIR impressed.
J. Meir, Tunstall. About 1820–1830.
A woman with a basket and a dog, seated beside a bridge over
a stream.

40. Miniature Plate 10.8 cms.
Mark: A2.
William Adams & Sons, Tunstall. About 1800–1815.
Basket and vase of flowers on a cellular ground.

41. Miniature Plate 12.4 cms.
Probably *Joseph Clementson, Hanley*. About 1847.
'Wild Goose Shooting' . This central pattern surrounded by
an inscription – 'Francis Clementson, Importer of China, Glass
and Earthenware, Saint John, NB'. Francis was the son of Joseph,
a Hanley potter, who set up his retailing business in St John,
New Brunswick, in about 1847, so this plate could have been a
trade card or hand-out to customers.
Loaned by Flora Rabinovitch.

Case 18 PEOPLE ON POTS

Transfer printed earthenware, with its history of more than
two hundred years, following or sometimes setting fashions,
serves as a social and historical guide to British life over that
period. Not only have we literary, historical, geographic and
topographical series, but we can also follow the changing ways
of life and the succeeding fashions by looking closely at the
people depicted on pots.

1. Slop Basin 15.8 × 7.9 cms.
Maker Unknown. About 1825–1835.
A rustic scene of a man carrying a spade being greeted by two
children and a woman at the door of a cottage.

2. Tea Bowl and Saucer 12.8 × 4.9 cms.
Maker Unknown. About 1800–1810.
'Milkmaid', showing two girls carrying pails on their heads,
within an unusual geometric border. The vignette inside the
bowl shows an animal stealing milk from a pail.
Footnote: The milkmaids with their pails may have been inspired
by a Hogarth print entitled 'The Enraged Musician', and also
appear on a Worcester tea pot of around 1765 (see *Hogarth's
China* by Lars Tharp, published by Merrell Holberton, 1997).

3. Coffee Pot with domed lid 23 cms.
Maker Unknown. About 1800–1810.
A pastoral scene with lovers seated beside a river, with what
appears to be a wharf opposite. The reverse shows two cows,
resting.

4. Coffee Pot with domed lid (see front cover) 30.4 cms.
Maker Unknown – both Ridgway and Davenport have been
suggested as the maker of this piece. About 1815–1825.
'Cottage Children' pattern (see Cat. Ref. Case 18/6).
Loaned by Terry Sheppard.

5. Slop Basin 16.3 × 8.5 cms.
Maker Unknown. About 1825–1835.

A rustic pattern featuring a boy with a bird cage and a woman
with a hay rake.

6. Tea Bowl and Saucer 13.3 × 5.1 cms.
Maker Unknown. About 1815–1825.
'Cottage Children', an uncommon pattern known also on a
coffee pot (see Cat. Ref. Case 18/4). Until ten years ago pigs
had not been recorded on blue printed earthenwares, but since
then several examples have come to light.

7. Jug 8.0 × 8.0 × 10.0 cms.
Maker Unknown. About 1820–1830.
Another unrecorded rustic scene, to be known as 'Distaff Lady'.

8. Bowl 15.7 cms
Maker Unknown. About 1795–1805.
On one side a partly-clothed couple (possibly a God and
Goddess) sit on rocks beneath a tree, while on the other a boy
attempts to spear a flying bird. Simple line engraving and
probably a fairly early date. The print is in a slate-blue shade.

9. Tea Bowl 12.5 × 9.5 cms.
Maker Unknown. About 1815–1825.
Part of a larger design known as 'Resting Soldier', in which the
soldier is seated below a large ruined church.

10. Jug 20 × 15.5 × 19 cms.
Maker Unknown. About 1820–1830.
'Gleaners III', one of three unrelated designs showing country
people gleaning ears of corn from the fields after the harvest
(see Cat. Ref. Case Kitchen/15 and 27/15).

11. Lobed Dessert Dish 22.2 × 20.6 cms.
J & W Ridgway, Shelton. About 1815–1820.
'Eastern Port', a view of 'Chios', a sea port on an island off the
coast of Asiatic Turkey. Ships' masts appear above the buildings
and soldiers and others walk or ride by a fence in the
foreground. The floral border, rather unusually, contains four
crowns. The source print is a 'View of SCIO anciently called
CHIOS, one of the most celebrated Cities in the Archipelago'
comes from Thomas Bankes' *New System of Geography* (printed
about 1790. Short title).

12. Saucer 13 cms.
Maker Unknown. About 1800–1810.
Three people in the dress of about 1800 walking in a townscape
including a domed building, steps, statues and a large urn.

13. Tea Canister with silver cover 7.6 × 11.4 cms.
Maker Unknown. About 1805–1810.
A pastoral scene showing a flock of sheep and goats and a
shepherdess holding a bunch of grapes out to a dandified gentleman in a wig. The silver cover is probably a later replacement.

14. Jug 22 × 13.5 × 21 cms.
Maker Unknown. About 1820–1830.
A previously unrecorded rustic scene, now to be called 'Family
at the Door'.

15. Sauce Boat 17.5 cms long.
Maker Unknown. About 1830–1845.
A vignette of two women in classical dress tending what appears
to be a sacred flame. Elaborate scroll and flower patterning as
a border.

16. Saucer 13.2 cms.
J & W Ridgway, Shelton. About 1815–1825.
'Girl with Lamb', a pattern which may be part of a series
including a 'Hare and Leverets' design (see Cat. Ref. Case 21/14).

17. Tea Bowl and Saucer.
Bowl 8 × 5.2 cms. Saucer 12.7 cms. diameter.
Mark: S1.
Shorthose & Co., Hanley. About 1820.
A hitherto unpublished design showing two people by a camp fire. Now to be called 'The Itinerants', but also known as 'Gipsy Fire' pattern.

18. Segment of a Supper Set and lid 33 × 17.6 cms.
J & W Ridgway, Shelton. About 1815–1825.
'Eastern Port' pattern (see Cat. Ref. Case 18/11)
Loaned by the City Museum and Art Gallery, Stoke-on-Trent.

19. Tea Bowl and Saucer.
Bowl 8 × 5.2 cms. Saucer 12.7 cms diameter.
Mark: S1.
Shorthose & Co., Hanley. About 1820.
'The Itinerants' pattern (see Cat. Ref. Case 18/17).

Case 19. BOTANICAL

Botany was among the Natural Sciences which became popular at the turn of the 18th century and furnished the pottery manufacturers with a wealth of subject matter. Wedgwood was the only factory to produce a major series in this genre, possibly this was connected with the fact that John Wedgwood was involved in the formation of the Horticultural Society in 1804.

1. Plate 24.8 cms.
Marks: W4 and two asterisks **.
Wedgwood, Etruria. About 1835.
Decorated with a pattern of 'Roses and Butterflies'.
Loaned by The Trustees of the Wedgwood Museum.

2. Coffee Pot with domed lid 25.3 cms.
Maker Unknown. About 1820–1830.
Wide band of large flowers including tulips, on a stippled background.

3. Plate 24.3 cms.
Maker Unknown. About 1820–1825.
Sheet pattern of fruit, leaves and stylised flowers, named the 'Medlar' pattern.

4. Moulded Jug (see figure 10) 14.8 cms high.
Maker Unknown. About 1790–1795.
Roses and other flowers in large sprays, printed alternately in blue and black.

5. Arcaded Plate 18.1 cms.
Maker Unknown. About 1820–1825.
Basket of fruit and flowers within a cellular border with floral reserves. Many makers used variations on this theme.
Loaned by Mervyn Gibbs.

6. Plate 24.8 cms.
Mark: W3.
Wedgwood, Etruria. About 1810–1830.
A striking flower with spiky leaves from the 'Botanical' series.

7. Custard Cup and cover 6.7 × 8.5 cms.
Maker Unknown. About 1795–1805.
Sprays of flowers and leaves within a geometric and floral border.
Footnote: Covered pots of this form were used in the 18th century in France at the table for serving meat juices accompanying the meat course. In contemporary England similar pots were called 'custard cups' and were used in the dessert service. The custard was very different to the modern concept.

A contemporary recipe suggests:
'To make fresh cruddes and creame. Take five whites of egges and two yolkes and beate them together then take a pinte of sweet creame and mingle it with them and streane them together and put them into a Skellet and put to it a branch of Rosemary and nutmege brused and a grane of muske put these in a lawne cloath and sett it upon the ffyre and stirre them well for burning when it begines to come put in the ieuse of an Orringe or Lemman and a little Rosewater and when it is well boyled take it of and let the whaye runne from it in a faire cloath then season it with sugar and boyle the Creame which you serve it up in with the yolkes of egges and Rosewater'.
(From Arcana Fairfaxiana Manuscript, a facsimile reprint of the original handwriting, Newcastle. 1890).

8. Soup Ladle 25.5 cms.
Wedgwood, Etruria. About 1815–1820.
Another design from the 'Botanical' series.
Loaned by The Trustees of the Wedgwood Museum.

9. Cup and Saucer. Cup 8.1 × 5.7 cms. Saucer 9.4 cms.
Mark: On the cup only; W1.
Wedgwood, Etruria. About 1815–1820.
A large Tiger Lily duplicated on cup and saucer with a different smaller flower on each. 'Botanical' series.

10. Coffee Can and Saucer (see figure 18). Can 6 cms. Saucer 13.2 cms.
Mark: On the saucer only; R2.
Job Ridgway, Shelton. About 1802–1808.
Sprays of roses on a cracked ice (or marbled) background.

11. Plate 25.1 cms.
Mark: H12.
Herculaneum Pottery, Liverpool. About 1815–1825.
'Flowers and Leaves'. A similar pattern was produced by Henshall & Co., Longport.

12. Sucrier with moulded ring handles 12 × 11.7 cms.
Wedgwood, Etruria. About 1820–1830.
A sheet pattern of stylised Chrysanthemums and small tendrils and leaves.
Loaned by The Trustees of the Wedgwood Museum.

13. Two-handled Cup (Loving Cup) 7.8 cms diameter.
Maker Unknown. About 1820–1830.
Band of flowers and large leaves, probably a border pattern.

14. Egg Cup Tulip-shape (see plate 4) 6.3 cms high.
Maker Unknown. About 1815–1830.
Tulip heads on a tulip-shaped item.

15. Dessert Dish with a moulded Flower Handle (see plate 4) 20.2 cms.
Mark: as X9.
Usually attributed to *Edward and George Phillips, Longport*, however, the same pattern border was produced by *William Ridgway, Shelton* and marked pieces of identical shape are known from the Ridgway factory. About 1830.
Single tulip with leaves, within a floral border (see Cat. Ref. Case 19/21).

16. Plate 24.8 cms.
Mark: W2 with two asterisks **.
Wedgwood, Etruria. About 1841.
'Fruit Basket' pattern.
Loaned by The Trustees of the Wedgwood Museum.

17. **Plate** 21.2 cms.
Mark: S18.
Bevington & Co., Cambrian Pottery, Swansea. About 1820.
All-over pattern of grapes on the vine.

18. **Plate** 25.2 cms.
Marks: W4 and 'HH' impressed.
Wedgwood, Etruria. About 1830.
'Garland' pattern.
Loaned by The Trustees of the Wedgwood Museum.

19. **Plate** 25 cms.
Mark: W4.
Wedgwood, Etruria. About 1825–1835.
A floral spray within an example of the 'Blue Rose Border'
pattern (see Cat. Ref. Case 24/28).
Loaned by The Trustees of the Wedgwood Museum.

20. **Patty Pan** (everted Lip) 5.5 × 4.3 cms.
Maker Unknown. About 1825–1840.
Oak leaf and acorn sheet pattern.

21. **Cup and Saucer** London-shape.
Cup 8.9 cms diameter. Saucer 14 cms.
Mark: as X9.
Attributed to *Edward and George Phillips, Longport.* About
1822–1834.
Central spray of flowers within a 'Union Spray Border' (Rose,
Thistle and Shamrock).
Footnote: The description 'Opaque China' was used by several
makers to indicate superior (China-like) quality.

Case 20 QUADRUPEDS

See essay on 'Sources of Design – Animal Patterns' by J.C. Holdaway
and Case 21 Zoological.

1. **Miniature Plate** 10 cms.
John Hall (& Sons), Burslem. About 1822–1832.
Centre: 'Hyena', from the 'Quadrupeds' series (see Cat. Ref. Case
20/6).
The border is as the series' border, but without vignettes. The
animal print is taken from Bewick (see Cat. Ref. Case 20/3).

2. **Tureen Stand** with handles 20 × 17 cms.
John Hall (& Sons), Burslem. About 1822–1832.
Centre: 'Fox', from a Church print (see Cat. Ref. Case 20/6).
The border is totally different and has no vignettes. It is possible,
but unlikely that a different border would have been introduced
for a specific shape or shapes. Another, larger stand, with the
same border and bearing the 'Quadrupeds' cartouche mark is
illustrated as Cat. Ref. Case 20/8.

3. **Two Small Plates** (see figure 22) a) 15 cms b) 13 cms.
Mark: H3.
John Hall (& Sons), Burslem. About 1822–1832.
a) Centre printed with 'The Dalmation, or Coach Dog'.
Vignettes: other animals.
b) Centre printed with 'The English Setter'. Vignettes: other
animals.
From the 'Quadrupeds' series (see Cat. Ref. Case 20/6).
These animals are taken from Thomas Bewick's *A General History
of Quadrupeds* (1790).

4. **Pierced Tureen or Basket Stand** 32 × 23 cms.
Mark: H3
John Hall (& Sons), Burslem.
About 1822–1832.

Centre: 'Pointer' (Hunter with Dog). Vignettes: Cow, Moose and
other animals.
From the 'Quadrupeds' series (see Cat. Ref. Case 20/6).

5. **Soup tureen stand** or **Platter** (see figure 19) 43 × 36 cms.
Mark: H3.
John Hall (& Sons), Burslem.
About 1822–1832.
Centre : 'Rhinoceros'. Vignettes: Horse, Nylghau and two others.
From the 'Quadrupeds' series (see Cat. Ref. Case 20/6).

6. **Plate** (see figure 20) 22 cms.
Mark: H3.
John Hall (& Sons), Burslem. About 1822–1832.
Centre: 'Otter'. Vignettes: Mole and Hedgehog, Rabbits, Seal,
Genet and Civet Cat.
From the 'Quadrupeds' series of more than thirty different
animal prints taken from Thomas Bewick's *A General History of
Quadrupeds* (1790) and J. Church's *Cabinet of Quadrupeds* (1805).

7. **Plate** (see figure 21) 19 cms.
Mark: H3.
John Hall (& Sons), Burslem. About 1822–1832.
Centre: 'Deer'. Vignettes: Wolf, Suricate or Four-toed weasel,
Raccoon, Ground Squirrel. From the 'Quadrupeds' series
(see Cat. Ref. Case 20/6).

8. **Tureen Stand** with handles 36 × 26 cms.
Mark: H3.
John Hall (& Sons), Burslem. About 1822–1832.
Centre: 'Hare', from a Church print.
From the 'Quadrupeds' series (see Cat. Ref. Case 20/6). Border
as Cat. Ref. Case 20/2.

9. **Platter** 52 × 42 cms.
Mark: M6.
Attributed to *Job Meigh & Son, Hanley.* About 1830–1834.
'Elephant' from the 'Zoological Sketches' series of at least ten
animal designs. This comes from a Church print
(see Cat. Ref. Case 20/6).

Case 21. ZOOLOGICAL

Various examples of animals used as decoration on transfer
printed earthenware. See also Case 20 Quadrupeds.

1. **Plate** 27 cms.
Mark: X4.
This series has been tentatively attributed to *Thomas Godwin,
Burslem* on the basis of tureen and platter shapes which match
marked pieces with different patterns, but another possibility is
George Phillips, Longport. About 1834–1840.
'Esquimaux Building a Snow Hut', from the 'Arctic Scenery' series
of at least nine different views taken from various sources. This is
from a print of this title in Sir Edward William Parry's *Journal of a
Second Voyage for the Discovery of a North-West Passage* (1824).
The border vignettes come mainly from Thomas Bewick's
General History of Quadrupeds (1790) or William Jardine's *Natural
History* (1833–1843).

2. **Platter** 38 × 28 cms.
Marks: M6 and an impressed 'Stone China' seal mark.
Attributed to *Job Meigh & Son, Hanley.* About 1830–1834.
'Hunting Leopard' from the 'Zoological Sketches' series
(see Cat. Ref. Case 20/9). This pattern is taken from Church (see
Cat. Ref. Case 20/6).

3. **Plate** 25.4 cms.
Toft & May, Hanley. About 1825–1829.
'Zebra' pattern, a close copy of the design first produced by the Rogers' partnership at Longport.

4. **Plate** 27 cms.
Mark: R16.
Robinson, Wood & Brownfield, Cobridge. About 1836–1841.
'Tiger Cages', pattern from the 'Zoological' series of views in the Zoological Gardens, London, which were first opened to the public in 1829.

5. **Lobed Dish** 24.7 × 17.7 cms.
William Adams, Stoke. About 1810–1819.
'Lions', taken from a print in *The Cyclopaedia of Arts, Sciences and Literature* (1807). The original was titled 'Felix Leo, Lion, Lioness and Young'.

6. **Tureen** and cover (see figure 31) 34 × 21 × 22 cms.
Maker Unknown. About 1795–1810.
'Sucatorio' pattern (see Cat. Ref. Case 21/9).

7. **Tea Pot** London-shape (no cover) 26 × 14 × 14 cms.
Marks: R13 and R15.
John Rogers & Son, Longport. About 1820–1825.
The 'Church Zebra' pattern, taken from J. Church's *A Cabinet of Quadrupeds* (1805).

8. **Vegetable Dish** and cover 23 cms square × 16 cms.
Mark: W20.
Enoch Wood & Sons, Burslem. About 1820–1830.
Inside dish: 'A Fox Carrying off a Duck'.
On cover: 'A Bear, a Wolf and a Fox'.
From the 'Sporting' series of at least sixteen patterns, some taken from Thomas Bewick prints. The subjects are all either hunting or hunted animals (see Cat. Ref. Case 30/9).

9. **Plate** 19 cms.
Maker Unknown. About 1795–1810.
Originally recorded as 'Spotted, Horned Animal', this design is now believed to represent the 'Sucatorio', an animal apparently to be found in the East Indies. Mention of this beast can be found between 1642 and 1820, but thereafter it disappears without trace (see J.C. Holdaway, 1987). The pattern is basically similar to the 'Buffalo' (see Cat. Ref. Case 8).

10. **Saucer** 12.4 cms.
Maker Unknown. About 1795–1805.
A small elephant with spots, with a chinaman in a typical chinoiserie landscape, all within a geometric border. The pattern is unrecorded, but a version is known, attributed to the Ferrybridge Pottery, where the elephant carries a howdah, but the overall layout is again very similar to that of the 'Buffalo' pattern (see Cat. Ref. Case 8).

11. **Cake or Cheese Stand** (see plate 16) 32.9 × 8.2 cms.
Maker Unknown. About 1810–1820.
'Giraffe and Obelisk' pattern, unrecorded until recently.
Loaned by Mervyn Gibbs.

12. **Frog Mug** (see figure 27) 13 × 9 cms.
Maker Unknown. About 1825.
Various animals, inside and outside, taken mainly from prints by Thomas Bewick.

13. **Plate** 27 cms.
Enoch Wood & Sons, Burslem. About 1820–1830.
'Stags', from the 'Sporting' series (see Cat. Ref. Case 21/8).
This pattern is taken from Luke Clennel's *Recreations in Natural History*.

14. **Saucer** 13.8 cms.
Mark: R2.
Probably *J & W Ridgway, Bell Works, Shelton.* About 1815–1830.
'Hare and Leverets'. Another very similar pattern but with a different border is known but remains unattributed (see Cat. Ref. Case 18/16).

15. **Jug** 16 cms.
Maker Unknown. About 1800–1810.
A standard chinoiserie landscape and border with the addition of three animals (Monkey, Lion and Zebra) around the handle terminals. Another monkey (Cercopithecus Talapoin) is printed on the base, where a maker's mark or pattern name might normally be found.

Case 22. SPODE

The Spode factory was one of the first in the blue and white field and today is one of the few pottery firms surviving from the 18th century, which still makes blue printed earthenware and, indeed, tends to make it a speciality, from time to time re-issuing patterns from 150 years ago.

1. **Coffee Pot** 25.3 cms high.
Attributed to *Spode, Stoke.* About 1800–1805.
'Tall Door', a somewhat cluttered chinoiserie pattern, also produced by at least one other (unidentified) maker.

2. **Coffee Pot** with domed lid 27 cms high.
Attributed to *Spode, Stoke.* About 1795–1810.
This pattern has several different names, the most commonly used being 'Trench Mortar' from what, at first, look like mortar barrels to the right of the house. Other titles are 'Malayan Village' (from a resemblance to a print in the British library) and 'Pearl River House', probably from an original Chinese version. Several manufacturers are known to have produced this pattern on both earthenware and porcelain.

3. **Coffee Pot** Vase-shape 26.1 cms.
Mark: S7.
Spode, Stoke. About 1816–1825.
'Italian Church', a view of the church opposite the Duke of Wellington's headquarters at Waterloo. The scene appears to have been taken, either directly or via a print, from a painting at Stratfield Saye, near Reading, Berkshire, the home of The Duke of Wellington.

4. **Trio of Plate, Saucer and Cup** Bute-shape.
Cup 8.4 × 6 cms. Saucer 14 cms. Plate 16.7 cms.
Mark: S7 (Cup and Saucer), S6 (Plate).
Spode, Stoke. About 1816–1820.
'Woodman' pattern (see Cat. Ref. Case 22/10).
Loaned by Mr. and Mrs. M. Houlden.

5. **Plate** 16.4 cms.
Mark: S6.
Spode, Stoke. About 1815–1820.
'Blossom', a boy and girl below an arched bridge. The design is very rare, and it was not until the late 1980's that it came to light.

6. **Pail Custard Cup** (missing pierced lid) 6.4 × 6.5 cms.
Mark: S5.
Spode, Stoke. About 1815–1820.
Part of the border from the 'Caramanian' series (see Cat. Ref. Case 15/13).
Footnote: The shape is recorded as Number 260 in the Spode records.

7. Egg Hoop 4.0 cms high.
Spode, Stoke. About 1815–1825.
Part of the border from the 'Caramanian' series (see Cat. Ref. Case 15/13).
The hoop or ring form of egg cup pre-dates the footed cup shape. The ring could usually be used either way up and sometimes offered different sizes, top and bottom.

8. Argyll, lid missing 13.5 cms high.
Mark: S7.
Spode, Stoke. About 1815–1825.
'Italian' pattern (see Cat. Ref. Case 37/4 for reference to the pattern and Cat. Ref. Case 1/19 for reference to the shape).

9. Pair of covered Custard Cups 9.5 cms high.
Mark: C17 (one cup only).
Spode, Stoke. About 1850–1870.
The 'India' pattern was introduced about 1816.
Loaned by City Museum and Art Gallery, Stoke-on-Trent.

10. Coffee Pot Vase-shape 26.1 cms high.
Mark: S7.
Spode, Stoke. About 1816–1825.
'Woodman' pattern was introduced about 1816 and copied in reverse by Thomas Fell of Newcastle-upon-Tyne.

11. Cup and Saucer Bute-shape.
Cup 9.2 cms diameter, Saucer 14.8 cms.
Spode, Stoke. About 1815–1820.
'Love Chase' pattern (see Cat. Ref. Case 22/12).

12. Tea Bowl 8.2 × 5.7 cms.
Spode, Stoke. About 1815–1825.
The 'Love Chase' pattern was still in use as late as 1910. It tells the story of Milanion, a Greek, who won the hand of Atalanta, daughter of Zeus, by defeating her in a foot race by causing her to stop to pick up golden apples which he had dropped.

13. Toast Rack Prow-ended 25.3 × 10.1 × 8.9 cms.
Mark: S6 and S7.
Spode, Stoke. About 1815–1830.
The central design is from the 'Union Wreath I' pattern, but the border is from 'Girl at the Well', otherwise known, from marked pieces, as 'The Font'. It is not uncommon to find some interchange of borders, especially when, as in this case, the correct border would have been too wide for the shape.
Loaned by Margaret and Peter Crumpton.

14. Vegetable Dish and cover 22.8 cms square × 12.7 cms.
Spode, Stoke. About 1815–1825.
'Gothic Castle', a Transitional pattern, with both Oriental and European features, introduced about 1812.

15. Bowl 34.2 × 10.1 cms.
Mark: C13 and C15.
Copeland and Garrett, Stoke. About 1833–1847.
'Cork Convent', a hitherto unrecorded pattern in the 'Byron Views' series (see Cat. Ref. Case 33/12).

16. Toast Rack 16.8 × 9.5 × 7.9 cms.
Mark: S7.
Spode, Stoke. About 1820–1835.
The border of a standard 'Broseley' design, which is derived from the 'Two Temples' and 'Standard Willow' patterns, and was used frequently on bone china.

17 and 17A. Pair of Pickle Dishes Leaf-shape
17) 11.4 cms. 17A) 12.7 cms.
Mark on 17: S6 and S7.

Mark on 17A: S6.
Spode, Stoke. About 1815–1825.
The pattern on 17 is part of the 'Common Wolf Trap' pattern from the 'Indian Sporting' series (see Cat. Ref. Case 14/6).
The design on 17A is a made-up print using parts from several views in the 'Caramanian' series (see Cat. Ref. Case. 15/13).

Case 23. WILLOW AND OTHER POPULAR PATTERNS

Of all the patterns made by many different manufacturers (as opposed to patterns which were copied only by a few, such as Spode's 'Italian'), 'Willow' is far and away the most prolific, having evolved from Chinese designs from 1780 onwards. 'Wild Rose' had a vogue between 1820 and 1850, when it was ousted by 'Asiatic Pheasants', a more indeterminate and pale blue pattern.

1. Oblong Vegetable Dish and cover 29.5 × 23.9 cms.
Mark: P3 printed and 'WEDGWOOD & CO.' impressed.
Wedgwood & Co., Tunstall. About 1860.
'Asiatic Pheasants', probably second only to 'Willow' as a long-running and popular pattern. It was first introduced, probably towards the end of the first half of the 19th century, by Podmore, Walker & Co., Tunstall, who were joined as a partner by Enoch Wedgwood, changed their name to 'Wedgwood & Co.' and used that as a mark. There was no connection between this firm and Wedgwood of Etruria. The printed pattern mark re-iterates the factory's claim to have initiated this pattern.
Loaned by the City Museum and Art Gallery, Stoke-on-Trent.

2. Gravy Boat and 2A. **Sauce Tureen**, Stand and Ladle.
2) 17.3 × 9.3 cms. 2A) 14 × 14 cms.
Maker Unknown. About 1850–1870.
'Asiatic Pheasants' (see Cat. Ref. Case 23/1).
Loaned by City Museum and Art Gallery, Stoke-on-Trent.

3. Plate 22.7 cms.
Mark: N1.
Thomas Nicholson & Co., Castleford, Yorkshire. About 1860.
'Wild Rose' pattern (see Cat. Ref. Case 23/18).

4. Pickle Dish 14.6 × 12.3 cms.
Maker Unknown. About 1825–1830.
'Wild Rose' pattern (see Cat. Ref. Case 23/18).
Loaned by David and Linda Arman.

5. Arcaded Plate 18.5 cms.
Probably *Herculaneum Pottery, Liverpool.* About 1800–1810.
'Two-Man, Two-Arch Willow'.
Loaned by Mervyn Gibbs.

6. Oblong Octagonal Platter 27.4 × 20.2 cms.
Mark: T6.
John Turner, Lane End. About 1785.
An extremely early design, having many of the basic features of the later Willow pattern. This piece supports the claim that John Turner I was the first Staffordshire potter to produce blue transfer printed earthenwares.

7. Pudding Plate (Fruit Dish) 16.5 cms.
Mark: S11.
Andrew Stevenson, Cobridge. About 1800–1805.
'Stevenson's Willow', which shows many variations from the standard pattern.

8. Segment of a Supper Set 32.9 × 10.1 cms.
Mark: H8.

Attributed to *Joshua Heath, Hanley*. About 1795–1800.
A Willow-style pattern with three men on the bridge.
Loaned by Flora Rabinovitch.

9. A curious **Dual-purpose Object**, possibly the centre of a
Supper Set with, on one side, a divided Tray (for Pickles) in three
sections and, on the other, what may be a stand for a heated vessel
15.75 × 3.7 cms.
Maker Unknown. About 1810–1820.
A non-Willow pattern in which an Apple tree has been
substituted for the Willow at the right hand end of the bridge.

10. **Tea Canister** with domed cover 10.2 × 8.2 × 14.1 cms.
Maker Unknown. Probably mid-19th century.
'Standard Willow' pattern.

11. **Mug** 8.9 × 11.4 cms.
Maker Unknown. About 1792.
'Willow Nankin', sometimes known as 'Caughley Willow',
reputed to have been a design first engraved by Thomas Minton
at the Caughley Porcelain Factory.

12. **Cow Creamer and Cover** (see plate 30) 18 × 13.2 cms.
Maker Unknown. About 1840–1860.
Part of the 'Standard Willow' pattern printed along each flank of
the animal.
Footnote: The cow cream jug was originally made in silver both
in England and Europe. These were quickly emulated by the
ceramic industry. They were manufactured in a wide range of
bodies and decorative finishes. Those of a larger size are
sometimes called a 'cow milk-jug'.

13. **Money box** 12.3 cms high.
Maker Unknown. About 1825–1840
'Broseley', a pattern obviously derived from the standard
'Willow' but a mirror image and usually printed in a pale blue.
The design was used extensively by porcelain manufacturers
including the Coalport factory.

14. **Plate** (possibly a Cup Plate) 10.1 cms.
Mark: A1.
William Adams, Stoke. About 1820–1840.
'Standard Willow' pattern.
Loaned by Dr. and Mrs. David Furniss.

15. **Two-handled Cup** (Loving Cup) 7 cms high.
Possibly *Spode, Stoke*. About 1800–1810.
'Standard Willow' pattern.

16. **Bowl** Cushion-shape 24.3 × 23.7 × 11.3 cms.
Mark: S6.
Spode, Stoke. About 1800–1815.
'Standard Willow' on outside, elongated version, with a usual
scene plus an additional vignette, on the inside.
Loaned by Mervyn Gibbs.

17. **Toast Rack** 21 × 10.5 cms.
Mark: M15 impressed and printed.
Minton & Co., Stoke. About 1860–1870.
'Standard Willow' pattern.
Loaned by Margaret and Peter Crumpton.

18. **Sauce Tureen,** Cover and Stand 21.2 × 15.8 cms.
Maker Unknown. About 1825–1830.
'Wild Rose', identified as a view of 'Nuneham Courtenay, near
Oxford', originally the seat of Lord Harcourt. The scene appears
to have been based on an engraving by W. Cooke from a drawing
by S. Owen published in 1811 under the title 'Nuneham
Courtenay, Bridge and Cottage'. The garden, landscaped by
Capability Brown, was one of the most famous of his works.

19. **Toast Rack** 20.3 × 10.1 × 11.4 cms.
Mark: X29. The 'Semi-China' mark was used by several
manufacturers, including J. & R. Riley and Minton & Co.,
without any further indication of origin.
Maker Unknown. About 1825–1845.
A 'Broseley' variant of the 'Willow' pattern in which elements
of the design have been reversed including the figures on the
bridge who now face the buildings.
Loaned by Margaret and Peter Crumpton.

20. **Toast Rack** 21.6 × 11.4 × 8.9 cms.
Mark: 'BB New Stone' impressed ('BB' indicates 'Best Body',
a mark used in the mid-19th century).
Minton, Stoke. About 1850–1860.
'Broseley' pattern (see Cat. Ref. Case 22/16).
Loaned by Margaret and Peter Crumpton.

21. **Toast Rack** 25.3 × 15.2 × 12.7 cms.
Maker Unknown. About 1835–1860.
A partial 'Broseley' pattern.
Loaned by Margaret and Peter Crumpton.

Case 24. WEDGWOOD

One of the most significant additions to Wedgwood
production in the first half of the 19th century was the
introduction of under-glaze blue printing in 1805. It seems
probable that the idea may have come from Thomas Byerley
(1747–1810), although the primary responsibility for its success
was probably due to the work of John Wedgwood (1766–1844).
Most of the blue prints were applied to Pearl Ware or the
Printing body, a slightly different body, the recipe for which
survives dated 1817. Although the Printing body and Pearl body
are not identical in composition they are sufficiently similar to
be difficult to visually differentiate between them.

Wedgwood's attempts to satisfy the different requirements
of the various markets is shown in a letter from York Street dated
October 1817: 'There is no making an universal one [colour] –
in the north they like a delicate faint pattern with a [good] blue
– in the south they are much divided, some dealers can sell
nothing but strong dark blues, the plate well covered – others
like to see a little of the ware, when it is a good glaze'.

Much of the responsibility for the success of Wedgwood's
blue print fell to Abner Wedgwood (d.1835), his contribution
was significant and he made himself one of the foremost
practitioners of printing. Josiah Wedgwood II (1769–1843) was
justifiably proud of his wares writing in 1813, 'There are no blue
printed plates like mine in Staffordshire. . . . I do not enter into
competition as to the cheapness, but as to quality'.

1. **Root dish** 18.4 × 33 × 16.5 cms.
Mark: W4 and two stars impressed.
Wedgwood Etruria. About 1815.
'Botanical Flowers' pattern, commonly known as 'Botanical' series.
Footnote: The engraving of the copper plates for these designs is
generally attributed to John Robinson and Thomas Longmore.
An invoice from J. Robinson dated November 1809 for
'Botanical Flowers' survives in the Wedgwood Archives
(Manuscript number L1–132) (see Cat. Ref. Case 19/8 & 9).
Loaned by Trustees of the Wedgwood Museum.

2. **Footbath** 48.3 × 36.1 × 24.1 cms.
Mark: W2.
Wedgwood Etruria. About 1810–1815.
'Botanical Flowers' pattern, with eight different sprays on the
interior, six of which are duplicated on the exterior. The form is
recorded in the 1802 Shape Book as number 1332
(see Cat. Ref. Case 24/1 and 19/8 & 9).
Loaned by Mr and Mrs J. Leatherland.

3. **Plate** 25 cms diameter.
Mark: W3.
Wedgwood Etruria. About 1830–1835.
Printed with a pattern of roses and a butterfly. The factory name for this has not yet been identified.
Loaned by Trustees of the Wedgwood Museum.

4. **Leaf Pickle Dish** 12.2 × 10.4 cms.
Mark: W2 and '2' impressed.
Wedgwood Etruria. About 1815–1830.
A botanical spray, similar to those in the 'Botanical' series but with a leaf and flower border added.

5. **Tea cup and Saucer**. Cup 7.8 cms diameter. Saucer 12.7 cms diameter.
Mark: on the cup only W4.
Wedgwood Etruria. About 1805–1815.
Bute shape. 'Blue Basket' pattern which was introduced into production in December 1805.

6. **Pair of Plates** (see figures 12–15) 24.7 cms diameter.
Mark: W3 and two stars impressed.
Wedgwood Etruria. About 1811–1820.
'Water Lily' (sometimes called 'Lotus') pattern.
Footnote: The 'Water Lily' pattern was introduced in 1808 when it was printed in brown and it was recorded in the pattern books as number 495. The copper plates were engraved originally by Semei Bourne in 1806 and re-engraved in various versions by John Robinson and William Hales. It was not printed in blue until 1811. For a further discussion of the design sources see the Botanical Patterns essay and *The Dictionary Volume I* page 394.
Loaned by Mervyn Gibbs.

7. **Water Jug** 23 cms high.
Mark: W1 and 'PEARL' and the date code 'HNW' impressed.
Wedgwood Etruria. 1868.
'Water Lily' pattern remained one of the most popular blue transfer printed patterns (see Cat. Ref. Case 24/6).
Loaned by Trustees of the Wedgwood Museum.

8. **Plate** 24.7 cms diameter.
Mark: W4.
Wedgwood Etruria. About 1822–1830.
'Blue Claude' pattern.
Footnote: The 'Blue Claude' pattern was engraved by Thomas Sparkes. The design was adapted from several paintings by Claude Lorraine. A copy of Claude's *Liber Verilatis*, published in three volumes between 1777 and 1819 was in Josiah Wedgwood II's library at Maer Hall and was probably used to provide the source material for this pattern. Introduced into production in 1822.
Loaned by Mervyn Gibbs.

9. **Plate** (with deep well) 22 cms diameter.
Mark: W4 and four triangles arranged in a cross impressed.
Wedgwood Etruria. About 1822–1825.
'Blue Claude' pattern (see Cat. Ref. Case 24/8).
Footnote: Impressed letters and symbols found before about 1860 are generally taken as workmen's marks (see *Proceedings of the Wedgwood Society Number 2*, 1957 for an article by Tom Lyth, pages 104–105).
Loaned by Trustees of the Wedgwood Museum.

10. **Soup Tureen,** lid and ladle 34 × 20.7 × 26.8 cms.
Ladle 28 cms long.
Mark: W3.
Wedgwood Etruria. About 1825–1830.
'Blue Claude' pattern (see Cat. Ref. Case 24/8). The tureen is recorded as shape number 77 in the 1802 Shape Book.
Loaned by The City Museum and Art Gallery, Stoke-on-Trent.

11. **Platter** 15.5 × 20.7 cms.
Mark: W5.
Wedgwood Etruria. About 1825–1830.
'Blue Claude' pattern (see Cat. Ref. Case 24/8).
Footnote: Wedgwood's Stone China was first introduced about 1820. Although manufactured over many years it appears to have been made in relatively small quantities.
Loaned by Trustees of the Wedgwood Museum.

12. **Plate** (see figure 16) 25.4 cms diameter.
Mark: W1.
Wedgwood Etruria. About 1807–1810.
'Hibiscus' pattern. Introduced into production in 1807. The copper plates for 'Hibiscus' were engraved by William Hale and Thomas Sparks (see Cat. Ref. Case 24/14).
Loaned by Trustees of the Wedgwood Museum.

13. **Knife Support** 10.2 cms.
Mark: W1.
Wedgwood Etruria. About 1815–1825.
Decorated with elements of the 'Hibiscus' pattern (see Cat. Ref. Case 24/12). The shape is recorded as number 1205 in the 1802 Shape Book.

14. **Soup Tureen** (see plate 22), Lid and Stand overall height 10.5 cms, 12 cms diameter.
Mark: W4.
Wedgwood Etruria. About 1815–1825.
'Peony' pattern.
Footnote: the 'Peony' pattern was introduced in 1806. The original copper plates are attributed to the work of William Hales and Thomas Sparks. Thomas Sparks (1773–1848) was an engraver in Hanley who supplied most of the major ceramic factories with patterns.
Loaned by Trustees of the Wedgwood Museum.

15. **Pair of Egg rings** 4.7 cms diameter, 4.4 cms height.
and 15A. **Pair of plate lifters** 6.1 × 5.2 cms.
Mark: on the plate lifters W1.
Wedgwood Etruria. About 1815–1830.
'Peony' pattern (see Cat. Ref. Case 24/14). The plate lifters are recorded as 'Dish Lifters', Shape number 1207 in the 1802 Shape Book. The egg rings are listed as 'Egg Cups', Shape 1232 in the same volume.

16. **Plate** 24.6 cms diameter.
Mark: W4 and 'H' impressed.
Wedgwood Etruria. About 1830–1835.
A capriccio Italian landscape with a dramatic repeated arch border. The landscapes are a version of the same view on the side of the dog pan (see Cat. Ref. Case 24/29).
Loaned by Trustees of the Wedgwood Museum.

17. **Bourdalou** 26.7 × 11.9 cms.
Mark: W1 and four squares in a square impressed.
Wedgwood Etruria. About 1825–1830.
Capriccio landscape views. The shape is recorded as number 1349 in the 1802 Shape Book (see Cat. Ref. Case 12/2 and 27/8).
Loaned by Trustees of the Wedgwood Museum.

18. **Breakfast Cup and Saucer.**
Cup 6.5 × 11 cms diameter. Saucer 17 cms diameter.
Mark: W4 on the cup and the outer flange of the saucer.
Wedgwood Etruria. About 1807.
'Peony' pattern picked out in gold (see Cat. Ref. Case 24/14 & 15).
Footnote: An interesting account of this pattern occurs in a plaintive yet mildly humorous account written by Thomas

Byerley, Wedgwood's London Showroom manager, in a memoranda dated 14th and 29th April 1807; 'Mrs Roberts, the famous swindler, has been with us, and got a set of blue Peony and gold edge, about 271 (pounds). We were all completely deceived by her address and her equipage, and our porters had not the smallest suspicion, finding 6 servants in Livery in the house. Our set and 12 more from other shops, the richest I daresay, she could lay her hands on, were all cleared off the premises, mostly converted into money instantly, and some taken in execution, as was the case with ours'. A few days later Byerley wrote again, 'I have bought back at Auction the Peony and gold ware we were swindled of. What we charge 171(pounds). I have got for 71 (pounds). It had never been used'.
Loaned by Trustees of the Wedgwood Museum.

19. **Sauceboat** overall length 15.5 cms.
Mark: W3.
Wedgwood Etruria. About 1830–1835.
A landscape scene with Storks or Cranes by a lake. The factory name for this design is not recorded.
Loaned by Trustees of the Wedgwood Museum.

20. **Soup Plate** 24.8 cms diameter.
Mark: W1 and 'HH' impressed.
Wedgwood Etruria. About 1825–1835.
Storks or Cranes in a landscape pattern
(see Cat. Ref. Case 24/19).
Loaned by Trustees of the Wedgwood Museum.

21. **Plate** 24.7 cms diameter.
Mark: W4 and three vertical lines bisected in the middle impressed.
Wedgwood Etruria. About 1823–1825.
'Blue Poppy' pattern.
Loaned by Trustees of the Wedgwood Museum.

22. **Small Plate** 16 cms diameter.
Mark: W1.
Wedgwood Etruria. About 1811–1815.
'Corinth' pattern (see Cat. Ref. Case 24/23).
Loaned by Trustees of the Wedgwood Museum.

23. **Plate** 24.7 cms diameter.
Mark: W1 and '4' impressed.
Wedgwood Etruria. About 1811–1820.
'Corinth' or 'Corinthian' pattern.
Footnote: This is probably the first landscape blue printed pattern to be produced. Josiah Wedgwood II produced 'Corinth' a capriccio view composed from various illustrations in Luigi Mayer's *Views in Egypt, Palistine and the Ottoman Empire* published in three volumes 1803–1804. The engraving of the Wedgwood design was in hand by March 1811 and in an account dated 1st May–23rd November it shows that John Robinson was responsible for much of it. The first orders were not taken until 4th October by Bateman (a company traveller), who was able to report that the new pattern was 'Very much liked'. Thomas Byerley in London commented in November, 'It is a beautiful pattern and will be much admired'.
     The erroneous name 'Absalom's Pillar' was first given to this design in 1943 by S.B. Williams as a result of his researches into Spode's 'Caramanian' series (see Cat. Ref. Case 15/13). Williams found that the most prominent part of the design came from a print in Volume 3 called 'The Sepulchre of Absalom' or 'Absalom's Pillar'. He also discovered that various other aspects of the pattern came from five different engravings in Volumes 2 and 3.
Loaned by Trustees of the Wedgwood Museum.

24. **Drainer** 36 × 25.3 cms.
Mark: W4.
Wedgwood Etruria. About 1822–1835.
The border design only from the 'Corinth' pattern.
Footnote: In 1814 Thomas Byerley suggested that the crocus border might be used with a botanical centre; 'I mean a large blue flower in the centre and the Corinth border round the rim'. Although no specimens have been found, it is evident that they were prepared to use just the crocus border and plates with plain (undecorated) centres are recorded.

25. **Vegetable tureen,** liner and cover (see plate 18)
25.5 cms diameter.
Mark: W3 on the liner only.
Wedgwood Etruria. About 1825–1835.
'View of Greenwich and the Thames', from the 'Blue Rose Border' series (see Cat. Ref. Case 24/26, 27, 28, 29 & 30).
The shape is recorded as number 83 in the 1802 Shape Book.
Loaned by John and Sally Storton.

26. **Tureen** on pedestal foot (cover missing)
21.5 × 34 cms diameter.
Mark: W4 and two sets of four small squares in a square and 'Y' impressed.
Wedgwood Etruria. About 1818–1821.
'View of the Tower of London' from the 'Blue Rose Border' series (see Cat. Ref. Case 24/25, 27, 28, 29 & 30).
Loaned by Trustees of the Wedgwood Museum.

27. **Drainer** 33.8 × 23.2 cms.
Mark: W4.
Wedgwood Etruria. About 1825–1835.
'Sailing ship and rowing boat' from the 'Blue Rose Border' series (see Cat. Ref. Case 24/25, 26, 28, 29 & 30).

28. **Pair of Preserve Pots** (see plate 11) 23.2 × 14.2 cms diameter.
Mark: W4.
Wedgwood Etruria. About 1830–1840.
'The Rookery, Surrey' from the 'Blue Rose Border' series of at least twelve different patterns, mostly landscapes of which a few have been identified. These were originally engraved by Allen and Hordsley, a local firm of engravers (see Cat. Ref. Case 24/25, 26, 27, 29 & 30).
The shape is recorded as number 1147 in the 1802 Shape Book.
Loaned by Flora Rabinovitch.

29. **Dog Pan** 30 × 20.7 × 15.5 cms.
Mark: W4 and a diamond shape impressed.
Wedgwood Etruria. About 1830–1835.
'Blue Rose Border' series with various landscapes (see Cat. Ref. Case 24/25, 26, 27, 28 & 30). The dog pan, on pedestal feet, is listed as shape number 1105 in the 1802 Shape Book.
Loaned by Trustees of the Wedgwood Museum.

30. **Plate** 26 cms diameter.
Mark: W3 and two sets of four small squares in a square impressed.
Wedgwood Etruria. About 1825–1830.
'Gothic Ruins' from the 'Blue Rose Border' series. The plate has a moulded border of scallops intersected by stylised acanthus leaves (see Cat. Ref. Case 24/25, 26, 27, 28 & 29).
Loaned by Trustees of the Wedgwood Museum.

31. **Divided dish** (probably the liner to a vegetable tureen)
27.8 × 20.6 cms.
Wedgwood Etruria. About 1805–1820.
'Blue Bamboo' pattern, sometimes called 'Chinese Vase'.
Footnote: This design is thought to be one of the first blue printed patterns to be introduced about 1805 at the Etruria

works. The engraving was executed by William Brookes, who was credited by Simeon Shaw with being the originator of the idea of using a standard border pattern for all plates but differentiating between sizes by altering the centre decoration (see Cat. Ref. Case 24/32 & 33).
Loaned by Flora Rabinovitch.

32. **Salad Dish** (see figure 11) 19.7 cms square.
Mark: W3.
Wedgwood Etruria. About 1805–1820.
'Blue Bamboo' pattern (see Cat. Ref. Case 24/31 & 33).

33. **Plate** 25 cms diameter.
Mark: W1.
Wedgwood Etruria. About 1805–1820.
'Blue Bamboo' pattern (see Cat. Ref. Case 24/31 & 32).
Loaned by Trustees of the Wedgwood Museum.

34. **Plate** 24.7 cms diameter.
Mark: W4 and 'H' impressed.
Wedgwood Etruria. About 1827–1830.
'Water Tower' pattern. The factory name for this design has not been identified from the records but it is now generally known by this name.
Loaned by Trustees of the Wedgwood Museum.

35. **Group of miniatures** comprising tureen and lid, plate and soup plate.
Tureen 12 × 7.5 cms; soup plate 9 cms diameter; plate 9.2 cms diameter.
Mark: W2 on the soup plate and plate.
Wedgwood Etruria. About 1830–1835.
'Willow' pattern (see Cat. Ref. Case 23).
Footnote: The Wedgwood version of the 'Willow' pattern was engraved by J. Mollart in 1806. The pattern for some unexplained reason was not put into production until 1818.
Loaned by Trustees of the Wedgwood Museum.

36. **Plate** 24.7 cms diameter.
Mark: W4 and 'H', 'H' impressed.
Wedgwood Etruria. About 1830–1835.
'Chinese Temples' pattern (see Cat. Ref. Case 24/37, 38 & 39 for similar versions of this design).
Loaned by Trustees of the Wedgwood Museum.

37. **Sucrier** (missing lid) 8 × 10.7 cms diameter.
Mark: W4.
Wedgwood Etruria. About 1828–1835.
An Oriental landscape with temples. The original factory name is not known but it is frequently referred to as the 'Chinese Temples' pattern (see Cat. Ref. Case 24/36, 38 & 39). The design was introduced into production in May 1818.
Loaned by Trustees of the Wedgwood Museum.

38. **Plate** 25 cms diameter.
Mark: W4 and two stars impressed.
Wedgwood Etruria. About 1828–1835.
An Oriental landscape with temples, sometimes called 'Chinese Temples' pattern (see Cat. Ref. Case 24/36, 37 & 39).
Loaned by Trustees of the Wedgwood Museum.

39. **Plate** 24.8 cms diameter.
Mark: W4 and 'H', 'H' impressed.
Wedgwood Etruria. About 1828–1835.
Chinese landscape with temples
(see Cat. Ref. Case 24/36, 37 & 38).
Loaned by Trustees of the Wedgwood Museum.

40. **Vase** 13 × 11.5 cms diameter.
Mark: W1 and four small squares in a square and 'O' impressed.
Wedgwood Etruria. About 1818–1820.
An Oriental floral pattern.
Loaned by Trustees of the Wedgwood Museum.

41. **Platter** 38 × 28 cms.
Mark: W1 and '2', '2' impressed.
Wedgwood Etruria. About 1830–1835.
Border pattern of 'Birds in a Net' pattern, the centre with Oriental vases (see Cat. Ref. Case 30/10).
Loaned by Trustees of the Wedgwood Museum.

42. **Plate** 26 cms.
Mark: W4.
Wedgwood Etruria. About 1830–1835.
The plate of scalloped shape has a moulded bead border. The central design of Oriental vases is an abbreviated version of Cat. Ref. Case 24/41. The shape is the same as Cat. Ref. Case 24/43.
Loaned by Trustees of the Wedgwood Museum.

43. **Plate** 26.6 cms diameter.
Mark: W1 and 'M' impressed.
Wedgwood Etruria. About 1835–1840.
The factory name for this pattern is not known but it is generally referred to as 'Swans'. The plate of scalloped shape has a moulded bead border, Cat. Ref. Case 24/42.
Loaned by Trustees of the Wedgwood Museum.

44. **Plate** 24.5 cms diameter.
Mark: W1 and two stars impressed.
Wedgwood Etruria. About 1841–1845.
The pattern is referred to as 'Fruit Basket'.
Loaned by Trustees of the Wedgwood Museum.

45. **Toast Rack** 19.1 × 10.2 × 6.4 cms.
Mark: W3 and 'A' impressed.
Wedgwood Etruria. About 1835–1845.
A 'Broseley' style border in pale blue with the upper side of the unusual, serpentine dividers picked out in a deeper cobalt blue. The shape is listed as number 1417 in the 1802 Shape Book.
Loaned by Peter and Margaret Crumpton.

Case 25. COUNTRY HOUSES

1. **Chestnut Basket** and stand. Basket 26 × 21.7 cms. Stand 25.5 × 21.7 cms.
Attributed to *J & W Ridgway, Shelton*. About 1815–1835.
Basket: 'Comb Bank'. Stand: 'Gunnersbury House'.
From the 'Angus Seats' series (see Cat. Ref. Case Kitchen/38)
Loaned by John and Sally Storton.

2. **Soup Tureen** (no cover) 30.5 × 18.8 cms.
Elkin & Co., Lane End. About 1822–1830.
'Blenheim Palace', from the 'Irish Scenery' series. This pattern has not been recorded previously in this series.
(see Cat. Ref. Case Kitchen/36).
Loaned by John and Sally Storton.

3. **Plate** 15.9 cms.
Mark: X10.
Attributed to *J & W Ridgway, Shelton*. About 1820–1830.
'Fisherman Casting', possibly a view of Stokesay Castle, from one of the 'British Scenery' series.
(see Cat. Ref. Case 31/15).

4. Sauce Tureen, cover and stand.
Tureen 18 × 20.5 cms. Stand 21.5 × 16.3 cms.
Mark: X2.
Maker Unknown. About 1820–1830.
'Arundel Castle, Sussex' from the 'Antique Scenery' series of about twenty-three English and Scottish views. Some of the patterns have been taken from *The Antiquities of Great Britain* (short title), published in two volumes in 1807; the engravings are by William Byrne from drawings by Thomas Hearne.
Loaned by John and Sally Storton.

5. Plate 22 cms.
Mark: A2 and A7.
William Adams, Stoke. About 1820–1830.
'Carstairs, Lanarkshire', from the 'Flowers and Leaves Border' series (see Cat. Ref. Case Kitchen/31).
Loaned by John and Sally Storton.

6. Vegetable Dish with cover 25 cms square.
Mark: A2 and as A5.
William Adams, Stoke. About 1820–1830.
'Kimberley Hall, Norfolk', a previously unrecorded pattern from the 'Flowers and Leaves Border' series (see Cat. Ref. Case Kitchen/31). The views on the outside appear to be of Stanmer Park, Sussex.
Loaned by John and Sally Storton.

7. Soup Tureen and cover 39.5 × 21 × 24 cms.
Mark: As H11.
Henshall & Co., Longport. About 1820–1828.
'Cashiobury' from the 'Fruit and Flower Border' series (see Cat. Ref. Case Kitchen/33). This pattern was previously unrecorded.
Loaned by John and Sally Storton.

8. Soup Tureen and cover 35.5 × 33 cms.
Mark: As C2.
T & J Carey, Lane End. About 1825–1830.
Tureen: 'Kilruddery Hall, Wicklow, Earl of Meath's Seat'.
Interior: 'Hollywell Cottage, Ireland'.
Cover: 'Shugborough Hall, Staffordshire, Viscount Anson's Seat'.
From the 'Titled Seats' series (see Cat. Ref. Case 25/9 & 10).
Loaned by John and Sally Storton.

9. Chestnut Basket 28.5 × 17.5 cms.
Mark: As C2
T & J Carey, Lane End. About 1825–1830.
'Luton Hoo, Bedfordshire, Marquis of Bute's Seat' from the 'Titled Seats' series of at least thirteen named Country Houses (see Cat. Ref. Case 25/8 & 10).
Loaned by John and Sally Storton.

10. Plate 22 cms.
Mark: C2.
T & J Carey, Lane End. About 1825–1830.
'Woburn Abbey, Duke of Bedford's Seat' from the 'Titled Seats' series of at least thirteen named country houses (see Cat. Ref. Case 25/8 & 9).
Loaned by John and Sally Storton.

11. Plate 22 cms.
Mark: S13 and as S14.
A. Stevenson, Cobridge. About 1820–1830.
'Barrington Hall', from the 'Rose Border' series (see Cat. Ref. Case Kitchen/34).
Loaned by John and Sally Storton.

12. Plate 14 cms.
J & R Riley, Burslem. About 1820–1825.
'Culzean Castle (S.E. View)' from the 'Large Scroll Border' series

of at least nineteen views, mainly taken from John Preston Neale's *Views of the Seats of Noblemen and Gentlemen in England and Wales, Scotland and Ireland* (1813–1829).
A pattern which has been previously unrecorded in this series.
Loaned by John and Sally Storton.

13. Soup Plate 25 cms.
Mark: X16.
Maker Unknown. About 1820–1830.
'Foremark, Derbyshire, The Home of Sir Francis Burdett Bart'.
Not previously identified as part of a series, but now incorporated in the 'Freesia Border' series of three views (see also Cat. Ref. Case 25/14).
Loaned by John and Sally Storton.

14. Oblong Handled Dish and cover 31 × 23.7 cms.
Mark: as X16.
Maker Unknown. About 1820–1830.
'Kirklees Hall, Yorkshire', a previously unrecorded pattern now incorporated in the 'Freesia Border' series (see Cat. Ref. Case 25/13).
Loaned by John and Sally Storton.

15. Plate 22 cms.
Mark: A2 and as A7.
William Adams, Stoke. About 1820–1830.
'Armidale, Inverness-shire', from the 'Flowers and Leaves Border' series (see Cat. Ref. Case Kitchen/31).
Loaned by John and Sally Storton.

Case 26. TOWNS AND CITIES

1. Platter 37 × 28.6 cms.
Mark: P2.
Pountney and Allies, Bristol. About 1820–1830.
'Clifton', from the 'Bristol Views' series of at least nine scenes, taken from various different print sources.
Loaned by John and Sally Storton.

2. Platter 42 × 31.5 cms.
Mark: As P2.
Pountney and Allies, Bristol. About 1820–1830.
'View near Bristol, River Avon', from the 'Bristol Views' series (see Cat. Ref. Case 26/1).
Loaned by Mervyn Gibbs.

3. Platter (Well and Tree) 52 × 41.8 cms.
Mark: X1.
Maker Unknown. About 1820–1830.
'North East View of Lancaster', from the 'Antique Scenery' series (see Cat. Ref. Case 25/4 and 27/7).

4. Platter 45 × 36.2 cms.
Mark: As A8.
William Adams, Stoke. About 1827–1830.
'The Regent's Quadrant, London', from the 'Regents Park' series of at least twenty views of that area of London. The main source for these scenes was Thomas Shepherd's *Metropolitan Improvements* (1827), but engravings from other sources were also used (see Cat. Ref. Case 35/2 & 3).
Loaned by John and Sally Storton.

5. Plate 22.3 cms.
Mark: G4 and 'T. & B. Godwin, New Wharf' impressed.
Thomas & Benjamin Godwin, Burslem. About 1825–1830.
'View of London', showing London Bridge and St Paul's Cathedral, taken from a print which has not yet been identified. The printed scroll mark (not previously recorded) appears to be

almost identical to that used on the 'British Scenery' series (Mark X10; see Cat. Ref. Case 25/3), which, after many years of anonymity, has been tentatively attributed to J. & W. Ridgway on the basis of shape comparisons. This attribution now needs to be re-examined.

6. **Platter** 53.9 × 43 cms.
Mark: G9 and the Staffordshire knot impressed.
Goodwins and Harris, Lane End. About 1831.
'View of Greenwich', from the 'Metropolitan Scenery' series of at least sixteen views around London. This view is looking from Blackheath Point. The source of some of the scenes in this series has been identified as *Twenty Views in the environs of London – Sketched from Nature and Drawn on Stone*, by T.M. Baynes (1823). It is interesting that copper plates entitled 'Metropolitan Scenery' were sold in 1828 after the closure of John Denton Bagster's pottery in Hanley.
Loaned by Terry Sheppard.

7. **Platter** 39.3 × 32.3 cms.
Mark: As G9.
Goodwins & Harris, Lane End. About 1831.
'View from Blackheath', from the 'Metropolitan Scenery' series (see Cat. Ref. Case 26/6).
Loaned by Terry Sheppard.

8. **Platter** 30.4 × 22.8 cms.
Mark: As G9 and the Staffordshire knot impressed.
Goodwins & Harris, Lane End. About 1831.
'Road from Blackheath', from the 'Metropolitan Scenery' series (see Cat. Ref. Case 26/6).
Loaned by Terry Sheppard.

9. **Plate** 19.5 cms.
Mark: T4.
S. Tams & Co., Longton. About 1825–1830.
'Bruce Castle, Tottenham', a previously unrecorded pattern in the 'Tams Foliage Border' series of at least seventeen views, mainly of London and Dublin.
Loaned by John and Sally Storton.

10. **Plate** 23 cms.
Mark: T4.
S. Tams & Co., Longton. About 1825–1830.
'The Guildhall, London', previously recorded as Maker Unknown but now identified as part of the 'Tams Foliage Border' series (see Cat. Ref. Case 26/9).
Loaned by John and Sally Storton.

11. **Plate** 15 cms.
Mark: T4.
S. Tams & Co., Longton. About 1825–1830.
'Royal Coburg Theatre, London' from the 'Tams Foliage Border' series (see Cat. Ref. Case 26/9).
Loaned by John and Sally Storton.

12. **Plate** 25 cms.
S. Tams & Co., Longton. About 1825–1830.
'Residence of Gen. Sir Herbert Taylor, Master of St. Katherine's Church, Regents Park' a previously unrecorded pattern in the 'Tams Foliage Border' series (see Cat. Ref. Case 26/9).
This scene is taken from Thomas H. Shepherd's *Metropolitan Improvements* (1827).
Loaned by John and Sally Storton.

13. **Platter** 55.5 × 43 cms.
Maker Unknown. About 1820–1830.
'Alexander Pope's Villa on the Thames at Twickenham', a view believed to be part of a series known as 'Tulip Border'. The

source is a print in *The Beauties of England and Wales* (short title) Volume 9, Part 2, page 203. Today the villa at Cross Deep has gone, but Pope's grotto remains.
Loaned by John and Sally Storton.

Case 27. MEDICAL

Like kitchen equipment, medical items of many different shapes and uses were produced in blue printed earthenware. Before the advent of modern plumbing, elaborate toilet sets graced bedrooms and dressing rooms, and the first wash basins and toilets often carried the same decoration. This relatively cheap method of disguising some of the less palatable realities of life was applied also to the sick room and the nursery.

1. **Veilleuse** (or Rechaud) see Glossary (see plate 32)
14.2 × 21.4 × 23.2 cms.
Mark: X14 (Base only).
Attributed to *Minton, Stoke.* About 1830–1840.
'Florentine' pattern. A vase of flowers within a flower and scroll border. The shape is rare in blue printed earthenware, especially when found complete with the 'Godet' or lamp, which provides the heat (missing from this example). The attribution is tentative on the basis of the mark, as an apparently identical mark has been noted on pieces made by George Gordon at Prestonpans.
Footnote: A veilleuse, food warmer or night lamp as it was variously called in the 18th and 19th centuries. They consisted of a cylindrical pedestal, into the top of which fits a flanged bowl which is intended to be filled with water, kept warm by the light below and in turn heat another bowl or kettle which fits into it in the manner of a 'bain marie'. When a kettle is used it becomes a tea-warmer or thèiere and it could also be used to make infusions (tisanes) of camomile or herbs when it was called a veilleuse-tisanière.

2. **Baby Feeding Bottle** (see plate 14) 19 × 9.5 × 4.5 cms.
Maker Unknown. Mid-19th century.
An all-over marble design.

3. **Upright Sucking Pot** (see plate 14) 9.5 cms high.
Mark: S6.
Spode, Stoke. About 1820–1830.
'Tower' pattern (see Cat. Ref. Case 27/4).

4. **Sucking Pot** 9.5 cms high.
Mark: S7.
Spode, Stoke. About 1825–1850.
'Tower', taken from a Merigot aquatint – 'The Bridge of Salaro near Porta Salara', a design first introduced about 1815.

5. **Pap-Boat** (see Glossary), for feeding infants or invalids
11.5 × 6.8 cms.
Attributed to *Wood & Challinor, Burslem.* About 1830–1840.
A floral pattern, probably a border pattern.

6. **Pap-Boat** (See Glossary) 5.7 × 3.2 × 3.2 cms.
Mark: F1.
Thomas Fell, Newcastle-upon-Tyne. About 1820–1830.
An unrecorded pattern showing a boy assisting a seated man who is obviously suffering either from an injured leg or from gout. On the reverse – a hay making scene.

7. **Bidet** and covered stand 52 × 29 × 10.5 cms.
Maker Unknown. About 1820–1840.
An unidentified view of a large cathedral or abbey church. From the 'Antique Scenery' series (see Cat. Ref. Case 25/4). The interior pattern is repeated twice. (Illustrated without stand.)
Loaned by Mr. and Mrs. M. Houlden.

8. **Bourdalou** or Lady's Coach Pot (See Glossary), (see plate 14) 22.8 × 10.1 × 10.7 cms.
J & W Ridgway, Shelton. About 1815–1830.
'Osterley Park' near Hounslow, Middlesex. A mansion built in 1577 by Sir Thomas Gresham and later largely rebuilt, between 1761 and 1780, by Robert Adam (1728–1792), for its then owner, Francis Child.

9. **Gentleman's Urinal** (see plate 14) 19.0 × 11.7 cms.
Maker Unknown. About 1835–1850.
A typical pale blue romantic design. This shape of urinal, as opposed to the normal bottle shape, may have been intended as the masculine equivalent of the Bourdalou
(see Cat. Ref. Case 27/8).
Loaned by Terry Sheppard.

10. **Spitting Pot** with funnel for emptying and cleaning 18 × 9 cms.
Mark: Unmarked but the standard series cartouche is shown in X30.
Attributed to *Andrew Stevenson, Cobridge.* About 1820–1825.
'Duck Shooting', from the 'Stafford Gallery' series of at least nine rural scenes possibly derived from a series of engravings of paintings in the possession of the Marquis of Stafford, published in several volumes in 1818 under the title *An Illustrated Series of the Collection of Paintings of the Marquis of Stafford.*

11. **Spitting Pot** with funnel 17.7 × 11.4 × 7.6 cms.
Spode, Stoke. About 1805–1815.
'Queen Charlotte', a standard chinoiserie pattern. The origin of the name has been lost but it may simply have been a factory name.
Loaned by Flora Rabinovitch.

12. **Vomit Pot** (see plate 14) 12.7 cms diameter.
Mark: Blue-painted '4'.
Maker Unknown. Second half of the 19th century.
'London Hospital' – A plain circular cartouche with a picture of the London Hospital (now 'The Royal London Hospital') and the words 'London Hospital Incorporated MDCCLVIII' (1758) (see footnote to Cat. Ref. Case 27/13).

13. **Vomit Pot** 12.5 × 8.6 cms.
Mark: B4.
G.F. Bowers, Tunstall. About 1845–1860.
'Vintage' pattern, showing fruiting vine and a basket.
Footnote: The shape seems to have derived from Oriental porcelain which had been specially commissioned through the East India Companies by European customers. Many objects were copied in this manner from prototypes and models in wood, metal or ceramics sent to the Far East. In excavated wrecks of cargo carrying boats such as the Dutch East Indiaman, the Geldermalsen (found 1984), there were a large quantity of handled bowls, which were initially thought to be children's chamber pots, recovered. The real function was discovered through the V.O.C. (Verenigde Oost-Indische Compagnie, the official title of the Dutch East India Company) records. From the late 1740's the V.O.C. had taken delivery each year of 'vomit pots'. As the trade with China decreased it is probable that the British earthenware manufacturers continued to supply the demand for these useful objects.
Loaned by Mervyn Gibbs.

14. **Toothbrush Holder** with hinged pewter lid (probably a travel item) 5.8 × 2.1 × 2.5 cms.
Maker Unknown. About 1840–1860.
A small part of a chinoiserie or Willow pattern, on an uncommon shape.
Footnote: In 1990 a similar item was the subject of a 'spoof' article in *World of Antiques* in which it was described as a 'Racing Mouse Box'.

15. **Toothbrush Box** from a Toilet Set 20.2 × 7.6 cms.
Maker Unknown. About 1820–1830.
Part of the 'Gleaners III' pattern (see Cat. Ref. Case 18/10).

16. **Slop Pail** with cover 35.4 × 30.3 cms.
Mark: B5.
Zachariah Boyle & Son, Stoke. About 1835–1845.
An early romantic pattern of Swiss-style lake scenery. A slop pail was often included in a toilet set.
Loaned by Terry Sheppard.

17. **Spitting Pot** with separate funnel (see plate 14) 14.5 cms diameter × 11.7 cms.
Mark: W2.
Wedgwood, Etruria. About 1810–1815.
'Water Lily' pattern (see Cat. Ref. Case 24/6).
Stevenson Collection.

Case 28. NAMED VIEWS

1. **Dish** 19 cms.
Mark: T2.
Tams, Anderson & Tams, Longton. About 1820–1830.
'Richmond Castle, Yorkshire', a previously unrecorded pattern believed to be part of a small series known as 'Floral City'.
Loaned by John and Sally Storton.

2. **Plate** 16.5 cms.
Mark: C9 and C10.
J & R Clews, Cobridge. About 1820–1830.
'Wingfield Castle, Suffolk' from the 'Bluebell Border' series (see Cat. Ref. Case 29/1).
Loaned by John and Sally Storton.

3. **Tureen Stand** 33 cms.
John Rogers & Son, Dale Hall, Longport. About 1825–1830.
'Byland Abbey, Yorkshire', from the 'Rogers Views' series. The usual series' border has been extended by the addition of a wide rim band of geometric moulding, picked out in part with a cellular blue transfer.

4. **Dish** Lobed Oblong 29.1 × 20.3 cms.
Mark: as X5.
William Mason, Lane Delph. About 1820–1825.
'Ly[n]mouth, North Devon', from the 'Beaded Frame' series, of which at least fifteen views, have recently been attributed to William Mason as an independent potter.

5. **Small Soup or Pudding Plate** 20.3 cms.
Mark: H10A.
Henshall & Co., Longport. About 1820–1828.
'Bradfield', from the 'Fruit and Flowers Border' series (see Cat. Ref. Case Kitchen/33). The view has not been identified with certainty since there are several villages of the same name.

6. **Drainer** 33 × 23.2 cms.
Attributed to *John Meir, Tunstall.* About 1820–1830.
'Barnard Castle', from the 'Pineapple Border' series (see Cat. Ref. Case Kitchen/21).

7. **Platter and Source Print.** Platter 36.2 × 27.9 cms.
Mark: S13 and as S14.
Andrew Stevenson, Cobridge. About 1820–1830.
'Tunbridge Castle, Surry (sic)', from the 'Rose Border' series (see Cat. Ref. Case Kitchen/34).
Source Print 'Tunbridge Castle, the Seat of Wm. Bailley, Esq.'. Drawn and engraved by T. Higham for *The Excursions Through Kent* (about 1818).
Loaned by Terry Sheppard.

Case 29. CHURCHES AND COLLEGES

Churches and abbeys, ruined or otherwise, formed the basis of several well-known series of views. More unusual, however, is the large series of views of 'Oxford and Cambridge Colleges', produced by J. & W. Ridgway in the 1820's. The provision of domestic china for universities and colleges was quite big business; bursars or in some instances the cooks themselves ordered for their own college.

1. **Soup Plate** 25 cms.
Mark: C9 and C10.
J & R Clews, Cobridge. About 1825–1830.
'Tintern Abbey, Monmouthshire', from the 'Bluebell Border' series of at least fourteen topographical views in England, Scotland and Wales. A similar series with an identical border was produced at about the same time by William Adams of Stoke, mainly for export. The Adams' series was larger, yet only one view appears in both series.
Loaned by John and Sally Storton.

2. **Platter** 27.0 × 19.7 cms.
Mark: as R3.
J & W Ridgway, Shelton. About 1820–1830.
'Library of Trinity College, Cambridge', from the 'Oxford and Cambridge Colleges' series (see Cat. Ref. Case 29/5).
Loaned by John and Sally Storton.

3. **Sauce Boat** 17.7 × 7.0 × 8.9 cms.
J & W Ridgway, Shelton. About 1820–1830.
'Sidney Sussex College, Cambridge' from the 'Oxford and Cambridge Colleges' series (see Cat. Ref. Case 29/5).

4. **Sauce Tureen**, cover and stand 20.3 × 10.1 × 15.2 cms.
Mark: as R3 (Tureen and Stand only).
J & W Ridgway, Shelton. About 1820–1830.
Tureen: 'Trinity Hall, Cambridge'.
Cover: 'Merton College, Oxford'.
Stand: 'Christ's Church, Oxford'.
From the 'Oxford and Cambridge Colleges' series (see Cat. Ref. Case 29/5).

5. **Dessert Dish** 20.3 cms.
Mark: as R3.
J & W Ridgway, Shelton. About 1820–1830.
'Clare Hall, Cambridge' from the 'Oxford and Cambridge Colleges' series of about twenty-two views of college buildings. Many of the views appear to have been taken from prints published over a period of twenty years in the *Oxford Almanack* and the *Cambridge University Almanack*.

6. **Footed Hexagonal Bowl** 25.4 × 15.2 cms.
Mark: C1.
T & J Carey, Lane End. About 1825–1830.
Views of Bristol Cathedral and Bath Abbey, a dual pattern labelled 'Bristol and Bath Cathedrals' in the 'Cathedral' series (see Cat. Ref. Case 29/7).
Loaned by Christopher Fiorini.

7. **Dessert Plate** 22.2 cms.
Mark: 'Chichester Cathedral' in a blue printed scrolled cartouche surmounted by a Bishop's mitre. This mark would normally include a ribbon inscribed 'Carey's Saxon Stone China'.
T & J Carey, Lane End. About 1825–1830.
'Chichester Cathedral' from the 'Cathedral' series of at least five views of various British cathedrals.

8. **Platter** 27.2 × 21.6 cms.
Mark: H5.

Ralph Hall, Tunstall. About 1825–1830.
'Norwich Cathedral', from the 'Picturesque Scenery' series of at least nineteen views in Europe. Printed in export blue.

9. **Square Vegetable Dish** and Cover.
24.1 cms square × 15.2 cms high.
Mark: as R3 (Dish only).
J & W Ridgway, Shelton. About 1820–1830.
Dish: 'Radcliffe Observatory, Oxford'.
Cover: 'Christ's Church and Cathedral, Oxford'.
From the 'Oxford and Cambridge Colleges' series (see Cat. Ref. Case 29/5).

Case 30.
NATURAL HISTORY, ORNITHOLOGICAL AND HUNTING/SHOOTING

Interest in the Natural Sciences was growing in the early part of the 19th century, and patterns of seashells, butterflies, birds and fruit were popular on ceramics. Hunting and shooting designs enjoyed considerable success, depicting as they did, recreational pursuits enjoyed by various sectors of society.

1. **Cup and Saucer** Porringer-shape.
Cup 10 cms diameter × 8.7 cms. Saucer 14.6 cms.
Possibly *Leeds Pottery.* About 1810–1815.
A central pattern and border showing various types of shells, seaweed and fish.

2. **Soup Plate** 40.1 cms.
Mark: H18.
Herculaneum Pottery, Liverpool. About 1830.
'Hunters with Pointers', from the 'Field Sports' series of at least six hunting and sporting patterns.

3. **Soup Plate** (see figure 6) 25.3 cms.
Mark: X17.
Maker Unknown. About 1820–1825.
'Game Keeper', a pattern found mainly on dinner wares and identified as taken from a print in a three-volume publication on rural sports by the Rev'd W.B. Daniel, published between 1805 and 1812. The original painting from which this print was engraved is by Landseer, but the engraver has added what appears to be a view of Goodwood House, Sussex.
This example also bears a tavern mark on the face – 'Eyre Tavern, St. John's Wood'.

4. **Tea Bowl** with brown rim 8.3 cms diameter.
Leeds Pottery. About 1805–1810.
A design of seashells and seaweed on a stippled ground, known also on a smoker's set and a marked tea pot.

5. **Dish** Small Twist-handled 12.1 cms.
Mark: S7.
Spode, Stoke. About 1816–1825.
'India' pattern, introduced about 1816, showing a large butterfly and other insects around flowers.

6. **Chestnut Basket** and Stand.
Basket 21.3 × 17.7 cms. Stand 24.8 × 21.2 cms.
Chetham and Woolley, Longton. About 1800–1810.
'Fruit' including grapes and a large pineapple.
Loaned by City Museum and Art Gallery, Stoke-on-Trent.

7. **Plate** 25.3 cms.
Attributed to *Joseph Stubbs, Longport, Burslem.* About 1825–1830.
A dark blue pattern with a group of dead game birds, apparently a still life, in a central reserve within a border of flowers, leaves and scroll cartouches containing landscape views.

8. **Octagonal Plate** 19 cms across.
Stevenson, Cobridge. About 1816–1825.
'Dusky Grebe or Black and White Dobchick' (*sic*), from the 'Ornithological' series of about eleven patterns featuring wild birds in their natural habitat, most of them identifiable. A source for at least some of the designs is Thomas Bewick's *British Birds* (1797–1804).

9. **Plate** 22 cms.
Mark: W20.
Enoch Wood & Sons, Burslem. About 1825–1830.
'Hunter Shooting Fox' from the 'Sporting' series of about sixteen hunting scenes both English and Indian. The scene is taken from Luke Clennell's 'Fox', in *Recreations in Natural History* (see Cat. Ref. Case 21/8).

10. **Pickle Dish** Leaf-shape overall length 15.2 cms.
Wedgwood, Etruria. About 1825–1830.
'Birds and Butterfly', one of two variations on this theme, from the series 'Blue Bird Cage' (sometimes known as 'Blue Birds and Net') of at least four different patterns (see Cat. Ref. Case 24/41).

11. **Curd Skimmer** 12.2 cms.
Stevenson, Cobridge. About 1816–1825.
'Grouse', from the 'Ornithological' series (see Cat. Ref. Case 30/8).
Loaned by City Museum and Art Gallery, Stoke-on-Trent.

12. **Tea Bowl and Saucer.** Bowl 5.1 cms. Saucer 12.0 cms.
Mark: X36.
Maker Unknown. About 1815–1820.
Different bird prints in reserves in a stylised floral border. The birds appear to be based on Thomas Bewick's *British Birds* (1797–1804).

13. **Plate** 20.7 cms.
Maker Unknown. About 1815–1830.
One of several patterns based on seashells, used mainly on tea wares and mostly unidentified. The seaweed background motif carries the design through to a logical conclusion.

14. **Plate** 25.2 cms.
Ralph Stevenson, Cobridge (attribution based on a marked piece). About 1825–1830.
'Springer Spaniel', based on a print in *The Sportsman's Cabinet* of 1803 (see Cat. Ref. Case 30/16).

15. **Plate** 25.0 cms.
Mark: D8.
Possibly *Davenport, Longport.* About 1825–1830.
'Hunting with Greyhounds', a hunting scene with a border of flowers and parrots.
Footnote: The retailers 'Hill and Henderson, New Orleans', whose mark appears on the reverse, are known to have imported wares from the Davenport factory. No other British connection has been found.

16. **Small Tray or Dish** 12.7 × 10.8 cms.
Attributed to *Ralph Stevenson, Cobridge.* About 1820–1830.
'Springer Spaniel', based on a print in *The Sportsman's Cabinet* of 1803 (see Cat. Ref. Case 30/14).

17. **Arcaded Plate** 20.4 cms.
Maker Unknown. About 1820–1840.
'Set Too' (*sic*) – a cock-fighting scene, from an original drawing by the artist and engraver Henry Alken I (1785–1851), whose name appears at the bottom left corner of the central print.

18. **Jug** 11.3 cms.
Maker Unknown. About 1820–1830.
A fox-hunting scene, with the fox sneaking away in the opposite direction to the huntsmen and hounds.

19. **Arcaded Plate** 18.8 cms.
Maker Unknown. About 1815–1825.
'Stag Hunt', in a central reserve with a wide border of flowers, leaves and berries.

20. **Sucrier** 18 × 11.5 × 13 cms.
Maker Unknown. About 1815–1830.
'Kingfisher', a previously unrecorded pattern. A tentative attribution to Enoch Wood & Sons has been made on the basis of shape, but similar shapes were also produced for export by the Mayer partnerships at Dale Hall, Burslem.

21. **Cup Plate** 10.2 cms.
Mark: C9.
J & R Clews, Cobridge. About 1825–1830.
'Hunter with Dog', from a small series of 'Hunting Views'. It is believed that cup plates were used to set down cups while drinking from saucers. It is, however, possible that they were coasters for general use, including glasses, as they have been found as part of dinner services.
Loaned by David and Linda Arman.

Case 31. RURAL VIEWS

Rural views, whether real or imagined, account for a very high proportion of the many thousands of designs recorded as having been used for the decoration of blue printed earthenware. There are many substantial series of views as well as hundreds of striking single patterns. Today it is often difficult to tell some of the designs apart, as both central patterns and borders were copied or plagiarised from factory to factory and frequently had no identifying marks at all. Milkmaids, shepherds and cattle were particularly popular.

1. **Coffee Pot** with domed lid 25.3 cms high.
Maker Unknown. About 1820–1830.
A group of travellers, one riding a mule with panniers, in rural scenery dominated by a large church. Similar in appearance to Davenport's 'Muleteer' series, but the border is different.

2. **Small Platter** 24 × 17.4 cms.
Mark: X13.
Now attributed to *T & J Carey, Lane End* on the basis of a piece bearing both an impressed factory mark and the series' cartouche. About 1820–1830.
'Man Filling Trough', from the 'Domestic Cattle' series of at least eight designs featuring domestic animals.

3. **Tea Bowl** 9.2 cms.
Possibly *Leeds Pottery.* About 1825–1835.
An unrecorded rustic view showing a woman milking a reindeer, while two children play around the animal's feet. Reindeer appear occasionally on British designs but it must be a possibility that this is a piece from the Swedish factory at Rorstrand, whose excellent blue printed earthenwares were made in the British style.

4. **Tea Bowl** 7.4 cms diameter.
Maker Unknown. About 1820–1830.
A man lying down playing a pipe to a kneeling milkmaid. The man and his companion carrying a hay fork, both wear large, plumed hats. Several different designs featuring milkmaids are

known. It is interesting to note that the contemporary novel *The Dairyman's Daughter* was also popular, emphasising the general interest in country pursuits.

5. **Mug** 10.2 × 12.7 cms.
Maker Unknown. About 1815–1825.
A man and a milkmaid sheltering with cows, beneath a tree. A dog is expecting them to throw sticks for him.
Footnote: The scene is copied from an engraving by Francis Vivares which was published in 1760 after a painting by Thomas Gainsborough (1727–1788) entitled 'The Rural Lovers'. This design is also known as an overglaze black print on porcelain attributed to the engraving of Robert Hancock.

6. **Sucrier** with cover 14.3 cms.
Maker Unknown. About 1820–1830.
'Milkmaid', this version of the pattern was used, with variations, by at least four different potters including Spode and Davenport.

7. **Jug** 11.5 cms.
Bovey Tracey Pottery. About 1800–1810.
'Two Kilns' – this may possibly be a view of the Bovey Tracey Pottery itself, and the two kilns referred to in the pattern name may, in reality, be three structures.

8. **Lobed Dessert Dish** 22 × 21.5 cms.
Maker Unknown. About 1810–1815.
'Driving the Cattle', one of a series of about eight patterns from the 'Durham Ox' series. The Durham Ox was a prize ox, bred near Darlington by Charles Willings and eventually owned by farmer John Day. He showed the animal throughout England and Scotland from 1801 and to 1807 when the ox fell and had to be destroyed. The carcass weighed over a ton. The only mark known on the series is 'Withers', which may refer to a retailer or to a College caterer.
Loaned by P.L. and A.E. Maclean-Eltham.

9. **Tankard** 9.7 × 15 cms.
Maker Unknown. About 1815–1825.
A horse grazing in the graveyard of a country church and a cow in a stream nearby. An unidentified view.

10. **Sauce Boat** 17.8 cms long.
Maker Unknown. About 1820–1830.
Two men fishing below a ruined church on a hill.

11. **Leaf-moulded Mug** 11 cms high.
Maker Unknown. About 1820.
A mixed group of sheep, cows and goats, with a child approaching a woman who stands beside a man reclining under a tree. A little imagination could interpret the scene as an illustration of the nursery rhyme 'Little Bo-Peep'.

12. **Jug** 11.5 cms high.
Mark: X7.
Maker Unknown. About 1825–1835.
A man driving a packhorse beside a lake or river with a bridge and a mansion in the background. There are sailing boats on the water and two men fishing on the bank. The view is recorded as 'Packhorse and Sailing boat', but it is marked 'British Scenery'. The border differs substantially from that on the large and well-known 'British Scenery' series now attributed to J. & W. Ridgway. In this case 'British Scenery' may be the proper name for this single pattern.

13. **Plate** 21.5 cms.
Maker Unknown. About 1820–1830.
A herd of reindeer in a field below a ruined classical temple.

14. **Comport** 24.1 × 20.3 × 10.2 cms.
Mark: S12.
Ralph Stevenson, Cobridge. About 1820–1830.
Decorated with two patterns – 'Milking the Goats' and 'Boy and Dogs', from the 'Semi-China Warranted' series of at least seven rural scenes.

15. **Chestnut Basket** 24.8 × 14.6 × 10.3 cms.
Mark: X10.
Attributed to *J & W Ridgway, Shelton* on the basis of a comparison of shapes. About 1820–1830.
'Lakeside Castle' from the 'British Scenery' series of at least thirteen rural scenes, some identified as actual views (see Cat. Ref. Case 26/5).

16. **Toast Rack** 17.7 × 8.9 × 7.2 cms.
Griffiths, Beardmore and Birks, Lane End. About 1830.
A scene identified as 'Castle Richard', from the 'Light Blue Rose Border' series of at least seven different named views.
Loaned by Margaret and Peter Crumpton.

17. **Vegetable Dish** and cover 23.4 × 20.2 × 12.0 cms.
J & W Handley, Hanley. About 1820–1830.
'Village Fishermen' pattern.

18. **Dessert Dish** Square with cut-out corners 25.3 cms square.
Mark: as M9.
Attributed to *John Meir, Tunstall* on the basis of shape.
About 1820–1830.
'Roche Abbey, Yorkshire', from the 'Pineapple Border' series (see Cat. Ref. Case Kitchen/21).

19. **Coffee Cup and Saucer.**
Cup 7 × 6.3 cms. Saucer 13.3 cms.
Maker Unknown. About 1815–1820.
A pastoral scene with cows, a man with a pitchfork and a milkmaid carrying buckets on a yoke, with a ruined church on a hill in the background.

20. **Chestnut Basket** 30 × 20.5 cms.
Maker Unknown. About 1815–1820.
An unusual rural scene, so far unrecorded, which shows a number of people picnicking with a large church in the background. One of the men has a long feather in his hat.

Case 32. HERCULANEUM AND THE NORTH WEST

Despite the favourable position of Liverpool, a major port with canal access, and its history as the home of delftware and porcelain potters, and as the cradle of printing on tiles, relatively little transfer printed earthenware was produced there. Only the Herculaneum Pottery (which also made porcelain) and John Gordon's Seacombe Pottery are worthy of note. There was also a flourishing pottery at Whitehaven, further north, but potting in the north-west was minimal by comparison with the north-east.

1. **Plate** 25.0 cms.
Mark: H12.
Herculaneum Pottery, Liverpool. About 1800–1810.
'Curling Bridge and Temple', also known as 'Chinese Garden Festival', the Liverpool Garden Festival of 1984 having been held very close to the site of the pottery.

2. **Plate** 25.1 cms.
Mark: H16 and H15.
Herculaneum Pottery, Liverpool. About 1815–1825.
'View of Lancaster', one of the views in the 'Cherub Medallion Border' series (see Cat. Ref. Case 32/3).

3. **Tureen**, cover and stand.
Tureen 19 × 11 cms. Stand 21 × 16.4 cms.
Overall height 17.9 cms.
Mark: Tureen H12 and H13, Stand H14.
Herculaneum Pottery, Liverpool. About 1815–1825.
Tureen: 'Cambridge'. The cover with the border design only.
Stand: 'Cluny Castle'.
From the 'Cherub Medallion Border' series of at least nineteen views of towns, cities and castles in the British Isles.

4. **Round Vegetable Dish** and cover 26.0 cms.
Mark: H12 and as H14 (dish only).
Herculaneum Pottery, Liverpool. About 1815–1825.
'Worcester' from the 'Cherub Medallion Border' series
(see Cat. Ref. Case 32/3).

5. **Coffee Pot** 20.3 cms.
Mark: H12.
Herculaneum Pottery, Liverpool. About 1800–1805.
'Laughing Dog' pattern.
The lug to secure the lid is an unusual feature.

6. **Oblong Tray** 25.3 × 19.0 cms.
Mark: H12.
Herculaneum Pottery, Liverpool. About 1815–1820.
A version of part of the 'View in the Fort, Madura' pattern, one of several dinner service designs generally known as the 'India' series. Most of the views are composite patterns incorporating a main feature and some subsidiary details taken from prints by Thomas and William Daniell in *Oriental Scenery* (1795–1808).

7. **Cup and Saucer.** Cup 8 × 5 cms. Saucer 12.7 cms.
Mark: H17 (saucer only).
Herculaneum Pottery, Liverpool. About 1815–1825.
'Mushroom Picker', a design showing a kneeling girl; with a border of leaves and flowers.

8. **Plate** 23 cms.
Whitehaven Pottery, Cumbria. About 1820–1830.
'Lowther', a view of the village of Lowther, near Penrith, which is still identifiable.
Loaned by Mr. and Mrs. D.T. Sibson.

9. **Jug** 17 × 17 cms.
Mark: W9.
Whitehaven Pottery, Cumbria. About 1825–1835.
'Pekin' pattern, an unusual combination of Chinese boats, figures and mountains with a very English-looking castle.
Loaned by Mr. and Mrs. D.T. Sibson.

10. **Set of Four Furniture Lifts**
6.4 cms square × 6.0 cms high.
Possibly from the *Whitehaven Pottery, Cumbria.* About 1820–1830.
An unidentified rural pattern on a very rare item. The lifts would have been used to protect furniture from a damp floor.
Loaned by Flora Rabinovitch.

11. **Sauce Tureen**, Cover and Stand 16 × 20 cms.
Mark: W10.
Whitehaven Pottery, Cumbria. About 1835–1845.
'Antiquities', a romantic pattern on a very ornate shape.
Loaned by Mr. and Mrs. D.T. Sibson.

12. **Plate** 22.5 cms.
Mark: W15.
Whitehaven Pottery, Cumbria. About 1825–1835.
'Minstrel' pattern, a rarely-seen design.
Loaned by Mr. and Mrs. D.T. Sibson.

13. **Plate** 25 cms.
Mark: W16.
Whitehaven Pottery, Cumbria. About 1845–1860.
'Charity', a typical Victorian scene, popular at the Whitehaven Pottery where it was frequently printed in black and white.
Loaned by Mr. and Mrs. D.T. Sibson.

14. **Small Tureen** and Cover 17.8 cms high.
Mark: X33.
J. Goodwin, Seacombe Pottery, Liverpool. About 1845–1855.
'Rousillon', a typical romantic scenery design.

15. **Tureen** and Cover 28 × 13 × 13 cms.
Mark: W14.
Whitehaven Pottery, Cumbria. About 1825–1835.
'May Field', an uncommon pattern of flowers and scrolls.
Loaned by Mr. and Mrs. D.T. Sibson.

Case 33. BIBLICAL AND LITERARY

Biblical themes ranging from texts to scenes from the Bible were used as a basis for decoration on earthenwares. These unusual patterns are possibly a response to a demand from a Nation who were regular Church attenders. Their secular counterparts consisted of both series and single designs from books, poems or plays, or landscape views connected with literary publications. Notable were series based on the works of Scott and Byron, the Dr. Syntax satirical cartoons, Don Quixote and even Aesop's Fables.

1. **Mug** 8.8 cms.
Mark: X18.
Maker Unknown. About 1835–1845.
'John Gilpin', illustrating a scene from William Cowper's poem *The Diverting History of John Gilpin*, first published in 1782. Gilpin attempts to reach the Bell Inn at Edmonton to celebrate his 20th wedding anniversary by having dinner with his wife, but his horse bolts and carries him many miles north to Ware. In this view the toll gate keepers wave him through, thinking he is in a race.

2. **Miniature Cup and Saucer** Bute-shape.
Cup 3.8 cms high. Saucer 9.6 cms.
Maker Unknown. About 1810–1815.
A scene representing 'The Cock and the Fox', one of Aesop's Fables in which the fox tries to trick the cock into descending from the tree but is himself tricked into running away.

3. **Plate** 16.5 cms.
Mark: R11 and R11A.
John & Richard Riley, Burslem. About 1815–1825.
'Europa', a given title for a scene which seems to represent the legend of Europa and the Bull.

4. **Child's Plate** with moulded rim 15.3 cms.
Maker Unknown. About 1815–1830.
'The Lord's Prayer' within a chain border.

5. **Small Plate** with vine-moulded rim 17.7 cms.
Mark: X26.
Maker Unknown. About 1820–1840.
'Sower', one of a series of five or six prints under the title 'Progress of a Loaf'. Each pattern contains an appropriate verse. Other designs are – Ploughman, Reaper, Thrasher, Miller and Baker. A similar, but more elaborate series, 'The Progress of a Quartern Loaf', was made by Brameld & Co., Swinton, Yorkshire.

6. **Child's Plate** 13.9 cms.
Mark: H12.
Herculaneum Pottery, Liverpool. About 1825–1840.
Within a floral circlet, an improving verse 'Against Idleness', from Isaac Watts' *Divine Songs for the use of Children.*

7. **Footed Bowl** 19.5 cms.
Maker Unknown. About 1810–1825.
'Christ's Ascension into Heaven', a pattern with a wide geometric and insect chinoiserie border, previously unrecorded. Several potters, including Thomas Mayer, Enoch Wood and the Pountney partnerships in Bristol, produced series based on scriptural subjects.

8. **Plate** 26.2 cms.
Mark: S15.
Ralph Stevenson & Son, Cobridge. About 1832–1835.
'Millennium', illustrating the period of one thousand years during which Christ shall reign on earth, as foretold in 'Revelations', Chapter 20, verses 1–5. A lion is pictured, lying down with a lamb, and being petted by a little girl.

9. **Plate** Feather-edged 20.9 cms.
Maker Unknown. About 1810–1830.
In an oval chain cartouche, an evangelical sentiment 'This is not the bread of life, but seek and ye shall find'.

10. **Tea Bowl and Saucer.** Bowl 5.7 cms. Saucer 12.7 cms.
Mark: X35.
Maker Unknown. About 1815–1825.
'Moses in the Bulrushes', a scene showing Miriam and the Pharaoh's daughter discovering the infant Moses in his basket among the rushes.

11. **Slop Bowl** 15.9 × 8.3 cms.
Maker Unknown. About 1815–1825.
External design of city walls and a flock of sheep, but the interior rim has a border which can only represent the shepherd boy, David, shielding his flock from a bear. A previously unrecorded pattern.

12. **Tureen Stand** 34.1 cms.
Mark: C13 and C14.
Copeland & Garrett, Stoke. About 1835–1846.
'Franciscan Convent, Athens', from the 'Byron Views' series of at least twenty-four scenes based on Finden's *Landscape and Portrait Illustrations to the Life and Works of Lord Byron* (three volumes 1832–1834).
Loaned by Mervyn Gibbs.

13. **Tea Cup** 9.8 cms diameter.
Maker Unknown. About 1835–1845.
Flowers and scrolls with reserves of:
a) John Wesley, MA. Born at Epworth 17th June 1703, died in London 2nd March 1791.
b) Centenary Hall and Mission House, London.
Inside the cup are several repeats of a dove with an olive branch and a picture of the Centenary Hall.

14. **Lobed Rectangular Dish or Stand** 24.8 × 15.3 cms.
Mark: C11.
J & R Clews, Cobridge. About 1825–1830.
'Death of Punch', one of the Doctor Syntax series of thirty-one patterns. Based on drawings by Thomas Rowlandson, originally published in the *Poetical Magazine* between 1809 and 1811 to illustrate doggerel verses by a long-term inmate of the Debtors' Prison. Between 1815 and 1821 the drawings were re-published in book form. Some of the patterns were re-issued by William Adams & Sons, Tunstall, early this century.
Loaned by The Strong Collection.

15. **Handled Dish** 21.0 × 15.2 cms.
Mark: G7.
John & Robin Godwin, Cobridge. About 1835–1850.
'Bride of Lammermoor', one of at least nine scenes taken from the Robert Cadell edition of Sir Walter Scott's works, published between 1827 and 1833. This series seems to have been produced at about the same time as a similar series made by the Davenport factory, but using a completely different border.

16. **Pickle Dish** 15.5 cms.
Mark: R10.
William Ridgway & Co., Hanley. About 1840–1845.
One of a series of views featuring the Dickens' character 'Little Nell'. 'Humphrey's Clock', the series title, comes from Dickens' original title for the projected set of stories 'Master Humphrey's Clock'. This then came to be used with the serial instalments of 'The Old Curiosity Shop' and 'Barnaby Rudge'.
Loaned by City Museum and Art Gallery, Stoke-on-Trent.

17. **Jug** (see plate 7) 14 × 13.7 cms.
Mark: X31.
Thomas Godwin, Burslem. About 1835–1845.
'Tam O' Shanter', scenes illustrating Tam's escape across the bridge as he flees a coven of witches. The story is told in Robert Burns' poem of the same name and the picture seems to have been taken from a print by J. Rogers from a painting by A. Cooper RA.

18. **Plate** 25 cms.
Jones & Son, Hanley. About 1826–1828.
'Alfred as a Minstrel' (Alfred in the camp of the Danes), one of a series of fifteen scenes from 'British History'. The source of all the scenes has been identified as Smollett's *England*, 1825 edition, part of Dolby's *Universal Histories*. The drawings are by W.H. Brooke and the engravings by H. White. The title backstamp on the ceramic pieces follows closely the shape of the design on the title page of the book.
Loaned by City Museum and Art Gallery, Stoke-on-Trent.

Case 34. CLASSICAL, GEOMETRIC AND NAUTICAL

The Classical taste for decoration on earthenware was set off at the end of the 18th century by Josiah Wedgwood I's use of Sir William Hamilton's collection as a design source. It reappears at intervals over the next hundred years. The Geometric fashion appears, as much as anything, to have been a manufacturers' ploy to save on design costs. The ongoing appeal of Nautical patterns mirrors a constant preoccupation of an island people with a great maritime tradition.

1. **Jug** 13.5 cms.
Mark: X3.
Maker Unknown. About 1830–1840.
'Arcadian Chariots', a design similar to the 'Triumphal Car' pattern made by several Scottish potters (see Cat. Ref. Case 12/2). This jug too, has the appearance of a Scottish piece.

2. **Octagonal Soup Plate** 25 cms.
Maker Unknown. About 1810–1820.
An unidentified scene from a series of classical patterns known as the 'Kirk' series because several have been traced to engravings in Thomas Kirk's *Outlines from the Figures and Compositions upon the Greek, Roman and Etruscan Vases of the late Sir William Hamilton* (1804) (see also Cat. Ref. Case 5/10).

3. **Plate** 18.6 cms.
Mark: A blue printed cartouche containing
'ANTIQUES – STONE CHINA'.
Maker Unknown but a Scottish origin has been suggested.
About 1830–1840.
'Antiques' pattern, showing three classical figures in an octagonal reserve, with a wide border of large urns, classical scenes and scrolls.

4. **Stand** for a Sauce Tureen or Boat. 20.5 × 15.5 cms.
Mark: W8.
Ralph Wedgwood & Co., Ferrybridge, Yorkshire. About 1800.
One of many designs, large and small, in the Ferrybridge 'Greek' series of Classical patterns few of which have been properly identified though some have been given names for record purposes.

5. **Jug** 12.8 cms.
Spode, Stoke. About 1820–1830.
Unidentified pattern from Spode's 'Greek' series of at least twenty-five classical tableaux. The complete pattern incorporated the border panels with further tableaux, sometimes parts of larger pictures (see Cat. Ref. Case 7/1).

6. **Ewer** 22.6 cms.
Mark: impressed 'E'.
J & G Rogers, Longport, Burslem. About 1815–1835.
'Galleon at Anchor' from 'Rogers' Views' series
(see Cat. Ref. Case 10/7).

7. **Plate** 26.4 cms.
Mark: A1 and A9.
William Adams & Sons, Tunstall. About 1840–1850.
'Columbus with Fleet (Two Figures)' also known as 'Fleet Scene – Two Companions'. This is one of at least eight scenes commemorating the landing of Columbus in the New World, under the series title 'Columbus Views'.
Loaned by Dr. and Mrs. David Furniss.

8. **Tea Bowl** 8.5 × 5.0 cms.
Maker Unknown. About 1805.
One side of the bowl shows a sea battle, the other what appears to be a funeral car with Neptune and sea horses. The piece is possibly a commemorative item following the death of Lord Nelson at the Battle of Trafalgar in 1805. Another, more elaborate pattern, again by an unknown maker, is recorded as 'Neptune' or 'The Apotheosis of Nelson'.
Loaned by Mervyn Gibbs.

9. **Sauce Boat** 16.8 cms.
Mark: X22.
Maker Unknown. About 1830–1840.
'Fort and Sailing boats', a fourth scene in a small series marked 'Italian Scenery'. There are at least three other series with the same title.

10. **Scalloped Vegetable Dish** (no cover) 32.5 × 24.7 cms.
Mark: Impressed 'J & G Alcock, Cobridge'.
J & G Alcock, Cobridge. About 1840–1845.
A shipping scene outside a harbour entrance with a lighthouse and a fort. A sailing ship appears to be on the rocks with flotsam in the water.

11. **Plate** 22.3 cms.
Maker Unknown. About 1815–1825.
'Frigate II' from the 'Shipping' series of at least fourteen nautical views within a seaweed and shell border.

12. **Desk Set** including Candlesticks, Ink Wells and Pounce Pot (see plate 25) 21 × 15 cms.
Mark: W4 and 3BM impressed coded date mark.
Wedgwood, Etruria. 1910.

'Ferrara', a design introduced in 1832 which remained in production into the 20th century, showing an Italian harbour scene, said to have been engraved by William Brookes.
Loaned by Mr. and Mrs. Maclean-Eltham.

13. **Trio comprising Tea Bowl, Coffee Cup and Saucer.**
Bowl 8.5 cms. Cup 6.9 cms and Saucer 13.3 cms.
Possibly *Spode.* About 1805–1810.
'Flower Cross', sometimes known as 'Persian Quatrefoil'. Spode is not the only recorded maker of this pattern, but there are significant differences (eg the stipple background) on these pieces which may indicate that the design has been copied by another maker. The ochre rims may also point to this conclusion.

14. **Plate** 20.6 cms.
Attributed to *Baddeley, Shelton.* About 1800–1805.
'Violin' pattern (see Cat. Ref. Case 34/15), sometimes known as 'Chinoiserie Wheel'.

15. **Tea Pot** with moulded gallery and swan knop (see plate 10) 26 × 17.5 cms.
Maker Unknown. About 1800–1815.
'Violin' pattern (see Cat. Ref. Case 13/5 & 34/14), is known to have been made by at least five different firms. As the swan knop and the moulded spout and body were used by many different makers these features do not help in the identification of this piece.

16. **Saucer Dish** 15.8 cms.
Mark: W7.
Wedgwood & Co. (Ralph Wedgwood of Burslem or Ferrybridge). About 1800.
Unnamed Greek design, thought possibly to be a version of 'Hephaestus (Vulcan) Presenting Arms to Aphrodite (Venus)'.

17. **Tea Bowl and Saucer.**
Bowl 10.4 × 6.4 cms. Saucer 15.3 cms.
Maker Unknown. About 1805–1810.
Basket weave with a central Sun medallion. Ochre painted rims.

18. **Tea Bowl and Saucer.**
Bowl 8.3 cms diameter. Saucer 15.9 cms diameter.
Maker Unknown. About 1800–1805.
A geometric sheet pattern with floral reserves and a scale background. Ochre painted rims.

19. **Tea Bowl and Saucer.**
Bowl 8.9 × 5.3 cms. Saucer 13.3 cms.
Maker Unknown. About 1805–1810.
'Violin' pattern (see Cat. Ref. Case 34/15).

20. Covered **Sucrier** with satyr-head handles 9.1 × 14 cms.
Maker Unknown. About 1820–1830.
A sheet pattern of leaves, scrolls and geometric inserts on a cellular ground.

Case 35. AMERICAN SUBJECTS AND THE AMERICAN EXPORT MARKET

From the second decade of the 19th century, the Staffordshire potters enjoyed a vast market opened up in the fast-growing 'Land of Opportunity' across the Atlantic. So voracious was the market that almost anything printed in blue could be sold there, but especially in demand were historical American views and, surprisingly, named British landscapes. These subjects, printed in strong dark blue to satisfy the American taste, were produced by every potter seeking export trade in the 1820's and 1830's and today form the basis of a large collectors' market which is just beginning to re-cross the ocean to the land of its birth.

1. **Plate** 17.7 cms.
Mark: A2 and A6.
William Adams, Stoke, Staffordshire. About 1820–1830.
'Moorland Castle, Staffordshire', from the 'Bluebell Border' series of at least twenty named British views, mostly castles and abbeys, made mainly for the American market. This pattern has only recently been recorded in Britain. J. & R. Clews produced a similar series with an almost identical border. Although both series were large only one view was duplicated.
Loaned by Dr. and Mrs. David Furniss.

2. **Plate** 21.5 cms.
Mark: A3 and A8.
William Adams, Stoke. About 1827–1830.
'Villa in the Regent's Park – the Residence of the Marquis of Hertford', from the 'Regent's Park' series (see Cat. Ref. Case 26/4). This building was designed by Decimus Burton.
Loaned by Dr. and Mrs. David Furniss.

3. **Small Platter** 37.1 × 29.1 cms.
Mark: W22 and W25.
Enoch Wood & Sons, Burslem. About 1827–1830.
'The Limehouse Dock, Regent's Canal', from the 'London Views' series of about nineteen views of London. The source for this pattern is a print from Thomas Sheppard's *Metropolitan Improvements* (1827), a source also used for the William Adams 'Regent's Park' series (see Cat. Ref. Case 26/4).

4. **Coffee Pot** with domed lid.
Spout to handle 25.4 cms. Height 27.9 cms.
Enoch Wood & Sons, Burslem. About 1825–1830.
'Lafayette at Franklin's Tomb'. A very similar pattern showing Lafayette at Washington's tomb was also produced. The Marquis de Lafayette fought under both men during the War of American Independence and visited their graves during his visit to America in 1824 (see Cat. Ref. Case 35/9).
Loaned by Flora Rabinovitch.

5. **Plate** (see plate 28) 24.3 cms.
Mark: H8.
Attributed to *Joshua Heath, Hanley.* About 1790.
A portrait medallion of 'Washington – President' and a matching medallion with the American Eagle, interspersed with sea shells, all within a cellular border. A very rare and early piece.

6. **Plate** 22.4 cms.
Mark: S13 and as S14.
A. Stevenson, Cobridge. About 1820–1830.
'Faulkborn Hall', one of at least four versions, some with added portrait medallions. The 'Rose Border' series, in its basic form, included about twenty-three different views while the adapted 'Four Portrait Medallions' series contained only about twelve. The portraits on this plate are of Jefferson, Lafayette, Washington and Clinton, while the scenic vignette is of 'The Entrance of the Erie Canal into the Hudson River at Albany'.
Loaned by David and Linda Arman.

7. **Sauce Boat** 19 cms length.
Mark: Pattern name printed in blue in a cartouche.
R. Stevenson, Cobridge. About 1825–1830.
'Catholic Church, New York', from the 'American Views – Vine Border' series of at least twenty-six scenes. The Cathedral was dedicated to St. Patrick.
Loaned by David and Linda Arman.

8. **Tea Bowl and Saucer.** Bowl 8.6 cms. Saucer 13.7 cms.
J. Rogers & Son, Longport. About 1825–1830.
'Boston Harbour', a marine view with a large eagle and a shield superimposed, within a border of flowers, leaves and scrolls.
Loaned by David and Linda Arman.

9. **Tankard** 9 × 12.4 cms.
J & R Clews, Cobridge. About 1825–1830.
'Landing of Lafayette, 1824' from the 'American Views – Scroll Border' series of at least seventeen views. The Marquis of Lafayette left France in 1777 to assist the American colonists. He was then about 20 years' old and fought at Yorktown in 1782. He returned to America in 1824 to tremendous popular acclaim, by then he was a distinguished General and politician in France (see Cat. Ref. Case 35/4).
Loaned by David and Linda Arman.

10. **Two Plates** (see plate 17) 25.3 cms.
Mark: as H11.
Henshall & Co., Longport. About 1820–1828.
Two patterns from the extensive 'Fruit and Flower Border' series (see Cat. Ref. Case Kitchen/33). Both scenes depict 'The Dam and Waterworks, Philadelphia', but one incorporates a paddle steamer with sails and the other a stern-wheeler.

11. **Pickle Dish** Shell-shape 11 cms.
J & R Clews, Cobridge. About 1825–1830.
'Landing of Lafayette' (see Cat. Ref. Case 35/9).
Loaned by David and Linda Arman.

12. **Basket** (see plate 15) 27.5 × 20.4 × 13.7 cms.
Mark: C7.
J & R Clews, Cobridge. About 1825–1830.
'Landing of Lafayette' (see Cat. Ref. Case 35/9).
Loaned by David and Linda Arman.

13. **Plate** 25.7 cms.
Maker Unknown. About 1820–1835.
'Standard Willow', with vignette of a steam boat and 'North River, James Kent'. The North River Steamboat Company was incorporated by act of the legislature of the State of New York on 10th March 1820.
Loaned by David and Linda Arman.

14. **Platter** 31.7 × 25.3 cms.
Mark: W22.
Enoch Wood & Sons, Burslem. About 1825–1830.
'Erith on the Thames', from the 'Shell Border' series of about twenty views from around the world including Africa, India, Ireland and England but not America.
Loaned by Terry Sheppard.

15. **Platter** 24.4 × 19.5 cms.
Mark: C9.
J & R Clews, Cobridge. About 1820–1830.
'Belton House, Lincolnshire', from the 'American Views – States Border' series of about ten different scenes, mostly unnamed. Not all of the views are American.
Loaned by David and Linda Arman.

16. **Footed Fruit Bowl** with handles 25.3 cms.
Mark: R4.
J & W Ridgway, Shelton. About 1820–1830.
a) Outside: 'Exchange Charleston' (South Carolina).
b) Outside: 'Bank, Savannah' (Georgia).
c) Inside: 'City Hall, New York'.
From the 'Beauties of America' series of at least eight named views (see Cat. Ref. Case Kitchen/39).
Loaned by David and Linda Arman.

Case 36. ROMANTIC DESIGNS – THE LAST 150 YEARS

From the 1840's onwards the potential market for blue printed earthenware broadened to cover practically every home in Great Britain and, as part of this process, prices dropped as the manufacturers found ways of reducing production costs. This they achieved by using simpler engravings needing less work and less ink. These left a pale blue and much more white on the finished article. In turn, this resulted in a totally new-look decoration which, from its use of fanciful, fictitious scenes or scrolled or geometric patterns is now known as the 'Romantic' style.

1. **Plate** 26 cms.
Mark: R9 and R9A.
Ridgway, Morley, Wear & Co., Shelton. About 1836–1842.
'Agricultural Vase', a large vase in front of a view of Lake Memphremagog, through which runs the American/Canadian border south of Montreal. The view is adapted from a W.H. Bartlett print.

2. **Water Jug** 15.5 × 24 cms.
Maker Unknown. About 1835–1850.
Cattle grazing opposite a ruined abbey. Not identified with any recorded pattern.

3. **Mug** 12.5 × 12.5 cms.
Mark: W11.
Whitehaven Pottery, Cumbria (John Wilkinson). About 1845–1855.
'Terrace', a view of a man, woman and peacock on the terrace of a grand romantic mansion.
Loaned by Mr. A. Kessel, Whitehaven.

4. **Water Jug** 16 × 22 cms.
Maker Unknown. About 1840–1850.
A romantic landscape with some Chinese influence and the large vase of flowers which figured in many patterns of the Mid-Victorian period.

5. **Soup Plate** 24 cms.
Mark: D6 and 'DAVENPORT' printed in blue.
Davenport, Longport. About 1853.
A standard romantic pattern unidentified by name.
Loaned by Mervyn Gibbs.

6. **Breakfast Cup and Saucer.**
Cup 11.9 cms diameter, saucer 16.6 cms diameter.
Mark: M10.
J. Meir & Son, Tunstall. About 1840–1850.
'Roselle', a typical pale blue romantic pattern. Cups of this size are not common in blue printed earthenware.
Loaned by City Museum and Art Gallery, Stoke-on-Trent.

7. **Tea Pot** London-shape with flared cape and elaborate handle 25 × 13.8 cms.
Mark: R8.
Maker Unknown, but possibly *Ridgway.* About 1830–1840.
'Indian Figure', an unrecorded design in an early romantic style, printed in pale blue. The description 'Pekin China' has not so far been attributed to any particular maker.

8. **Small Plate** 17 cms.
Mark: F2 and 'Athens' in a blue printed cartouche.
T. Fell & Co., Newcastle-upon-Tyne. About 1845–1855.
'Athens', a romantic classical landscape including a ruined temple.

9. **Plate** 26.2 cms.
Mark: W28.
Wood & Challinor, Tunstall. About 1835–1840.

'Pheasant', a pattern showing pheasants in a romantic landscape including the usual urn of flowers, all within an extremely ornate border which is basically geometric but has a complicated scrolled outer edge and three scrolled cartouches containing the pheasants.

10. **Two-handled Mug** (Loving Cup) 12 × 12 cms.
Maker Unknown. About 1845–1860.
An unidentified romantic design incorporating a large fountain and a statue on a column.
Loaned by Mervyn Gibbs.

11. **Miniature Cup and Saucer.**
Cup 7.2 cms. Saucer 11.7 cms.
Mark: M16.
Robert May, Hanley. About 1830.
'Juvenile Sports', a kneeling boy playing with a top is watched by a girl in long frilly drawers. Possibly one of a series on the subject of children's play. Several potters produced patterns in this genre.

12. **Plate** 24.8 cms.
Mark: X30.
Andrew Stevenson, Cobridge (Marked piece found in 1992). About 1820–1830.
'The Trio', from the 'Stafford Gallery' series (see Cat. Ref. Case 27/10).

13. **Soup Plate** 23.4 cms.
Mark: M2.
John Marshall & Co., Bo'ness, Scotland. About 1855–1860.
'Bosphorus', one of the many romantic patterns with a Middle-Eastern flavour. Other makers also used this name.

14. **Tureen or Comport** Diamond-shape (lidless) 29.2 × 19.0 × 12.7 cms.
Mark: C8.
J & R Clews, Cobridge. About 1820–1830.
'River Scene with Fort', an Italianate view of bridge, obelisk, tower and church. An early forerunner of the romantic style which swept the market from the 1840's onwards.

15. **Tea Bowl and Saucer.**
Bowl 8.3 × 5.6 cms. Saucer 12.7 cms.
Mark: F2.
T. Fell & Co., Newcastle-upon-Tyne. About 1835–1850.
A typical romantic pattern, not so far identified with any of the named patterns known to have been used at the factory. Now called 'Swans and Vase'.

Case 37. EMULATION IS THE SINCEREST FORM OF FLATTERY

Until legislation to protect designs was enacted, a pattern was a free-for-all and in many fields of production including ceramics, plagiarism and blatant copying took place, in the sources of design as well as in designs already marketed. Consequently, as many as ten or more versions of a pattern can be found over the period of the 1820's and 1830's.

1. **Plate** 23.5 cms.
Spode, Stoke. About 1795–1805.

1A. **Plate** 23.5 cms.
Mark: W18.
Thomas Wolfe, Stoke. About 1795–1800.
'Buddleia' pattern. Both pattern and border are very similar to each other and the dating is not exact enough to answer the question 'Who copied whom?'.

2. **Rectangular Dish or Stand** 23.2 × 17.6 cms.
Mark: R13.
John Rogers & Son, Dale Hall Burslem. About 1820–1825.

2A. **Mustard Pot** with Pewter Lid 9cms high.
Mark: W6.
Wedgwood, Etruria. About 1890–1910.
'Fallow Deer', one of several patterns featuring deer in a landscape. The design originated with Rogers and was later copied at Wedgwood, who gave it the name.
Loaned by City Museum and Art Gallery, Stoke-on-Trent.

3. **Plate** 17.8 cms.
Mark: S6, S7 and as S9.
Spode, Stoke. About 1815–1825.

3A. **Plate** 22.8 cms.
Maker Unknown. About 1820–1830.
'The Hog at Bay', from the 'Indian Sporting' series (see Cat. Ref. Case 14/6). The piece by an unknown maker has a completely different border and the scene itself has been changed in several important details.
Loaned by Terry Sheppard.

4. **Footed Bowl** 29.5 × 12.7 cms.
Mark: X8.
Attributed to *John Mare, Shelton* (matching print on marked piece). About 1820.
A copy of Spode's 'Italian' pattern, printed with a cobalt blue pigment prepared from cobalt mined in Great Britain, which tended to be of higher quality than that obtained from the continent.

4A. **Plate** 24.8 cms.
Mark: S6 and S7.
Spode, Stoke. About 1820.
Spode's 'Italian' pattern, still in production today, 180 years later. At least six other makers are known to have copied this pattern.
Loaned by City Museum and Art Gallery, Stoke-on-Trent.

5. **Plate** 23.5 cms.
Mark: T8.
W & J Turner, Lane End. About 1800–1810.
Two variants of the 'Willow' pattern. The border corresponds quite closely. 'Turner's Patent' covered new recipes for earthenware and porcelain, both containing a 'new' ingredient referred to as 'Tabberner's Mine Rock', which came from Cornwall.

5A. **Plate** 23.5 cms.
Mark: M3 and M4.
G.M. & C.J. Mason, Lane Delph. About 1820–1830.

6. **Sauce Tureen**, cover and stand 17.5 × 11.1 × 6.7 cms.
Mark: F3 and F4.
Stephen Folch, Stoke. About 1820–1830.
'Blue Pheasants' pattern. The Folch factory lasted from about 1819–1830.
Footnote: Stephen Folch is said to have been, at one time, dancing master to two of the daughters of Josiah Wedgwood II.
Loaned by Jennifer Moody.

6A. **Small Sauce Boat Stand,** spearhead shape
16.2 × 11.1 cms.
Mark: M5.
G.M. & C.J. Mason, Lane Delph. About 1820–1825.

7. **Moulded Oval Dish** 36.7 × 32.9 cms.
Mark: T6.
William Turner, Lane End. About 1815–1820.

7A. **Platter** 41.8 × 31.7 cms.
Mark: H9.
Charles Heathcote & Co., Lane End. About 1818–1824.
'The Villager', with slight variations. At least three potters produced this pattern, an example being known marked 'Marsh', presumably Jacob Marsh, Burslem (about 1804–1818).

CENTRAL CASES

Case 38. Large Milk or Water Jug (see plate 9)
21.4 × 39.5 cms.
Maker Unknown although it has been attributed to Swansea in the past. About 1795–1800.
English view of a man driving cattle beside a stream in front of a farm house and outbuilding. The view is enclosed in a circular border of arrow heads and a chinoiserie border appears on the rim. This is the only 18th century example known of a jug of this size and is a very early instance of the use of European scenes on printed blue and white earthenware.

Case 39. Harvest Jug (see plate 8)
22.5 × 34.5 cms.
Attributed to *Wood and Brettell, Tunstall*. About 1820.
'Bird's Nest' pattern. These large jugs were used to carry ale or cider to groups of people at work, usually in the fields. Also known as Bellringers' Jugs.
Loaned by Anna Wolsey.

Case 40. Garden Seat 47 × 32.9 cms.
Mark: S6.
Spode, Stoke. About 1815–1825.
'Gothic Castle', a transitional pattern, repeated twice and interspersed with floral sprays (see Cat. Ref. Case 22/14).
Loaned by Terry Sheppard.

DINING ROOM

1 Esholt House

2 Holyrood House

3 Taymouth Castle

4 Wardour Castle

5 Warwick Castle

6 Wellcombe

7 Barlborough Hall

8 Cashiobury

9 Cave Castle

10 Compton Verney

11 Maxstoke Castle

12 Belvoir Castle

13 Castle Forbes

14 York Cathedral

15 Dunraven

16 Hagley

17 Shirley House

18 Luscombe

19 Greenwich

20 Harewood House

21 Hollywell Cottage   22 Wellcombe   23 Canterbury   24 Sproughton Chantry

25 Gubbins   26 Rivenhall Place   27   28

29   30   31   32

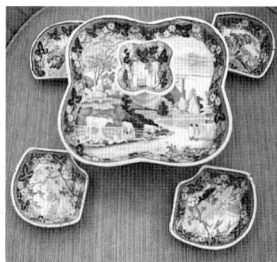

33   34   35 Dorney Court

TEA ROOM

1

2

3

4

5

6

7

8

TECHNIQUES

1

2

3

3a

Case 1. EARLY DESIGNS WITH DIRECT CHINESE INFLUENCE

1

2

3

4

5

6

7

8

9

10

11

12

13

14

15

16

17

18

19

20

97

21

22

23

24

25

26

27

28

29

30

31

32

Case 2. EUROPEAN INTERPRETATIONS OF THE CHINESE

1

2

3

4

5

6

7

8

9

10

11

12

13

14

15

16

17

18

19

20

21

22

23

24

25

26

27

28

Case 3. THE TRANSITIONAL PERIOD AND LATER REVIVED CHINOISERIE

1

2

3

4

5

6

7

8

9

10

11

12

13

14

INDIAN QUEEN

14a

KITCHEN

1

2

3

4

5

6

7

8

9

10

11

12

13

14

15a

15b

16

17

18

19

20

21

22

23

24

25   26   27   28

29   30   31   32

33   34   35   36

37   38   38   39

40   41   42   43

44

45

46

47

48

Case 4. NAMED AND DATED PIECES

1

2

3

4

5

6

7

8

9

Case 5. COMMEMORATIVE WARES

1

2

3

4

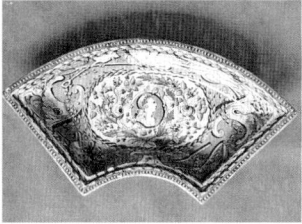

5

6

7

8

9

10

Case 6. SINGLE PATTERNS

1

2

3

4

5

6

7

8

9

Case 7. ARMORIAL PATTERNS

1

2

3

4

5

6

7

Case 8. BOY ON A BUFFALO

1   2   3   4

5   6

Case 9. SMOKING

1   2   3   4   5

Case 10. RILEY, ROGERS & WOOD

1   2   3   4

5   6   7   8

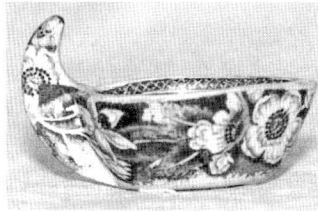

9   10   11

Case 11. DON AND DAVENPORT

1   2   3   4

5   6   7   8

9

10

11

12

13

14

15

Case 12. SCOTTISH AND WELSH POTTERIES

1

2

3

4

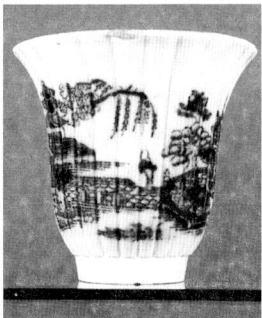

5

6

7

8

9

10

11

12

13

14

15

Case 13. YORKSHIRE AND THE NORTH EASTERN POTTERIES

1

2

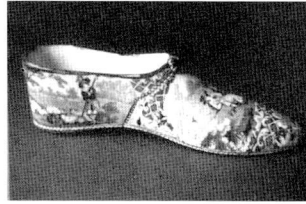

3

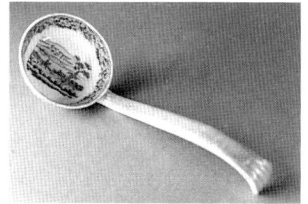

4

5

6

7

8

9   10   11

12   13   14

15   16   17

Case 14. INDIAN SPORTING

1   2   3   4

5

6

7

8

9

10

11

12

13

14

15

Case 15. MIDDLE EASTERN VIEWS

1

2

3

4

112

5

6

7

8

9

10

11

12

13a

13b

13c

13d

Case 16. EUROPEAN VIEWS

1

2

3

4

5   5a   6   7

8   9   10

11   12

Case 17. MINIATURES

1   2   3   4

5   6   7   8

9

10

11

12

13

14

15

16

17

18

19

20

21

22

23

24

25

26

27

28

29

30

31

32

33

34

35

36

37

38

39

40

41

1

2

3

4

5

6

7

8

9

10

11

12

13

14

15

16

17   18   19

Case 19. BOTANICAL

1   2   3   4

5   6   7   8

9   10   11   12

13

14

15

16

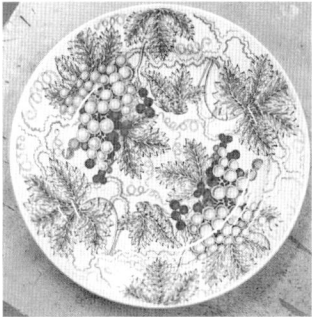

17

18

19

20

21

Case 20. QUADRUPEDS

1

2

3

4

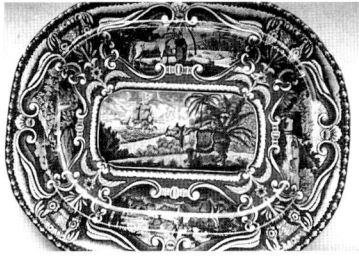

5

6

7

8

9

Case 21. ZOOLOGICAL

1

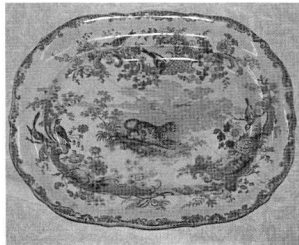

2

3

4

5

6

7

8

9

10

11

12

13

14

15

15a

Case 22. SPODE

1

2

3

4

5

6

7

8

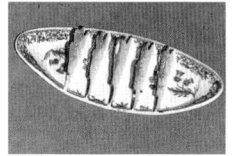

9   10   11   12   13

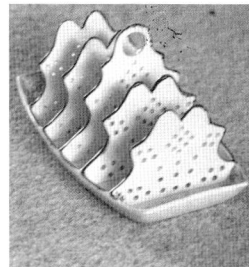

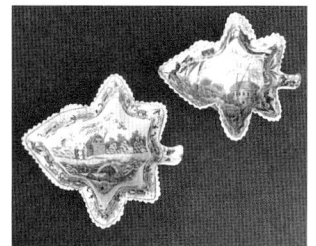

14   15   16   17 and 17A

Case 23. WILLOW AND OTHER POPULAR PATTERNS

1   2   2a   3

4   5   6   7

8

9

10

11

12

13

14

15

16

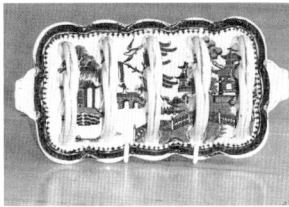

17

18

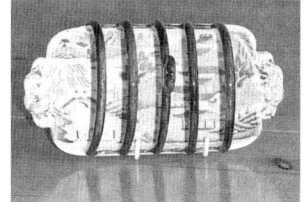

19

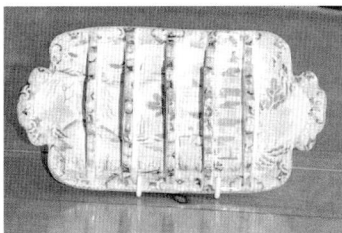

20

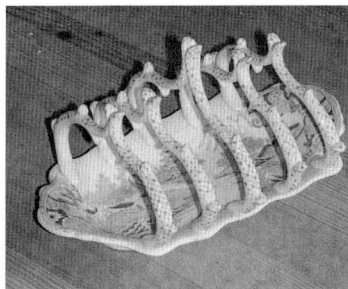

21

Case 24. WEDGWOOD

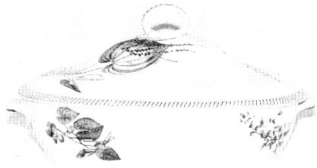

1

2

3

4

5

6

7

8

9

10

11

12

13

14

15 and 15a

16

17

18

19

20

21

22

23

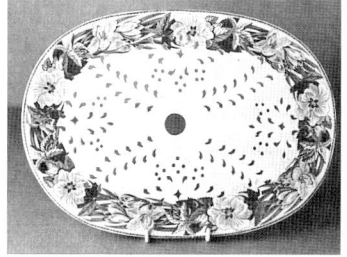

24

25

26

27

28

29

30

31

32

125

33

34

35

36

37

38

39

40

41

42

43

44

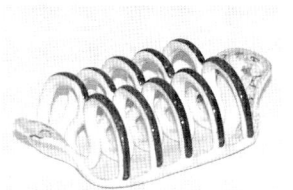

45

Case 25. COUNTRY HOUSES

1

2

3

4

5

6

7

8

9

10

11

12

13

14

15

Case 26. TOWNS AND CITIES

1

2

3

4

5   6   7   8

9   10   11   12   13

Case 27. MEDICAL

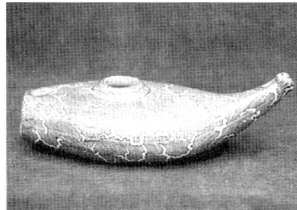

1   2   3   4

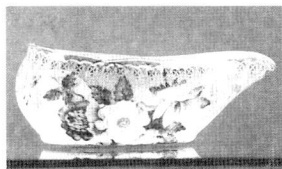

5   6   7   8

9   10   11   12   13

14   15   16   17

Case 28. NAMED VIEWS

1   2   3   4

5   6   7   7a

Case 29. CHURCHES AND COLLEGES

1   2   3   4

5   6   7   8   9

Case 30. NATURAL HISTORY, ORNITHOLOGICAL AND HUNTING/SHOOTING

1   2   3   4   5

6   7   8   9

10

11

12

13

14

15

16

17

18

19

20

21

Case 31. RURAL VIEWS

1

2

3

4

5

6

7

8

9

10

11

12

13

14

15

16

17

18

19

20

1

2

3

4

5

6

7

8

9

10

11

12

13

14

15

1

2

3

4

5

6

7

8

9

10

11

12

13

14

15

16

17

18

Case 34. CLASSICAL, GEOMETRIC AND NAUTICAL

1

2

3

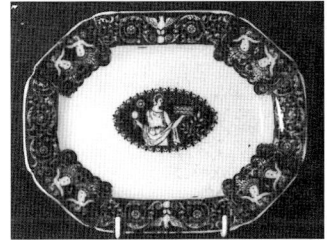

4

5

6

7

8

9

10

11

12

13

14

15

16

17

18

19

20

Case 35. AMERICAN SUBJECTS AND THE AMERICAN EXPORT MARKET

1

2

3

4

5

6

7

8

9

10

11

12

13

14

15

16

Case 36. ROMANTIC DESIGNS – THE LAST 150 YEARS

1

2

3

4

5

6

7

8

9   10   11   12

13   14   15

Case 37. EMULATION IS THE SINCEREST FORM OF FLATTERY

1   1a   2   2a

3   3a   4   4a

5   5a   6   6a

7   7a

CENTRAL CASES

CASE 38   CASE 39   CASE 40

APPENDIX A
Synopsis of the Major Potters and Factories Manufacturing
Blue Printed Earthenware During the 18th and 19th Centuries.
by Laurie Fuller

Major Staffordshire Potters:

ADAMS A large and important family of potters which, at the beginning of the 19th century, counted among its number three cousins, all named William:

William Adams, 1746–1805, worked Greengates Pottery, Tunstall, from 1779 until his death. He was an early manufacturer of blue printed earthenwares, among other products. The factory was subsequently continued by his younger son Benjamin until 1820, when it was sold.

William Adams, 1748–1831, ran the family's Brick House Works, Burslem, for a few years from 1773, along with another pottery at Cobridge. He then transferred all his potting interests to Cobridge and, by 1820, had given up production. He was said to have been among the earliest to introduce the blue printing process.

William Adams, 1772–1829, much the youngest of the three, took over the Cliff Bank Works at Stoke in 1804 and gradually made blue printed earthenwares a major part of his output.

In due time he took his three sons into partnership and, when he died in 1829, the business comprised several potteries in Stoke and was still expanding. Notable among his blue and white production is a series portraying villas in Regent's Park and other views in London, a series of castles, abbeys and stately homes with a border of bluebell flowers and a similar series with a border of flowers and leaves. A large part of his output was exported to North America.

BAGSTER John Denton Bagster ran the Church Works, Hanley, from about 1823 to 1828. A series bearing a cartouche containing a Staffordshire Knot, the series title 'Vignette', and the makers initials, IDB, shows small central reserves portraying rural scenes within a broad distinctive border of flowers and scrolls.

BARKER The brothers John, Richard and William Barker, were in partnership in a family business at Lane End from about 1786 to about 1800. Early blue printed earthenwares known are impressed BARKER.

BATHWELL & GOODFELLOW T. Bathwell and Thomas Goodfellow potted in partnership at the Upper House Works, Burslem, from about 1818 to about 1823. Between 1820 and 1822, they also worked a pottery at Tunstall. A series marked 'Rural Scenery' in a cartouche includes the impressed makers' names in an oval.

CAREY Thomas and John Carey were in partnership at the Anchor Works, Lane End, from 1823 to 1842. By the end of the partnership they may have been working two additional potteries – one at Middle Fenton and a second at Lane End. The single word, CAREY'S, is found impressed

or as part of a printed cartouche.

CHESWORTH & ROBINSON This partnership operated at Lane End between 1825 and 1840. A printed mark, C & R, may refer to this firm or to that of Chetham & Robinson, q.v.

CHETHAM & WOOLLEY James Chetham and Richard Woolley ran a pottery at Commerce Street, Longton, between about 1796 and 1809, when James Chetham died.

CHETHAM/CHETHAM & ROBINSON James Chetham's widow, Ann, continued to run the pottery at Commerce Street after her husband's death and the ending of the partnership with Richard Woolley. She took her son into the business as Chetham & Son (1810–1834) and the impressed mark CHETHAM is recorded.

From 1822 to 1837 the firm, however, was known as Chetham & Robinson and the printed mark, C & R, may refer to this partnership.

CLEWS Ralph and James Clews rented the Cobridge Works, Cobridge, from William Adams in 1817. Blue printed earthenwares of fine quality formed a large part of their output and they are particularly well known for the dark blue wares which they exported to North America. Blue printed stone china was also produced. The name CLEWS appears in various printed and impressed marks throughout the life of the firm, which went bankrupt in 1834.

COPELAND & GARRETT William Taylor Copeland became a partner at Spode when he joined his father and Josiah Spode in 1824. With the death of the senior partners in 1826 and 1827, William Taylor Copeland carried on alone until 1833, when he took his London agent into partnership and the firm became Copeland & Garrett (1833–1847). The fine quality of Spode's blue printed earthenwares continued during this period.

DAVENPORT John Davenport started his pottery at Longport in 1794 and it remained in the family as a working pottery until 1887. John himself retired from the firm in 1830. Large quantities of blue printed earthenwares were produced during his years in charge. Early Davenport pieces usually have a lustrous glaze. He is credited with producing the earliest example of a view of a stately home - 'Bisham Abbey' (c.1810).

ELKINS & CO. A firm with this title operated a pottery at Lane End from 1822–1830. It seems that there were two potters called Elkin and a third named John King

Knight. Between 1822 and 1844, these three men are recorded in several different business partnerships with each other at the Foley Potteries, Fenton:

Elkin, Knight & Co. 1822–1826
Knight, Elkin & Co. 1826–1840
(also known as Knight & Elkin)
Knight, Elkin & Knight 1841–1844
(also known as Knight, Elkin & Co.).

Initial marks are found for the different partnerships; sometimes the full title appears. A partnership of Elkin, Knight & Bridgwood (initial mark EKB) is also recorded, from about 1827–1840, at the Foley Potteries. A series of views called 'Irish Scenery' is known, marked Elkins & Co., although only English and Welsh views have, so far, been identified. A series of named views in England and Wales, the titles appearing on a ROCK CARTOUCHE, is also known, at least one example bearing the impressed mark ELKIN KNIGHT & CO. in two lines below an impressed crown.

GARNER Robert Garner operated a pottery at Lane End in 1786 but died in 1789, when his son, also Robert Garner, took over. The impressed name, GARNER, is found on early plates in 'Buddleia' pattern.

GODWIN Thomas and Benjamin Godwin were in partnership at the New Basin Pottery, Burslem, and later at the New Wharf Pottery, Burslem, possibly from 1809–1834. After 1834, Thomas Godwin continued to work the pottery alone. Printed initial marks of T & B G and T G are known, and also the full name, sometimes with the words WHARF or NEW WHARF. Thomas Godwin produced a series of American Views.

GOODWINS & HARRIS John Goodwin entered into a number of partnerships at Lane End between 1827 and 1840, one of which, Goodwins & Harris, 1831–1838, produced a series of blue printed views around London, called 'Metropolitan Scenery'.

HALL John and Ralph Hall were partners at the Sytch Pottery, Burslem, from about 1803 to 1822, and also, for a time, up to 1822, at the Swan Bank Works, Tunstall. They then dissolved the partnership.

John Hall remained at Burslem, took his sons into the business, and they became major exporters, both to Europe and to North America. Nonetheless, the business failed in 1832.

Notable series of blue printed patterns are 'Oriental Scenery', and 'Quadrupeds'. Printed marks I.HALL OR I.HALL & SONS are found.

Ralph Hall took over the Swan Bank Works, Tunstall, in 1822 and he, too, was engaged in a large export trade to America. Among the blue printed earthenwares exported was a series called 'Select Views', and another called 'Picturesque Scenery'. While the views in both these series are mainly of places in Britain, there are also a number of continental scenes. Ralph Hall died in 1836 but the firm continued until 1849, when it was taken over by Podmore, Walker & Co.

HAMILTON Robert Hamilton started potting on his own at Stoke in 1811 and continued until 1826. The extent and variety of the blue printed wares he produced is still being realised.

HARLEY Thomas Harley manufactured earthenwares at Lane End between 1802 and 1808. Blue printed tewares, particularly teapots, are known.

HARRISON George Harrison was an early manufacturer of blue printed earthenwares at Lane Delph and Fenton in the 1790's.

HARVEY Charles Harvey operated the Stafford Street Works, Longton, and another pottery in Great Charles Street, between 1799 and possibly 1818, when he retired from potting, having taken his sons into the business. The firm continued as Charles Harvey & Sons until 1835. A series of blue printed views of English and Scottish cities and towns is known, a few examples of which bear the impressed mark HARVEY.

HEATH Several potters called Heath are known to have produced blue printed earthenwares:

Joseph Heath & Co., of Newfield Pottery, Tunstall, made blue printed wares between 1828 and 1841.

Another Joseph Heath potted at High Street, Tunstall, from 1845 to 1853.

Joshua Heath of Hanley potted between about 1770 and 1800 and made early blue printed earthenwares from about 1785. Wares marked I.H. impressed are attributed to him. He is important because wares by Joshua Heath are almost certainly 18th century.

Thomas Heath potted at the Hadderidge Pottery, Burslem, from 1812 to 1835.

HEATHCOTE Charles Heathcote & Co. of Lane End made good quality blue printed earthenwares between 1818 and 1824.

HENSHALL Henshall & Co. of Longport covers a number of different partnerships between approximately 1790 and 1828. Henshall & Clowes; Henshall, Williamson & Co.; Henshall & Williamson at which point, 1828, Henshall is no longer mentioned. The only relevant mark found is HENSHALL & CO. impressed and this is rare. Their blue printed wares are of the finest quality and include a series of views in Britain and Europe using a border of fruit and flowers. Some American views also make use of the same border.

HICKS & MEIGH This partnership operated two factories in High Street, Shelton, from 1806–1822 and made very high quality stone china which is sometimes confused with Mason's Ironstone.

HICKS MEIGH & JOHNSON This partnership succeeded Hicks & Meigh at High Street, Shelton, between 1822 and 1836, continuing the same fine stone china wares. Initial marks HMJ and HM&J refer to this partnership.

JONES Elijah Jones of the Villa Pottery, Cobridge, operated between 1831 and 1839. Blue printed wares marked E.J. or just JONES probably refer to this firm.

JONES & SON This mark is known on a series of blue printed wares with the title 'British History' which numbers at least fifteen different scenes. Little is known about the firm, which operated at Hanley from 1826 to 1828.

KEELING Excavations on the site of James Keeling's pottery at New Street, Hanley, have provided sherds to identify a number of shapes and patterns produced by this potter, who operated from about 1790 to 1832.

LAKIN & POOLE Thomas Lakin and John Poole were in partnership at the Hadderidge Pottery, Burslem, from 1791 to 1795. They produced early chinoiserie blue printed wares.

LAKIN Thomas Lakin reappeared in about 1810 at Stoke, where he potted until c.1817.

MASON George Miles Mason, Charles James Mason and their elder brother, William, took over the running of their father's Minerva Pottery at Lane Delph when Miles Mason retired from the business in 1813. The Patent Ironstone China must have been fully developed at this point, since Charles Mason promptly took out the famous patent for the ironstone recipe. He, George and William had already bought the Fenton Stone Works, and George and Charles produced the new patent ironstone china there until George retired in 1829.

Charles continued the pottery as C.J. Mason & Co. until 1845, and then, by himself, until his bankruptcy in 1848.

William Mason potted at Lane Delph from 1811 until 1822. The printed mark W MASON is known but is rare.

MAYER Thomas Mayer operated Cliff Bank Works, Stoke, from about 1825 to 1835, when he moved for a few years to Longport. He is chiefly known for his export wares to North America.

MEIGH Charles Meigh, of the Old Hall Pottery, Hanley, 1835–1849, had joined the firm in about 1812 when his father, Job Meigh, who ran the pottery, took him into partnership. The firm was then styled J. Meigh & Son. Job Meigh died in 1817, but the firm's name seems to have remained unchanged until 1835, when it finally became simply Charles Meigh. Marks include C.M.; MEIGH; OLD HALL; and J.M. & S. (although these initials usually apply to J. Meir & Son). An impressed mark including the words IMPROVED STONE CHINA is also known.

MEIR John Meir took over at Greengates Pottery, Tunstall, in about 1820. In 1837, the style became John Meir & Son. Marks include MEIR impressed, and the printed initial marks I.M. & S; J.M. & S; J.M.& SON.

MINTON Thomas Minton started to operate his own pottery at Stoke in 1793. Early blue printed earthenwares were not marked and it is only recently that attributions are beginning to be made. Printed marks, including a cursive capital 'M', are found from the 1830's.

PHILLIPS Edward and George Phillips potted at Longport from approximately 1822 to 1834, at which point Edward had disappeared from the scene and George continued in sole charge until 1848. Blue printed earthenwares were produced throughout the period.

RIDGWAY The brothers, Job and George Ridgway, potted at the Bell Works, Shelton, from about 1792 until 1802, where they were early makers of blue printed earthenwares. They then dissolved the partnership and Job set up at the Cauldon Place Works, Shelton, leaving George to run the Bell Works alone until 1814, when he retired. Blue printed wares attributable to George Ridgway include the important 'Angus Seats' series.

Meanwhile, in 1808, Job Ridgway took his sons, John and William, into the Cauldon Place factory, which became theirs on the death of their father in 1814.

John and William Ridgway also took over the Bell Works when their uncle George retired in 1814 and ran both factories until they dissolved the partnership in 1830. Theirs was a most successful business and included the manufacture of very high quality blue printed earthenwares, of which the best known is probably the 'Oxford and Cambridge College' series. They had a thriving export trade with America.

In 1830, John remained at Cauldon Place while William retained the Bell Works. Both firms continued to make blue printed wares.

RILEY John and Richard Riley potted at the Nile Street Works, Burslem, from about 1802–1814. The firm then moved into the rebuilt Hill Works, Burslem, and continued until 1828, when John died, Richard having pre-deceased him in 1823.

An extensive series of British and Irish views has a wide border of flowers and large leafy scrolls and may well have been produced primarily for export to America.

ROGERS John and George Rogers potted at Dale Hall, Longport, from about 1784 to 1815, when George died. John then took his son, Spencer Rogers, into partnership and, when John died in 1816, Spencer continued to pot until 1842. Early marked blue printed earthenwares by Rogers are rare but, from c.1815 onwards, many marked pieces are to be found. Notable is their only American view, the 'Boston State House', used to decorate a dinner service and other items, and a series called 'The Drama', which shows scenes from popular plays with details of act and scene printed on the front under the picture and the series name printed on the back. At least twenty-four different scenes are known. Throughout the duration of the firm the impressed mark ROGERS in small capitals was used.

SPODE Arguably the yardstick by which all other blue printed earthenwares are judged. Josiah Spode I is reputed to have introduced underglaze blue transfer printing at his pottery in Stoke in 1784, the first in Stoke to do so. He died in 1797, to be succeeded by his son, Josiah Spode II who saw the firm through the next thirty years. Blue printed earthenwares were produced throughout. Two well known and very extensive dinner services were produced from about 1810: the 'Caramanian' and the 'Indian Sporting'. Blue printing continued during the Copeland & Garrett period of the firm, 1833–1847.

STEVENSON Two potters named Stevenson were potting at Cobridge in the early 19th century.

Andrew Stevenson was sole proprietor of a Cobridge pottery from about 1816 to 1830. He made large quantities of blue printed earthenwares, much of it for export to America, including a series of American views.

Ralph Stevenson potted at the Lower Manufactory, Cobridge, from approximately 1810 to 1832. He was joined for a short time about 1825 by a man called Williams, and this is reflected in the mark at that time. In about 1832, the style of the firm became Ralph Stevenson and Son. Ralph Stevenson was another major exporter to America and made several series of American views. Initial marks: R.S.; R.S. & S.; RSW.

TURNER John Turner of Lane End was an early producer of blue printed earthenwares. On his death in 1787, he was succeeded by his sons, John and William, until John left in 1804, by which time they had a second pottery. William continued but was made bankrupt in 1806, seemingly at the original pottery, because he continued to pot at Lane End, at a site in the High Street, until 1829. William Turner was responsible for introducing an early stone china formula for which a patent was taken out in 1800.

WEDGWOOD For a major manufacturer of long standing, Wedgwood of Etruria came late to underglaze blue printing, producing the first pattern in 1805. Josiah Wedgwood I would have none of it and it took ten years after his death, in 1795, for his two older sons, John and Josiah II, to realise that the factory needed to take up this type of decoration if it were to survive.

Famous among Wedgwood's underglaze blue output is the series of botanically accurate prints of flowers applied to the stylish Wedgwood shapes.

WOLFE Thomas Wolfe, an early manufacturer of blue printed earthenwares at his pottery at Church Street, Stoke, operated from about 1784 until his death in 1818. Between 1800 and possibly 1811, he was in partnership with Robert Hamilton. The impressed mark Wolfe is found, but very rarely, on early wares.

WOOD Enoch Wood, who came from a large and important family of potters, went into partnership with James Caldwell about 1790 at Fountain Place, Burslem. The partnership continued until 1818, when Caldwell

retired from the business and Enoch Wood's three sons then joined their father. The firm of Enoch Wood & Sons continued until 1846, although the father died in 1840. The output of blue printed earthenwares from this firm was phenomenal, much of it aimed at the American market. Most notable is the 'Grapevine Border' series, which comprises at least 64 different views, mostly of castles and stately homes, making it by far the most extensive series made by any potter.

Potters and Factories outside Staffordshire:

Bristol
POUNTNEY AND ALLIES, POUNTNEY AND GOLDNEY The partnership of John Pountney and E. Allies operated the Bristol Pottery, Temple Backs, Bristol, between 1816 and 1835. The partnership was superseded by another between John Pountney and Gabriel Goldney which lasted until 1849. Some of the patterns produced spanned both partnerships.

Liverpool
HERCULANEUM The pottery founded by Richard Abbey in 1793 was sold in 1796 to Samuel Worthington and partners, who named it Herculaneum, following the example of Wedgwood (Etruria). Blue printed earthenware formed a good part of the output throughout the period of this major pottery outside Staffordshire. After a change of ownership in 1833, to Thomas Case and John Mort, the factory continued until 1841. Notable are the 'Cherub Medallion Border' series of views, mainly of cities, and the 'India' series of views from Thomas & William Daniell's 'Oriental Scenery' aquatints. Marks include HERCULANEUM and the Liver Bird (from Liverpool's Arms) impressed.

North East
Sunderland
DIXON AUSTIN The Garrison Pottery, Sunderland, was operated between about 1820 and 1840 by the partnership, Dixon, Austin & Co., and this mark impressed is found on blue printed earthenwares.

TYNESIDE. FELL St Peter's Pottery was established in 1817 and traded as Thomas Fell & Co., whose mark, impressed curving over an anchor, is commonly found.

TYNESIDE. SEWELL St Anthony's Pottery passed into the hands of Joseph Sewell in 1804. He retired in 1819. SEWELL impressed is found on blue printed wares.

Scotland
BO'NESS. JAMIESON Bo'ness Pottery was acquired in 1836 by James Jamieson who ran the factory with others as James Jamieson & Co. until his death in 1854.

GREENOCK. MUIR The Clyde Pottery, Greenock, was built in 1816 by Andrew James Muir who operated it until probably 1840, trading as Andrew Muir & Co. It was then acquired by Thomas Shirley, who worked it until 1857.

PORTOBELLO. RATHBONE Portobello Pottery was acquired in 1810 by Thomas Rathbone who operated as Thomas Rathbone & Co. until about 1845.

GLASGOW. BELL The Glasgow Pottery was founded by John and Matthew Bell in about 1842. They are best known for their pattern 'Triumphal Car' of which there are numerous versions, some by other potteries. The factory continued until 1928.

GLASGOW. VERREVILLE GEDDES Verreville Pottery, Glasgow, was sold to John Geddes in 1806, and he remained in charge until 1834. Blue printed earthenwares are known.

Wales
CAMBRIAN POTTERY, SWANSEA George Haynes joined the Cambrian Pottery, Swansea, in about 1782, as factory manager, and proceeded to modernise and enlarge it. Blue printed earthenwares were first manufactured in the 1790's. The impressed mark SWANSEA is found.

In 1802, Lewis Weston Dillwyn joined the other partners, and the style became Haynes, Dillwyn & Co. until 1810, when Haynes left.

Two employees in the firm, Timothy Bevington and his son, John, then became partners and the style changed to Dillwyn & Co.

When Dillwyn retired in 1817, this left the Bevingtons, with others, and they traded as T. & J. Bevington & Co. until 1821. At this point the Bevingtons carried on alone until 1824.

In 1824, Lewis Weston Dillwyn took over again until 1836 when his son, Lewis Llewelyn Dillwyn took control until 1850. During this period the firm again traded as Dillwyn & Co.

GLAMORGAN POTTERY SWANSEA
BAKER, BEVANS & IRWIN This pottery adjoined the Cambrian. George Haynes, formerly of the Cambrian, joined William Baker, William Bevan, Thomas Irwin and others in 1813, and between them they acquired the premises in order to start a rival pottery, the Glamorgan Pottery Co., known locally as Baker, Bevans & Irwin. The partnership continued until 1838, when the Dillwyns at the Cambrian, finding the competition too great, bought the partners out and closed the pottery down.

Yorkshire
LEEDS OLD POTTERY Leeds Old Pottery, Jack Lane, Hunslett, famous for its creamware, was operated between 1771 and 1820 by various partnerships, giving the mark, Hartley, Greens & Co., as well as the factory name. Blue printed earthenwares were introduced in the 1790's.

LEEDS. RAINFORTH Samuel Rainforth of Holbeck built Hunslett Hall Pottery in 1800 and worked it until 1814. Blue printed earthenwares are known.

LEEDS. PETTY In about 1814, Samuel Petty and Samuel Hewitt took over and ran the Hunslett Hall Pottery until 1824 as Petty & Co. It became known as Petty's Pottery to avoid confusion with another pottery opposite.

SWINTON. BRAMELD Swinton Old Pottery had been amalgamated with Leeds Old Pottery in 1785 and John Green of the Leeds partnership of the time seems to have run both potteries. John Green withdrew, bankrupt, in 1800, however, and the connection was eventually broken in 1806, when the lease on the Swinton Pottery ran out. It was renewed by John Brameld, a partner in the firm, and his eldest son, William. Blue printed earthenwares carry the impressed mark, BRAMELD, often followed by a numeral or sign.

The firm prospered again with help from their landlord, Earl Fitzwilliam but, by 1826, was again in trouble. The Earl was again prevailed upon to help, but required conditions. The factory was renamed the Rockingham Works and the griffin of Earl Fitzwilliam became incorporated in the new mark.

SWINTON. DON The Don Pottery was set up by some of the Green family from the Leeds Pottery c.1790, and they were prominent in the partnerships which ran the pottery until 1834 when it was put up for sale. Notable among the blue printed earthenwares produced is the series of 'Named Italian Views', comprising at least thirty-five different scenes. Engravings of this series were sold in 1835 to Joseph Twigg and examples marked TWIGG are sometimes found.

CASTLEFORD POTTERY David Dunderdale and John Plowes founded the Castleford Pottery in 1790. They traded as David Dunderdale & Co., and the style remained the same throughout, although Dunderdale's partners changed. In 1820 the then partnership was dissolved and the firm ended.

KNOTTINGLEY/FERRYBRIDGE The Knottingley Pottery was built in about 1793 and traded as Tomlinson, Foster & Co., there being five partners in all. In 1798 the partners attracted Josiah Wedgwood's nephew, Ralph, to the firm, and began to mark their ware WEDGWOOD & CO.

Ralph had previously potted at Burslem and was known as talented and inventive. Unfortunately for his new partners 'his experiments and peculiar mode of firing' caused a lot of breakage and, on 1st January 1801, they let him go. Financially depleted, the pottery was mortgaged but struggled on and, in 1804, the name of the works was changed to the Ferrybridge Pottery. Blue printed wares marked FERRYBRIDGE impressed are known.

HULL The pottery, afterwards called Belle Vue Pottery, Hull, was established in 1802 by two local potters, James and Jeremiah Smith, Joseph Hipwood, also of Hull, and Job Ridgway from Staffordshire. Early wares seem not to have been marked. In 1826 William Bell bought the works and gave it the name, Belle Vue Pottery, whose printed mark is known. The pottery closed in 1841.

Stilt marks, workmen's marks and similar painted marks, size marks and those without identity significance have not been recorded. Unless otherwise stated, all marks have been applied before the glazing process has been carried out and all printed and painted marks are in blue. Where marks have been described in the main catalogue section it should be assumed that the original was not sufficiently clear to be photographed. This is found mainly where impressed marks have been incorrectly applied or have been obscured by the glaze.

Abbreviations used:
imp – impressed into the clay.
tp – printed by transfer.
st – printed by stamp.

Note: Some of the simpler printed marks may have been stamped rather than transferred. It is not easy to tell the difference.

Use of this section:
The marks are identified by maker. Indication of the method by which the mark has been applied is given in column 2 and the marks are cross-referenced to the catalogue entries in column 3.

William Adams and William Adams & Sons:
A1	imp	2/14, 23/14, 34/7.
A2	imp	Kitchen 30, 31, 32; 16/2, 17/40, 25/5, 25/6, 25/15, 35/1.
A3	imp	35/2.
A4	tp	Kitchen 31 and 32.
A5	tp	16/2.
A6	tp	35/1.
A7	tp	25/5, 25/6, 25/15.
A8	tp	Kitchen 30, 26/4, 35/2.
A9	tp	34/7.
A10	tp	3/1.

Maker Unknown:
B1	imp	16/11.

John Denton Bagster:
B2	tp

J. & M. P. Bell & Co.:
B3	tp	12/2.

G. F. Bowers:
B4	tp	27/13.

Z. Boyle & Sons:
B5	tp	27/16.

Brameld & Co.:
B6	imp	16/1.

T. & J. Carey:
C1	imp	29/6.
C2	tp	25/8, 25/9, 25/10.

Edward Challinor:
C3	tp	14/1, 14/2.
C4	tp	17/13.

Chetham:
C5	imp

Chetham & Robinson:
C6	tp

J. & R. Clews:
C7	imp	35/12.
C8	imp	36/14.
C9	imp	Kitchen 24, 28/2, 29/1, 30/21, 35/15.
C10	tp	28/2, 29/1.

A1 A2 A3 A4 A5 A6 A7 A8 A9

A10 B1 B2 B3 B4 B5 B6 C1 C2

C11   tp   33/14.
C12   tp   Kitchen 24.

Copeland & Garrett:
C13   imp   1/26, 16/3, 22/15, 33/12.
C14   tp   33/12.
C15   tp   22/15.
C16   st-slate grey 1/26.

W. T. Copeland:
C17   tp   22/9.

Davenport:
D1   imp   2/15, 11/9.
D2   imp   11/7.
D3   imp   Kitchen 8, 5/5, 11/6, 11/8.
D4   imp   11/1.
D5   tp
D6   tp & imp 36/5.
D7   tp
D8   tp   30/15.

Davies, Cockson & Wilson:
D9   imp   13/4.

Dawson & Co.:
D10   imp   17/2.

Don Pottery:
D12   imp   16/6.

David Dunderdale & Co., Castleford:
D13   imp   13/15.

Elkins & Co.:
E1   tp   Kitchen 36.

Thomas Fell:
F1   imp   27/6.
F2   imp   36/8, 36/15.

Stephen Folch:
F3   tp   37/6.
F4   tp   37/6.

Unidentified:
G1   tp   17/9.

John Geddes:
G2   imp   12/1.

Glamorgan Pottery Co.:
G3   tp   12/3.

T. & B. Godwin:
G4   imp   26/5.
G5   tp   15/8.
G6   tp/st 17/11.

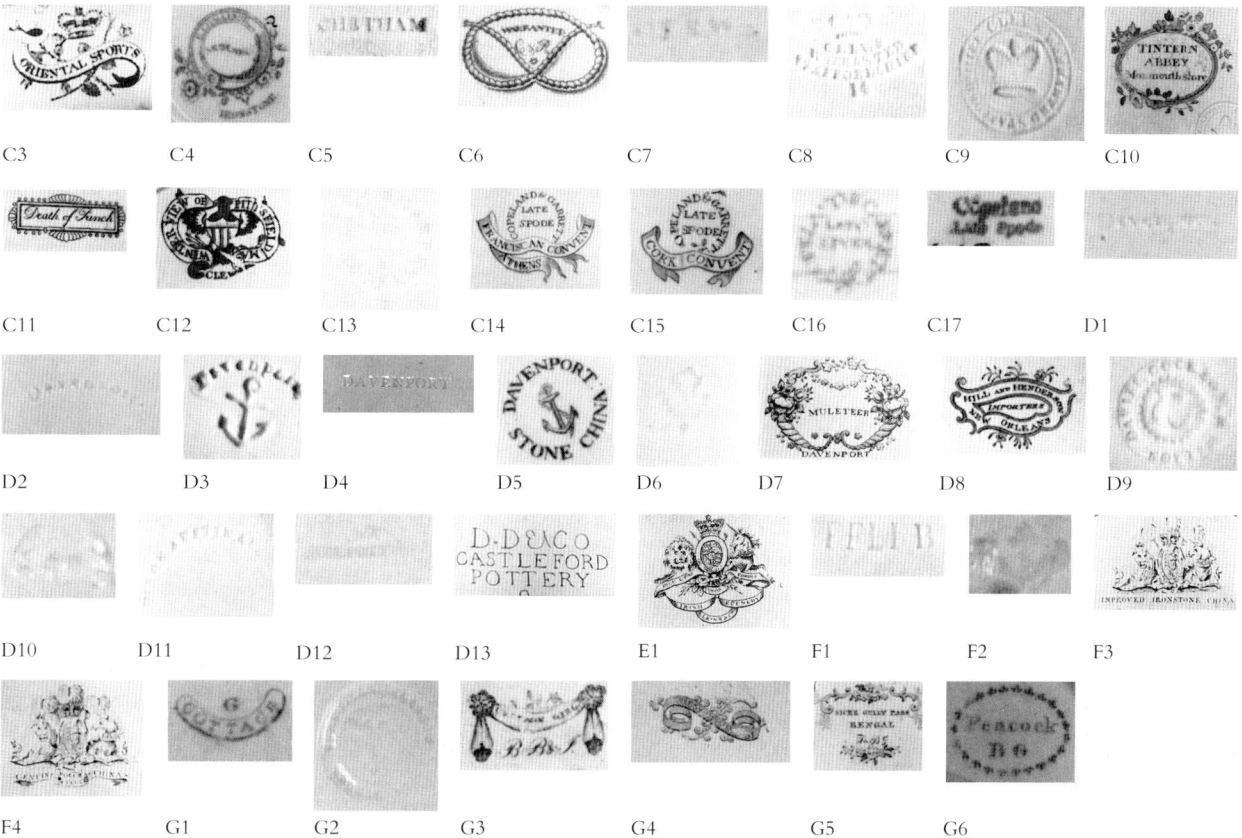

C3   C4   C5   C6   C7   C8   C9   C10

C11   C12   C13   C14   C15   C16   C17   D1

D2   D3   D4   D5   D6   D7   D8   D9

D10   D11   D12   D13   E1   F1   F2   F3

F4   G1   G2   G3   G4   G5   G6

J. & R. Godwin:
G7   tp   33/15.
G8   tp   17/10.

Goodwins & Harris:
G9   tp   26/6, 26/7 and 26/8.

William Hackwood:
H1   tp&st   Kitchen 7.

J. Hall:
H2   imp   Case 20 & 21.
H3   tp   Case 20 & 21.

R. Hall:
H4   tp   Kitchen 37.
H5   tp   29/8.

Robert Hamilton:
H6   imp   2/2.

G. Harrison:
H7   imp   1/25, 1/31.

Joshua Heath:
H8   imp   23/8, 35/5.

Heathcote & Co.:
H9   imp   37/7a.

Henshall & Co.:
H10   tp   Kitchen 17.

H10   a   tp   28/5.
H11   tp   Kitchen 16, 33; 25/7, 35/10.

Herculaneum Pottery:
H12   imp   19/11, 32/1, 32/3, 32/4, 32/5, 32/6, 33/6.
H13   tp   32/3.
H14   tp   32/3, 32/4.
H15   tp   Kitchen 29, 32/2.
H16   imp   32/2.
H17   imp   Kitchen 29, 32/7.
H18   imp   30/2.

T. & J. Hollins:
H19   imp   1/11.

J. Keeling & Co.:
K1   tp   15/7.

Lakin & Poole:
L1   imp

T. Lakin:
L2   imp   7/3.

Leeds Pottery:
L3   imp   13/1, 13/2.
L4   imp

Lockett & Hulme:
L5   tp   16/5.

J. Marshall & Co.:
M2   tp   36/13.

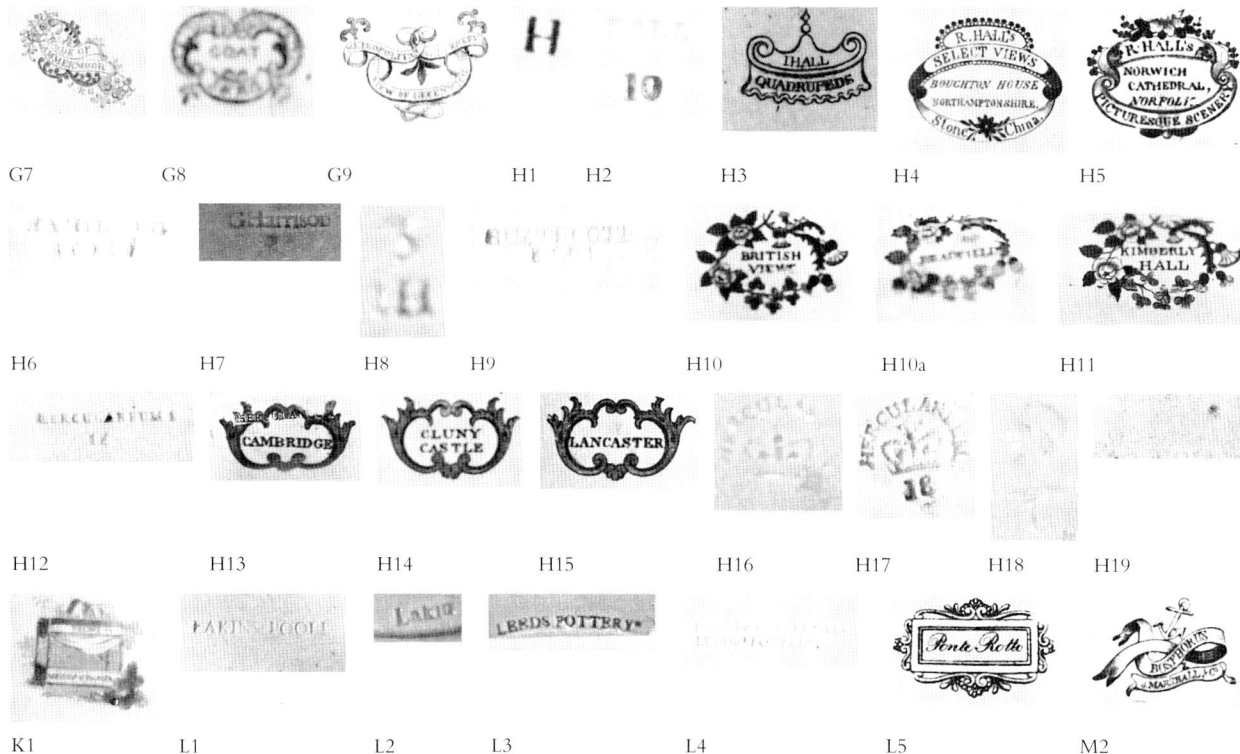

G7   G8   G9   H1   H2   H3   H4   H5

H6   H7   H8   H9   H10   H10a   H11

H12   H13   H14   H15   H16   H17   H18   H19

K1   L1   L2   L3   L4   L5   M2

G. M. & C. J. Mason:
M3 imp 37/5a.
M4 tp 37/5a.
M5 tp 37/6a.

Job Meigh & Son:
M6 tp 21/2.

J. Meir:
M7 tp Kitchen 22.
M8 tp
M9 tp Kitchen 21, 31/18.
M10 tp 36/6.

Middlesbrough Pottery:
M11 imp 13/9.

Minton:
M12 imp 23/17.
M13 tp 2/4.
M14 tp 17/20.
M15 tp 23/17.

Robert May:
M16 tp 36/11.

T. Nicholson & Co.:
N1 tp 23/3.

E. & G. Phillips:
P1 imp

Pountney & Allies:
P2 tp 26/1, 26/2.

Wedgwood & Co., Tunstall:
P3 tp 23/1.

Rainforth & Co.:
R1 imp

Ridgway:
R2 imp 19/10, 21/16.
R3 tp 29/2, 29/5, 29/9.
R4 tp Kitchen 39, 35/16.
R5 tp
R6 tp 15/4.
R7 tp 15/9.
R8 tp 36/1.
R9 imp 17/8, 36/1.
R10 tp 33/16.

J. & R. Riley:
R11 tp 33/3.
R11a imp 10/8, 33/3.
R12 imp 10/9, 10/11.
R12a tp 10/9.

J. & G. Rogers:
R13 imp 5/7, 10/7, 17/18, 21/7, 37/2.
R14 tp Kitchen 23.
R15 tp 21/7.

M3   M4   M5   M6   M7   M8   M9

M10   M11   M12   M13   M14   M15   M16   N1

P1   P2   P3   R1   R2   R3

R4   R5   R6   R7   R8   R9   R9a

R10   R11   R11a   R12   R12a   R13   R14   R15

Robinson, Wood & Brownfield:
R16   tp   21/4.

Shorthose & Co.:
S1   tp   18/17, 18/19.

J. Shorthose:
S2   tp   16/4.

Spode:
S3   imp
S4   imp   Dining room 7, 15/2, 15/3.
S5   tp   Dining room 7, 15/12, 22/6.
S6   imp   Dining room 7, Tea room 7, 7/5, 7/6, 14/3,
               14/4, 14/5, 14/6, 14/7, 14/8, 14/9, 14/10,
               14/11, 17/34, 17/35, 22/4, 22/5, 22/13,
               22/17, 23/16, 37/3, 37/4a, 40/1.
S7   tp   7/5, 7/6, 14/3, 14/4, 14/5, 14/6, 14/7, 14/8,
               14/9, 14/10, 14/11, 17/4, 17/34, 17/35,
               22/3, 22/4, 22/8, 22/10, 22/13, 22/16,
               22/17, 27/3, 27/4, 30/5, 37/3, 37/4a.
S8   tp   7/1, 15/11.
S9   tp   14/3, 14/4, 14/5, 14/6, 14/7, 14/8, 14/9,
               14/10, 37/3.
S10   tp   14/11.

A. Stevenson:
S11   imp   23/7.
S12   tp   Kitchen 18, 31/14.
S13   imp   Kitchen 35, 25/11, 28/7, 35/6.
S14   tp   Kitchen 34 and 35, 25/11, 28/7, 35/6.

R. Stevenson & Son:
S15   tp   33/8.

Swansea:
S16   imp
S17   tp   12/15.
S18   imp   19/17.

W. Smith & Co.:
S19   tp   13/16.
S20   tp&imp   13/17.
S21   tp   13/10.

South Wales Pottery:
S22   imp   17/14.

Tams, Anderson & Tams:
T1   imp   16/12.
T2   tp   28/1.

S. Tams & Co.:
T3   tp
T4   imp   26/9, 26/10, 26/11.
T5   tp   16/12.

J. Turner:
T6   imp   1/16, 23/6, 37/7.
T7   imp
T8   tp   37/5.

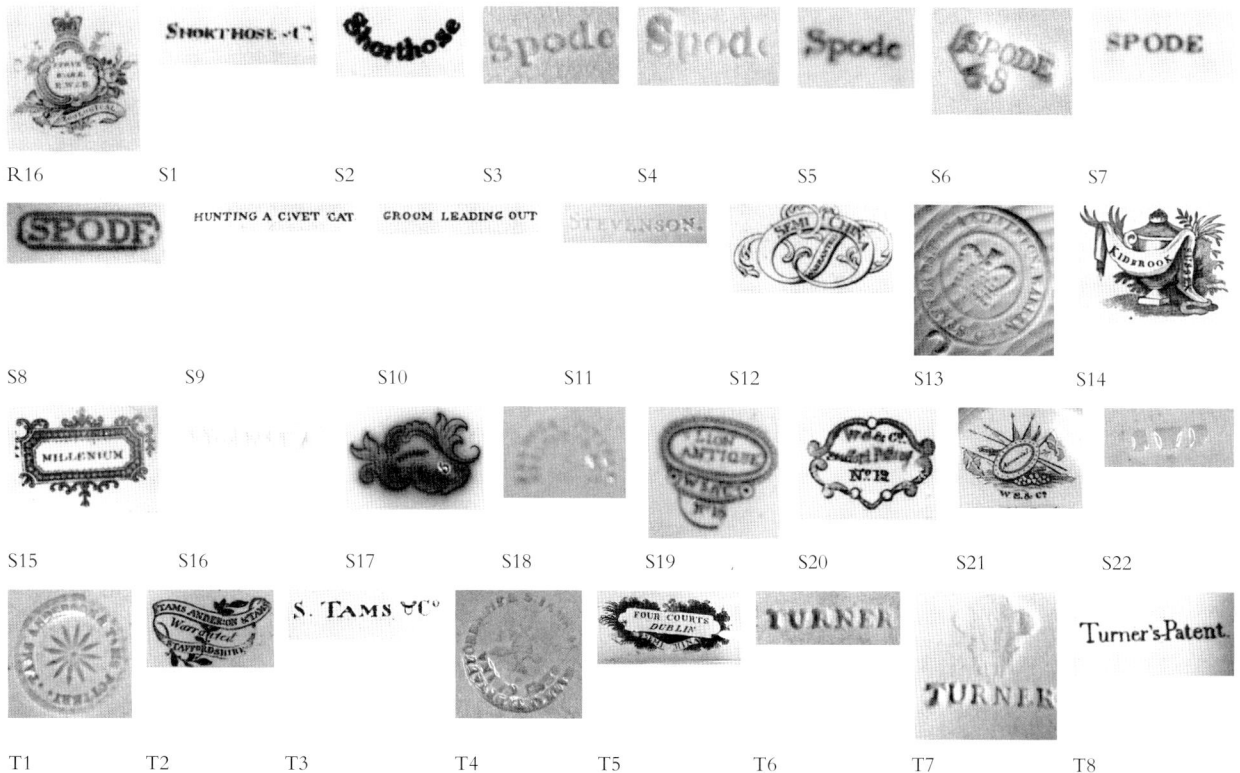

R16   S1   S2   S3   S4   S5   S6   S7

S8   S9   S10   S11   S12   S13   S14

S15   S16   S17   S18   S19   S20   S21   S22

T1   T2   T3   T4   T5   T6   T7   T8

Turpin & Co.:
T9   imp

Carr & Patton (attributed):
V1   tp   13/11.
V1a imp 13/11.

Wedgwood:
W1   imp   19/9, 24/4, 24/7, 24/12, 24/13, 24/15,
           24/17, 24/20, 24/22, 24/23, 24/24, 24/33,
           24/40, 24/41, 24/43, 24/44.
W2   imp   19/16, 24/2, 24/35, 27/17.
W3   imp   19/6, 24/3, 24/6, 24/10, 24/19, 24/25,
           24/30, 24/32, 24/45.
W4   imp   19/1, 19/18, 19/19, 24/1, 24/5, 24/8, 24/9,
           24/14, 24/16, 24/18, 24/21, 24/26, 24/27,
           24/28, 24/29, 24/34, 24/36, 24/37, 24/38,
           24/39, 24/42, 34/12.
W5   tp   24/11.
W6   tp   37/2a.

Wedgwood & Co.:
W7   imp   3/12, 34/16.
W8   imp   34/4.

Whitehaven Pottery:
W9   tp   32/9.
W10 tp   32/11.
W11 tp   36/3.

Wedgwood (continued)
W12 tp   3/2.
W13 tp   Kitchen 27.
W14 tp   32/15.
W15 tp   32/12.
W16 tp   32/13.
W17 tp

T. Wolfe:
W18 imp   37/1a.

E. Wood & Sons:
W19 imp   Dining room 10.
W20 imp   21/8, 30/9.
W21 imp
W22 imp   35/3, 35/14.
W23 tp
W24 tp   Kitchen 26, 10/1.
W25 tp   35/3.
W26 tp   10/2.

Wood & Challinor:
W27 tp
W28 tp   36/9.

Unidentified Makers and Miscellaneous:
X1   tp   26/3.
X2   tp   25/4.
X3   tp   34/1.
X4   tp   Kitchen 40, 21/1.

T9   V1   V1Aa   W1   W2   W3   W4

W5   W6   W7   W8   W9   W10   W11

W12   W13   W14   W15   W16   W17   W18

W19   W20   W21   W22   W23   W24   W25

W26   W27   W28   X1   X2   X3   X4

X5	tp	28/4.
X6	tp	Kitchen 46.
X7	tp	
X8	tp	37/4.
X9	tp	19/15, 19/21.
X10	tp	Dining room 9, 25/3, 31/15.
X11	tp	
X12	tp	
X13	tp	31/2.
X14	tp	27/1.
X15	tp	
X16	tp	25/13, 25/14.
X17	tp	30/3.
X18	tp	33/1.
X19	imp	1/9.
X20	imp	

X21	tp	
X22	tp	34/9.
X23	tp	Kitchen 11.
X24	tp	
X25	tp	5/1.
X26	tp	33/5.
X27	tp	Kitchen 44.
X28	tp	
X29	tp	23/19.
X30	tp	27/10, 36/12.
X31	tp or st	33/17.
X32	tp	
X33	tp	32/14.
X34	tp or st	1/3,1/7.
X35	imp	33/10.
X36	st	30/12

X5

X6

X7

X8

X9

X10

X11

X12

X13

X14

X15

X16

X17

X18

X19

X20

X21

X22

X23

X24

X25

X26

X27

X28

X29

X30

X31

X32

X33

X34

X35

X36

APPENDIX C
Patent Office Registration Marks
Rosalind Pulver

From 1842 until 1883 manufacturers marked their wares with a 'diamond' shaped mark to indicate that the design, shape or pattern was recorded at the British Patent Office. The ceramic category in this system was denoted by 'Class IV'. The registration by a manufacturer gave exclusive use and copyright protection for a period of three years.

The date given by decoding the diamond registration mark only indicates when the patent was lodged at the Registration Office. A popular pattern could continue in production for many years. From 1884 this method of dating registrations ceased and designs were numbered consecutively; for example Rd. 1234, or Rd. 1235.

Mark Used 1842–1867   Mark Used 1868–1883

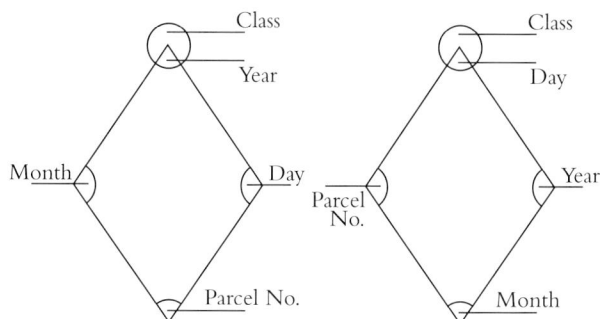

Year Letters 1842–1867

1842 X	1849 S	1856 L	1863 G
1843 H	1850 V	1857 K	1864 N
1844 C	1851 P	1858 B	1865 W
1845 A	1852 D	1859 M	1866 Q
1846 I	1853 Y	1860 Z	1867 T
1847 F	1854 J	1861 R	
1848 U	1855 E	1862 O	

Year Letters 1868–1883

1868 X	1872 I	1876 V	1880 J
1869 H	1873 F	1877 P	1881 E
1870 C	1874 U	1878 D	1882 L
1871 A	1875 S	1879 Y	1883 K

1840	J. Clementson 'Diomed', 'Classical Antiquities'
June 1841	Wedgwood 'Zodiac'
2.9.41	Edwards, James & Thomas 'Boston Mails'
9.42	Wedgwood 'Goats'
2.12.42	Clementson 'Rustic Scenery'
20.7.44	John Ridgway & Co. 'Doria'
14.10.44	Copeland 'Statice'
.44	Copeland & Garrett 'Louis Quatorze' border to 'Continental Views'
.44	Dimmock Thos. & Co. 'Lily'
.44	Knight Elkin & Co. 'Cobham Hall' ('Baronial Halls' series)
.45	William Adams & Sons 'Habana'
.45	Copeland 'Ivy'
.45	Thomas Fell & Co. 'Corinth'
25.4.45	Copeland 'Raphaelesque'
5.45	Francis Morley & Co. 'Cleopatra'
19.6.45	George Phillips 'Lobelia' (purchased later by Copeland)
26.7.45	William Adams & Sons 'Habana'
21.10.45	Copeland & Garrett 'Continental Views'
30.6.46	J. Goodwin 'Morea'
3.8.46	J. Wedgwood 'Bouquet'
14.9.46	Copeland & Garrett 'Field Sports'
21.11.46	T. Furnival 'Eagle on Globe'
16.12.46	J. Goodwin 'Rousillon'
9.1.47	Copeland 'Rose and Sprigs'
5.7.47	Mellor Venables & Co. 'Medici'
9.9.47	Copeland & Garrett 'Piccadilly'
9.9.47	W.T. Copeland 'Rose Wreath'
16.9.	Copeland 'Lily & Rose'
2.10.47	J. Ridgway & Co. 'Vintage' (grey-blue)
1.1.48	Barker & Till 'Laconia'
30.6.48	Copeland 'Alhambra'
23.8.48	John Wedge Wood 'Columbia'
26.8.48	John Meir & Son 'Roselle'
15.9.48	Copeland 'Ruins' or 'Melrose' pattern
30.9.48	J. Ridgway & Co.
3.1.49	William Adams & Sons 'Athens'
13.3.49	Clementson, Joseph 'Classical Antiquities' border segment and 'Phoemius'
2.4.49	Podmore Walker 'California'
17.8.49	Copeland 'Garland'
17.8.49	Copeland 'Convolvulus'
27.8.49	Mellor Venables 'Windsor'
22.11.49	Copeland 'Mock Orange' (Syringa)
50	J.M.P. Bell 'Iona'
9.3.50	Copeland 'Japonica'
8.4.50	Clementson 'Siam'
5.6.50	Barker & Son 'Missouri'
19.9.50	Copeland 'Rural Scenes'
20.12.50	Copeland 'Lotus'
11.6.51	Copeland 'Ionian'
19.6.51	Copeland 'Byron'
1.52	Edward Challinor 'Union'
17.2.52	Venables & Baines 'Union'
16.5.52	Copeland 'Fleur-de-Lys' (green)
14.6.52	Copeland 'Tuscan'
4.8.52	Copeland 'Fleur de Lys'
1.10.52	Copeland 'Strawberry'
30.10.52	Marple Turner 'Athena'
4.11.52	J. Holland 'Carrara'
3.1.53	Copeland 'Honeycomb'
10.2.53	Wooliscroft, George 'Eon'
24.6.53	Wolliscroft
8.8.53	A. Shaw 'Peruvian Horse Hunt'
7.4.55	Copeland 'Honeysuckle Empire'

GLOSSARY OF TERMS
by John Potter

ACANTHUS Plant with spiked leaves, used from Classical times as a decorative motif.

ANTHEMION Stylised decorative motif, based on the honeysuckle plant.

ARMORIAL WARE Ceramic items decorated with a family crest or coat-of-arms.

ASHET/ACHETTE Scottish term for a dish or platter.

ASPARAGUS HOLDER/SERVER Small flat, tapered trough with upturned sides and open ends, used for conveying asparagus stalks from a serving dish.

BACK STAMP Colloquial term for a maker's mark on the reverse of a ceramic item (see 'Marks').

BALL CLAY Clay, obtained mainly from S.W. England, which fires to a light colour and gives strength and plasticity to a ceramic body.

BALUSTER Shape, used for vases and similar objects, taken from the upright supports of a balustrade.

BAT PRINTING A method of transfer printing developed in about 1774. A copper-plate engraving forms the source of the design but instead of transferring coloured ink directly by means of tissue paper the outlines of the pattern are transferred, by means of a gelatine bat, in oil over which the appropriate colour is then dusted (see 'Transfer Printing').

BISCUIT Ceramic ware which has been fired once to induce permanent chemical changes in the clay, thus rendering it suitable for glazing and/or decorating.

BLUE Colour derived from cobalt oxide. The first colour to be controlled to withstand high temperature firing.

BODY The mixed material, containing various clays and additives, from which each different type of ceramic ware is fashioned, eg porcelain, earthenware, stoneware, etc. The many slightly changed recipes enabled manufacturers to market their products under different trade names.

BORDER That part of a design which decorates the outside edges or rim of an item of ware. Series of central patterns were frequently linked by a common border.

BOURDALOU Ladies' comfort pot, narrow oval in shape, originating in France and named, according to legend, after a French cleric notorious for his long sermons. Also known as 'coach pot', for use on long journeys.

BUTE Name given to a specific shape of cup, thought to have been named after the Earl of Bute and in general use from about 1795–1820.

CABARET SET A set of ceramic ware comprising tray, teapot, sucrier, cream jug and one cup and saucer (solitaire) or two cups and saucers (tête-a-tête).

CACHEPOT French term for a plant pot holder.

CARTOUCHE Scrolled ornamental panel often used as a frame for a mark on ceramics.

CASTING Method of forming a pot shape by pouring liquid clay (slip) into a plaster mould, which absorbs water from the solution and builds up a deposit of clay on its inner surface. When this deposit has reached an appropriate thickness, the surplus slip is poured off and the clay left to harden before the mould is removed.

CHEESE HARD The consistency of clay after some of its moisture has been evaporated, leaving it still workable. Sometimes called 'leather hard'.

CHINA A term used originally to describe porcelains imported from China, but now taken to mean any porcelain body.

CHINA CLAY The English term for kaolin, a white clay derived from decomposed granite. The main English deposits are in Cornwall.

CHINOISERIE Designs on printed ceramics, derived directly from Oriental sources or done in the Oriental style to include pseudo-Chinese figures, pagodas landscapes, etc, sometimes entering the realms of fantasy. Around 1800 patterns on earthenwares entered a phase known as 'transitional' in which the basic Oriental appearance was retained but European elements such as figures, dress, buildings or landscapes were incorporated.

CLOBBERING The addition of enamel colours painted overglaze on blue and white transfer printed earthenwares.

COBALT OXIDE The source of the blue colouring used initially in the Middle East and China as a ceramic stain and copied on early European ceramics (see 'Zaffre').

154

COMPORT A form of dessert dish, usually on a stem or pedestal base.

COSTREL See 'Pilgrim Bottle'.

COW CREAMER A Staffordshire form of milk or cream jug, popular in the 18th and 19th centuries, in the shape of a cow. The jug is filled by means of a lidded opening in the back and the contents poured through the animal's mouth, using the tail as a handle.

CRABSTOCK A Staffordshire design for handles (also used for spouts), in the form of knotted and twisted tree branches.

CRAZING Fine surface cracks in glazes, usually caused by different shrinkage rates between body and glaze.

DECORATION The improvement of the appearance of a ceramic item by the application of colour, gilding, etc, by painting or printing or the use of different coloured clay or glaze.

DESSERT SERVICE A set of plates, serving dishes, bowls, etc specially adapted for serving desserts and usually separate from the dinner service.

DRAINER A flat, pierced tray which rests on the bottom of a dish or plate and allows the juices of meat or fish to drain through and remain in the main vessel (see 'Well and Tree').

EARTHENWARE Pottery made from common clays and fired to a point at which it is hard and opaque but neither vitrified nor porous, thus rendering glazing necessary for use with liquids.

ENGRAVING The incising of a design into a copper plate so that it may be transferred to the surface of another object, generally by the use either of tissue paper or a bat of gelatine. The transfer medium, eg ink or oil, is forced into the grooves of the engraving and lifted out under pressure by means of the paper or bat (see 'Transfer printing'). The reproduction of designs improved substantially between the 1760's and 1820. Early transfer printing relied entirely on single line engraving, being improved towards the end of the 18th century by cross-hatching. Around 1800, the introduction of stippling (punching small dots into the copper plate) facilitated the use of perspective, which was again improved by the addition of partial etching, where the grooves in the copper plate were shallower and produced a fainter image.

ENAMEL A pigment of a vitreous nature, usually derived from metallic oxide, applied as decoration.

EVERTED Turned outwards – often used to describe the rims of holloware items.

EWER Large jug used for holding water and other liquids (see 'Toilet set').

FETTLING A pottery manufacturing process to remove (by hand) from unfired ware such blemishes as marks left by the removal of moulds.

FINIAL Term usually used for the knop or handle of a tea or coffee pot lid.

FIRING The process of hardening objects from the raw clay state by exposure in a kiln to the temperature appropriate to the type of ware.

FLATWARE Shallow articles such as dishes, plates, saucers etc (see 'Hollow Ware').

FLOWER BRICK Rectangular container used for floral arrangement.

FLOW(N) BLUE Cobalt oxide colour induced to flow into the surrounding glaze by firing in a chlorinated atmosphere. Popular during the second half of the 19th century, especially in America.

FOOT RIM The raised ring on which an object such as a cup or plate stands in order to keep it level, or to reduce the area which actually touches the surface beneath and thus avoid heat damage.

FROG MUG A drinking vessel in which a frog is modelled on the base inside so it either appears as the liquid is consumed or in some cases actually spits liquid at the drinker. Popular in the 18th and 19th centuries in Staffordshire and sometimes extended to include toads, newts etc.

GADROON An ornamental edge of repeated fluting, much in vogue on silverware. Not introduced in ceramics until the early 1820's.

GARNITURE A set of vases or ornaments usually to decorate a mantelpiece.

GILDING Decoration with applied gold.

GLAZE A glass-like mixture of variable constituency, applied by dipping or spraying to give a smooth brilliant surface which also protects against porosity.

HARDENING-ON Firing underglaze decoration at a low temperature sufficient to fix the design before glazing.

HOLLOW WARE Hollow articles such as cups, jugs, bowls etc (see 'Flatware').

IMPRESSED Describes a mark indented into unfired clay by means of a stamp.

IRONSTONE Term first used by C.J. Mason in 1813 to describe a type of opaque stone china. Subsequently used in many other trade names as an indication of durability, together with similar terms such as 'granite'.

JIGGER Mechanical method of forming flatware (see 'Jolley').

JOLLEY Mechanical method of shaping hollow ware (see 'Jigger').

KAOLIN White clay consisting almost entirely of aluminium silicate; an essential ingredient of true (Oriental) porcelain.

KNOP The knob on a lid (see 'Finial').

LANGE LIJSEN Literally 'slender maidens' – tall slender female figures appearing on Oriental porcelain and copied in Holland. In English – 'Long Elizas'.

LONDON SHAPE A style of tea ware first introduced around 1815 and in general use until about 1840. Probably the most common cup shape of the 19th century, with a very distinctive square hooked handle.

LOVING CUP A two-handled beaker (see 'Tyg').

MARKS Symbols (numbers, letters, words and simple pictures) appearing on ceramic pieces to denote such things as manufacturer, pattern, and other information relating to the production of the item.

MONTEITH A deep bowl with a scalloped edge on which wine glasses may be hung for cooling in iced water. It has also been suggested that the vessel could possibly be used for warming brandy glasses.

MOULD A form in which items may be shaped identically, from either solid or liquid clay. Often made of Plaster-of-Paris, which absorbs moisture from the clay.

MURRAY-CURVEX A modern method (patented in 1955) of printing directly onto ceramic ware from a design engraved on a copper plate.

NANKIN A term sometimes used in Staffordshire to describe a pattern or border in an Oriental style.

OPAQUE PORCELAIN A completely contradictory term used by Staffordshire makers to impute quality to an earthenware article. One of the usual qualities of porcelain is of course its translucency.

OVERGLAZE Decoration applied to an article which has already been glazed and fired.

PAINTED Decoration applied by hand with a brush. This may be over or under the glaze.

PAP BOAT A small boat-shaped vessel to hold a warm milk drink. Apparently used not only for babies' food but also for drinks fortified with alcohol.

PEARLWARE White earthenware with a glaze which has been artificially whitened by the addition of cobalt, sometimes leaving pools of colour inside footrims.

PILGRIM BOTTLE A flat, circular water bottle with lugs at the neck to take a carrying cord.

PIPKIN A small cooking dish with one or two lug handles, usually used for sauces, also can refer to a small pot, usually circular, used for warming brandy and other spirits.

PLINTH The base or foot of a vase or similar ornament.

PORCELAIN A form of ceramic body whose main usual property is translucency. True (Oriental) porcelain is a mixture of china clay and china stone, both derived from decomposed granite, but the term is also applied to other variant recipes including such ingredients as felspar, steatite or calcined animal bone (bone china). The Oriental style of porcelain is referred to as hard-paste and the other types as soft-paste, the descriptions implying respectively a higher and a slightly lower degree of firing.

POTTERY Now used as a generic term for all ceramic wares, but more specifically to denote wares other than porcelain.

PUZZLE JUG A novelty shape popular in the 18th century. The jug rim and handle are hollow with spouts and external holes and the objective was to drain the vessel without pouring the liquid over oneself. In order to do this it was necessary to know which holes needed to be stopped up with the fingers so that the liquid would emerge through one of the spouts.

QUINTAL A fan-shaped flower container, sometimes known as a finger-vase.

RESERVE A blank space within a decorated surface, usually intended for a name or some other wording, or perhaps a crest or coat-of-arms.

SAGGAR A box of coarse clay into which items for firing were placed for protection from the direct flame of the kiln. Believed to be derived from safeguard.

SALT A small open pot, often circular or block shaped to hold salt for table use. A table setting of the late 18th century would normally include individual salts for each place.

SHEET PATTERN An all-over design without a border. Such patterns could be used for pieces of all shapes or sizes and eliminated the need to make separate engraved copper plates according to the size of the object concerned.

SLIP Clay or clay based mixtures suspended in water to give a creamy consistency.

SPARROW-BEAK A pointed, triangular jug lip ideally suited to pouring liquids.

SPILL VASE Vase-like pot, usually cylindrical, to hold spills or tapers.

STILT MARKS Small dotted imperfections found on the base or upper rim of plates, etc. where the item concerned has been supported in the kiln by small pegs of refractory clay.

STONE CHINA See 'Stoneware'.

STONEWARE Wares formed from a mixture of various clays and additives such as calcined flint and fired to a higher temperature than earthenware, to the point of vitrification and sometimes, if thinly potted, translucency.

STRINGING Narrow bands of decoration used on the outer edge of pieces, or sometimes as a division between sections of a design.

SUCRIER French term for a sugar bowl, basin or box.

TEA BOWL A handleless cup, as originally used in China and Japan.

TERMINAL The joint at the lower end of a handle, sometimes ornamented with moulding or sprigged decoration.

THROWING The formation of a pot by working the clay by hand on a rotating wheel.

TOILET SET A set of pieces designed for use on a wash-stand, and usually including such items as washbowl, ewer, slop-pail, soapdish, razor box and toothbrush holder.

TRANSFER PRINTING The process of decorating a ceramic object by the transfer of a design engraved into a copper plate. The standard method of transferral was by the use of ink and tissue paper (see 'Bat Printing' and 'Engraving').

TRANSITIONAL See 'Chinoiserie'.

TURNING The process of smoothing or incising decoration on a pot on a lathe.

TWIFFLER Term for a small plate, usually about 8 inches in diameter, and having a slightly raised rim.

UNDERGLAZE Decoration applied to a pot before the glazing process, which then acts as a protective coating to the design.

UNDERGLAZE COLOURS Metal oxide colours which are able to withstand the heat of the firing of the glaze. Originally only cobalt (blue) was used, but many other oxides followed later, eg manganese (black), copper (red or green) and chrome (green).

WELL & TREE A system of channelling often found in large meat or fish dishes, in which a frond or branch pattern of grooves feeds into a central channel down the length of the dish, thus draining the juices into a well at one end.

ZAFFRE An impure cobalt oxide which can be used for colouring but is usually refined to produce a better result.

Selected Reading

This is not a comprehensive bibliography of works on the subject of blue and white transfer printed earthenware, but is intended as a list of suggested further reading.

Baker, John C. *Sunderland Pottery.* Tyne & Wear County Council Museums, Sunderland. 1983.

Barber, Edwin Atlee. *Anglo-American Pottery.* 1899. Indianapolis.

Berthoud, Michael. *A Compendium of British Cups.* Micawber Publications, Broseley, Shropshire. 1990.

Blake Roberts, Gaye. *Mason's, The First Two Hundred Years* – Exhibition Catalogue. 1996. Merrell Holberton Publishers Ltd, London.

Collard, Elizabeth. *The Potters' View of Canada.* McGill-Queen's University Press. Montreal, 1983.

Collard, Elizabeth. *Nineteenth Century Pottery and Porcelain in Canada.* McGill University, Montreal, 1967 (pp. 212–13).

Copeland, Robert. *Spode's Willow Pattern & Other Designs after the Chinese.* Studio Vista Cassell, London, 1980, 1990.

Copeland, Robert. *Blue and White Transfer-Printed Pottery.* Shire Album 97, Buckinghamshire. 1982.

Copeland, Robert. *Spode & Copeland Marks.* Studio Vista, 1993.

Coysh, A.W. *Blue and White Transfer Ware, 1780–1840.* David & Charles, Newton Abbot. 1970.

Coysh, A.W. *Blue and White Transfer Ware, 1800–1850.* David & Charles, Newton Abbot. 1972.

Coysh, A.W. and Henrywood R.K. *The Dictionary of Blue and White Printed Pottery, 1780–1880.* Volume I, Antique Collectors' Club, Woodbridge. 1982. Volume II, Antique Collectors' Club, Woodbridge. 1989.

Cushion, J.P. & Margaret. *A Collector's History of British Porcelain.* Antique Collectors' Club, Woodbridge. 1992.

Cushion, J.P. and Honey, W.B. *Handbook of Pottery & Porcelain Marks.* Faber & Faber, 1983.

Deane, Phyllis. *The First Industrial Revolution.* Cambridge University Press, Cambridge. 1965.

Drakard, D. & Holdaway, P. *Spode Printed Ware.* Longmans, London, 1983.

Drakard, D. *Teaware of Josiah Spode I.* The Spode Society Recorder, Volume 1, 7–11. 1988.

Dudson, Audrey M. *Dudson, A Family of Potters since 1800.* Dudson Publications Ltd., Hanley, Staffordshire. 1985.

Edmundson, R.S. *Bradley & Co: Coalport Pottery: 1796–1800.* Northern Ceramic Society Journal Volume 4, 127–156. 1981.

Ewins, Neil. *Supplying the Present Wants of Our Yankee Cousins . . . Staffordshire Ceramics and the American Market 1775–1880.* Journal of Ceramic History Volume 15. City Museum & Art Gallery, Stoke-on-Trent. 1997.

des Fontaines, U. *The Darwin Service and the First Printed Floral Patterns at Etruria.* Proceedings of The Wedgwood Society Number 6, 69–90. 1966.

des Fontaines, U. *Early printed Patterns at Etruria.* Proceedings of The Wedgwood Society Number 9, 1–21. 1975.

Friends of Blue Bulletins and Occasional Papers.

Godden, Geoffrey A. *Caughley & Worcester Porcelains 1775–1800.* Herbert Jenkins, London. 1969.

Godden, Geoffrey A. *Encyclopedia of British Pottery and Porcelain Marks.* Barrie & Jenkins, 1977.

Halfpenny, Pat. *Penny Plain, Twopence Coloured.* Exhibition Catalogue. City Museum & Art Gallery, Stoke-on-Trent. 1994.

Hampson, Rodney. *Longton Potters, 1700–1865.* City Museum & Art Gallery, Stoke-on-Trent. Journal of Ceramic History Volume 14, 1990.

Holdaway J.C. *The Influence of 18th Century Naturalists in Ceramic Decoration.* English Ceramic Circle Transactions Volume 12 part 1, 1–5. 1984

Holdaway J.C. *Explorers as a Source of Ceramic Design.* English Circle Transactions, Volume 13, part 1, 36–40. 1987.

Holdaway J.C. *Bewick Vignettes on Ceramics.* English Circle Transactions, Volume 13, part 3, 172–175. 1989.

Holdaway J.C. *A Popular Source of Animal Prints, circa 1805.* English Circle Transactions. Volume 14, part 3, 283–292. 1992.

Holdaway J.C. Derby Porcelain International Society Journal 3. 1996.

Holdaway, W.A.M. *Late 18th Century Earthenwares, Blue-printed Buffalo pattern.* Morley College Ceramic Circle Bulletin, Volume 1, Number 3. 1980.

Holdaway, W.A.M. *The Wares of Ralph Wedgwood,* English Ceramic Circle Transactions, Volume 12, Part 3, 255–264. 1986.

Holdaway, W.A.M. *The Influence of Contemporary Porcelain on late 18th Century Blue-printed Earthenware Designs.* English Ceramic Circle Transactions, Volume 14, Part 2, 199–208. 1991.

Holdaway, W.A.M. *Eighteenth Century Blue-printed Earthenware Designs.* English Ceramic Circle Transactions Volume 12, Part 3, 199–209. 1991.

Holdaway, W.A.M. *Rogers Blue Printed Earthenwares 1780+ to 1842.* Friends of Blue Occasional Papers, Number 2, 1–22. 1992.

Jewitt, Llewellynn. *Ceramic Art of Great Britain.* J.S. Virtue & Co., Limited, London. 1883.

Kelly, A. *Wedgwood Ware.* Ward Lock, London & Sydney. 1970.

Lawrence, Heather. *Yorkshire Pots and Potteries.* David & Charles, 1974.

Larsen, Ellouise Baker. *American Historical Views on Staffordshire China.* Garden City, New York, 1939 (Reprinted in 1950).

Ledger, A. *Derby Botanical Dessert Services 1791–1811.* Derby Porcelain International Society Journal II, 79–102. 1991.

Little, W.L. *Staffordshire Blue.* B.T. Batsford, Ltd. 1969.

Lockett, Terence A. and Godden, Geoffrey A. *Davenport China, Earthenware and Glass, 1794–1887.* Barrie & Jenkins, 1989.

Mantoux, Paul. *The Industrial Revolution in the Eighteenth Century.* 1964. First published in English in 1928 by Jonathan Cape; Revised 1961. 1966 edition used; University Paperbacks, Methuen & Co. Ltd., London.

May, J. & J. *Commemorative Pottery.* Heinemann, London. 1972.

Miller, George L. *Marketing Ceramics in North America. An Introduction.* Winterthur Portfolio Volume 19, No. 1. Spring 1984. Henry Francis du Pont Winterthur Museum, by University of Chicago Press.

Miller, George L.; Martin, Ann S. and Dickinson, Nancy S. *Changing Consumption Patterns. English Ceramics and the American Market from 1770 to 1840.* From 'Everyday Life in the Early Republic'. Winterthur Museum. Delaware. 1994.

Miller, Philip and Berthoud, Michael. *An Anthology of British Teapots.* Micawber Publications, Broseley, Shropshire. 1985.

Northern Ceramic Society Newsletters and Journals.

Pomfret, Roger. *John & Richard Riley, China & Earthenware Manufacturers.* City Museum & Art Gallery, Stoke-on-Trent, Journal of Ceramic History Volume 13, 1988.

Reilly, Robin. *Wedgwood* (2 Volumes). Stockton Press, London, 1989.

Reilly, Robin and Savage, George. *The Dictionary of Wedgwood.* Antique Collectors' Club, Woodbridge. 1980.

Rogers, Connie. *Willow Ware Made in the USA. An Identification Guide.* Published by the author. 1733 Chase Avenue, Cincinnati, Ohio 45223. 1995/1996.

Roussel, Diana Edwards. *The Castleford Pottery, 1790–1821.* Wakefield Historical Publications, Wakefield. 1982.

Shaw, Simeon. *History of the Staffordshire Potteries.* 1829.

Shaw, J.T. (edited by). *The Potteries of Sunderland and District.* Sunderland Public Libraries, Museum & Art Gallery, 1968.

Slosson, Annie Trumbull. The China Hunters Club. New York, 1878.

Smith, Alan. *The Illustrated Guide to Liverpool Herculaneum Pottery.* Barrie & Jenkins, 1970.

Tippett, Paul. *Blue & White China, The Connoisseur's Guide.* Christie's Collectables. Little, Brown & Co., London. 1997.

Trevelyan, G.M. *English Social History.* Longmans Green, London. 1944.

Watney, B. *English Blue & White Porcelain of the Eighteenth Century.* Faber & Faber, London, 1973.

Whiter, L. *Spode.* Barrie & Jenkins, London, 1970.

Williams, Petra. *Staffordshire Romantic Transfer Patterns. Cup Plates and early Victorian China.* Fountain House East, Jeffersontown, Kentucky. 1978.

Williams, Petra. *Flow Blue China. An aid to identification.* Fountain House East, Jeffersontown, Kentucky. 1971.

Williams, Petra. *Flow Blue China. An aid to identification.* Revised Edition. Fountain House East, Jeffersontown, Kentucky. 1981.

Williams, S.H. & Price, P.D. *Swansea Blue & White Pottery.* 1972. Antique Collecting Volume 7, Numbers 1, 2 and 3.

Williams, Sydney B. *Antique Blue and White Spode.* Omega Books, Batsford, London. 1943 (Reprinted in 1987).

Index of Named Manufacturers Included in the Exhibition

Maker	Case Number	Maker	Case Number
B. Godwin	17	Ridgway, Morley, Wear & Co.	36
J. & R. Godwin	17, 33	Job Ridgway	1, 19
Thomas Godwin	Kitchen, 15, 21, 26, 33	J. & W. Ridgway	Kitchen, Dining room, 15, 18, 21, 25, 27, 29, 31, 35
Goodwins & Harris	26		
J. Goodwin	32	W. Ridgway	17, 33
Griffiths, Beardmore & Birks	31	J. & R. Riley	3, 10, 25, 33
William Hackwood	Kitchen	Robinson, Wood & Brownfield	21
J. Hall (& Sons)	20	J. Rogers & Son	5, 10, 15, 17, 21, 28, 34, 35, 37
Ralph Hall	Kitchen, 29		
Robert Hamilton	Techniques, 2	Scottish makers	12
J. & W. Handley	31	Sewell & Donkin	13
G. Harrison	1	John Shorthose	16
J. Heath	1, 23, 35	Shorthose & Co.	9, 18
C. Heathcote & Co.	17, 37	William Smith & Co.	13
Henshall & Co.	Kitchen, 25, 28, 35	South Wales Pottery	17
Herculaneum Pottery	Kitchen, 15, 19, 23, 30, 32, 33	Spode	Dining room, Tea room, 1, 2, 7, 8, 14, 15, 17, 22, 23, 27, 30, 34, 37, 40
T. & J. Hollins	1		
Jones & Son	33		
James Keeling & Co.	Dining room, 15	Andrew Stevenson	Kitchen, 23, 25, 27, 28, 30, 35, 36
Thomas Lakin	7		
Leeds Pottery	Dining room, 13, 17, 30, 31	Ralph Stevenson	Kitchen, 30, 31, 33, 35
Lockett & Hulme	16	Joseph Stubbs	30
Robert Maling	13	Swansea	1, 3, 4, 12
John Mare	37	Swinton	13
John Marshall	36	S. Tams & Co.	26
G.M. & C.J. Mason	2, 37	Tams, Anderson & Tams	16, 28
William Mason	28	John Thomson	5
Robert May	36	Toft & May	21
Job Meigh & Son	20, 21	W. & J. Turner	1, 37
J. Meir (& Son)	Kitchen, 17, 28, 31, 36	J. Turner	23
		Joseph Twigg	3
David Methven & Sons	12	Enoch Wedgwood	23
Middlesbrough	13	Wedgwood, Etruria	19, 24, 27, 30, 34, 37
Minton	2, 7, 17, 23, 27	Ralph Wedgwood	3, 13, 34
Thomas Nicholson & Co.	23	Welsh makers	12, 17
North-Eastern makers	13	Whitehaven Pottery	Kitchen, 3, 5, 32, 36
North-Western makers	32	Thomas Wolfe	37
Patterson & Co.	6	Enoch Wood & Sons	Dining room, Kitchen, 10, 16, 21, 30, 35
Edward & George Phillips	19		
Pountney & Allies	7, 26		
Pountney & Goldney	Kitchen	Wood & Brettell	Kitchen, 39
Rainforth & Co.	2	Wood & Challinor	27, 36
Thomas Rathbone & Co.	12	Yorkshire makers	13

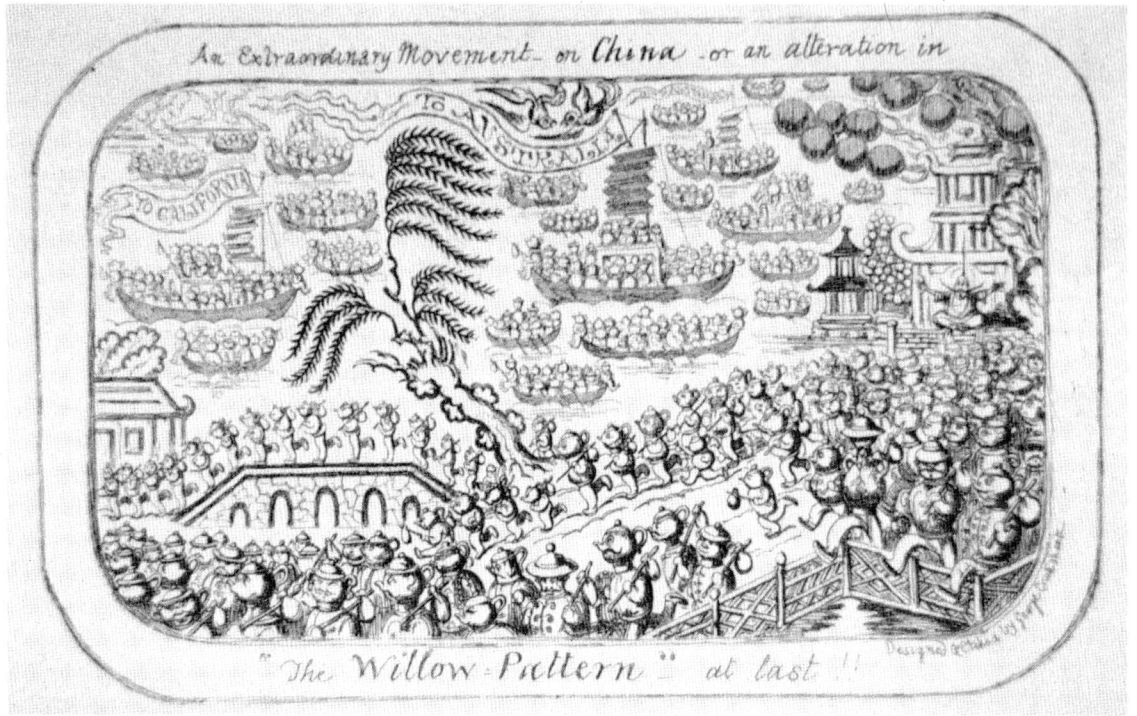

An Extraordinary Movement on China – or an alteration in "The Willow Pattern" at last!!